Study Guide & Working Papers

for use with

College Accounting

CHAPTERS 1-30

Twelfth Edition

John Ellis Price
University of North Texas – Dallas Campus

M. David Haddock, Jr.
Professor of Accounting, Emeritus
Chattanooga State Technical Community College
Directory of Training
Lattimore Black Morgan & Cain, PC

Michael J. Farina
Cerritos College

Boston Burr Ridge, IL Dubuque, IA New York San Francisco St. Louis
Bangkok Bogotá Caracas Kuala Lumpur Lisbon London Madrid Mexico City
Milan Montreal New Delhi Santiago Seoul Singapore Sydney Taipei Toronto

The McGraw-Hill Companies

Study Guide & Working Papers for use with
COLLEGE ACCOUNTING, Twelfth Edition
Chapters 1-30
John Ellis Price, M. David Haddock, Jr., and Michael J. Farina

Published by McGraw-Hill/Irwin, an imprint of The McGraw-Hill Companies, Inc., 1221 Avenue of the Americas, New York, NY 10020.

1 2 3 4 5 6 7 8 9 0 QPD/QPD 0 9 8

ISBN: 978-0-07-336569-5
MHID: 0-07-336569-6

www.mhhe.com

Table of Contents

Chapter 1	Accounting: The Language of Business	1
Chapter 2	Analyzing Business Transactions	5
Chapter 3	Analyzing Business Transactions Using T Accounts	21
Chapter 4	The General Journal and the General Ledger	41
Chapter 5	Adjustments and the Worksheet	73
Chapter 6	Closing Entries and the Postclosing Trial Balance	103
MINI-PRACTICE SET 1	Service Business Accounting Cycle	137
Chapter 7	Accounting for Sales and Accounts Receivable	151
Chapter 8	Accounting for Purchases and Accounts Payable	177
Chapter 9	Cash Receipts, Cash Payments, and Banking Procedures	207
Chapter 10	Payroll Computations, Records, and Payment	251
Chapter 11	Payroll Taxes, Deposits, and Reports	265
Chapter 12	Accruals, Deferrals, and the Worksheet	283
Chapter 13	Financial Statements and Closing Procedures	313
MINI-PRACTICE SET 2	Merchandising Business Accounting Cycle	353
Chapter 14	Accounting Principles and Reporting Standards	381
Chapter 15	Accounts Receivable and Uncollectible Accounts	401
Chapter 16	Notes Payable and Notes Receivable	421
Chapter 17	Merchandise Inventory	433
Chapter 18	Property, Plant, and Equipment	445
Chapter 19	Accounting for Partnerships	469
Chapter 20	Corporations: Formation and Capital Stock Transactions	491
Chapter 21	Corporate Earnings and Capital Transactions	511
Chapter 22	Long-Term Bonds	537
MINI-PRACTICE SET 3	Corporation Accounting Cycle	553
Chapter 23	Financial Statement Analysis	575
Chapter 24	The Statement of Cash Flows	597
MINI-PRACTICE SET 4	Financial Analysis and Decision Making	611

Chapter 25	Departmentalized Profit and Cost Centers	623
Chapter 26	Accounting for Manufacturing Activities	637
Chapter 27	Job Order Cost Accounting	663
Chapter 28	Process Cost Accounting	677
Chapter 29	Controlling Manufacturing Costs: Standard Costs	699
Chapter 30	Cost-Revenue Analysis for Decision Making	711

CHAPTER 1

Accounting: The Language of Business

STUDY GUIDE

STUDY GUIDE

Understanding the Chapter

Objectives

1. Define accounting. **2.** Identify and discuss career opportunities in accounting. **3.** Identify the users of financial information. **4.** Compare and contrast the three types of business entities. **5.** Describe the process used to develop generally accepted accounting principles. **6.** Define the accounting terms new to this chapter.

Reading Assignment

Read Chapter 1 in the textbook. Complete the textbook Section Self Review as you finish reading each section of the chapter, and the Comprehensive Self Review at the end of the chapter. Refer to the Chapter 1 Glossary or to the Glossary at the end of the book to find definitions for terms that are not familiar to you.

Activities

- ❑ **Thinking Critically** — Answer the *Thinking Critically* questions for Google and Managerial Implications.
- ❑ **Discussion Questions** — Answer each assigned discussion question in Chapter 1.
- ❑ **Critical Thinking Problem** — Complete the critical thinking problem as assigned.
- ❑ **Business Connections** — Complete the Business Connections activities as assigned to gain a deeper understanding of Chapter 1 concepts.

Practice Tests

Complete the Practice Tests, which cover the main points in your reading assignment. Compare your answers with those in the Practice Test Answer Key for Chapter 1 at the end of this chapter. If you have answered any questions incorrectly, review the related section of the text.

STUDY GUIDE

Part A True-False *For each of the following statements, circle T in the answer column if the answer is true or F if the answer is false.*

T	F	**1.** In a large company, the auditing process is completed by bookkeepers.
T	F	**2.** The American Institute of Certified Public Accountants is a governmental agency.
T	F	**3.** Employees should have no particular interest in the financial information about the business for which they work.
T	F	**4.** Shares of stock represent ownership in a corporation.
T	F	**5.** There is little difference between a corporation and other forms of business entities.
T	F	**6.** A sole proprietorship is a form of business entity owned by two or more people.
T	F	**7.** Because of the difference in the structures of the three types of business entities, certain aspects of their financial affairs are accounted for in different ways.
T	F	**8.** All accounting principles are established by law.
T	F	**9.** Because of the separate entity assumption, the personal financial activities of the owner of a sole proprietorship are combined with the financial affairs of his or her business in the accounting records of the business.
T	F	**10.** The Financial Accounting Standards Board issues income tax rules.
T	F	**11** The Securities and Exchange Commission often relies on pronouncements of the Financial Accounting Standards Board.
T	F	**12.** The Securities and Exchange Commission has a great deal of power to dictate accounting methods used by companies whose stock is traded on the stock exchanges.
T	F	**13.** Passing a test called the Uniform CPA Examination is required for one to become a certified public accountant.

STUDY GUIDE

Part B Completion *In the answer column, supply the missing word or words needed to complete each of the following statements.*

______ **1.** The ______ was created to review and oversee the accounting methods of publicly owned corporations.

______ **2.** ______ are developed by the Financial Accounting Standards Board.

______ **3.** The ______ is a national association of professional accountants.

______ **4.** The ______ is an organization of accounting educators.

______ **5.** Major areas of accounting are public accounting, managerial accounting, and ______.

______ **6.** The IRS and the ______ have large numbers of accountants on their staff and use them to uncover possible violations of the law.

______ **7.** ______ is the study of accounting principles used by different countries.

______ **8.** Many people call accounting the ______.

______ **9.** Periodic reports prepared from accounting records are called ______.

______ **10.** The accounting process involves ______, ______, summarizing, interpreting, and communicating financial information about an economic or social entity.

______ **11.** An economic entity is an organization whose major purpose is to produce a profit, whereas a(n) ______ is a nonprofit organization.

______ **12.** The three major types of business entities are sole proprietorships, corporations, and ______.

______ **13.** Ownership in a corporation is evidenced by ______.

______ **14.** Corporate owners are called ______.

______ **15.** The ______ and other tax authorities are interested in financial information about a firm.

WORKING PAPERS

Name

CRITICAL THINKING PROBLEM 1.1

Chapter 1 Practice Test Answer Key

Part A True-False

1. F
2. F
3. F
4. T
5. F
6. F
7. F
8. T
9. F
10. F
11. T
12. T
13. T

Part B Completion

1. SEC
2. generally accepted accounting principles
3. AICPA
4. AAA
5. governmental accounting
6. FBI
7. international accounting
8. language of business
9. financial statements
10. recording, classifying
11. social entity
12. partnerships
13. shares of stock
14. stockholders or shareholders
15. IRS

CHAPTER 2

Analyzing Business Transactions

STUDY GUIDE

STUDY GUIDE

Understanding the Chapter

Objectives

1. Record in equation form the financial effects of a business transaction. **2.** Define, identify, and understand the relationship between asset, liability, and owner's equity accounts. **3.** Analyze the effects of business transactions on a firm's assets, liabilities, and owner's equity and record these effects in accounting equation form. **4.** Prepare an income statement. **5.** Prepare a statement of owner's equity and a balance sheet **6.** Define the accounting terms new to this chapter.

Reading Assignment

Read Chapter 2 in the textbook. Complete the textbook Section Self Review as you finish reading each section of the chapter, and the Comprehensive Self Review at the end of the chapter. Refer to the Chapter 2 Glossary or to the Glossary at the end of the book to find definitions for terms that are not familiar to you.

Activities

❑ **Thinking Critically** — Answer the *Thinking Critically* questions for Southwest Airlines and Managerial Implications.

❑ **Discussion Questions** — Answer each assigned discussion question in Chapter 2.

❑ **Exercises** — Complete each assigned exercise in Chapter 2. Use the forms provided in this SGWP. The objectives covered by an exercise are given after the exercise number. If you need help with an exercise, review the portion of the chapter related to the objective(s) covered.

❑ **Problems A/B** — Complete each assigned problem in Chapter 2. Use the forms provided in this SGWP. The objectives covered by a problem are given after the problem number. If you need help with a problem, review the portion of the chapter related to the objective(s) covered.

❑ **Critical Thinking Problems 2.1 and 2.2** — Complete Critical Thinking Problems 2.1 and 2.2 as assigned. Use the forms provided in this SGWP.

❑ **Business Connections** — Complete the Business Connections activities as assigned to gain a deeper understanding of Chapter 2 concepts.

Practice Tests

Complete the Practice Tests, which cover the main points in your reading assignment. Compare your answers with those in the Practice Test Answer Key for Chapter 2 at the end of this chapter. If you have answered any questions incorrectly, review the related section of the text.

Part A True-False *For each of the following statements, circle T in the answer column if the answer is true or F if the answer is false.*

T F 1. Revenue decreases owner's equity.

T F 2. Expenses decrease owner's equity.

T F 3. The collection of cash from accounts receivable increases owner's equity.

T F 4. The net income or net loss for the period is shown on both the income statement and the statement of owner's equity.

T F 5. The net income or net loss for the period is shown in the Assets section of the balance sheet.

T F 6. The balance sheet shows the financial position of a business on a specific date.

T F 7. Profit and loss statement is another name for the income statement.

T F 8. A net loss results if total expenses exceed total revenue.

T F 9. The balance sheet is prepared at the end of the accounting period to show the results of operations.

T F 10. When equipment is purchased for cash, there is no change in the total value of the firm's property.

Part B Matching *For each numbered item, choose the matching term from the box and write the identifying letter in the answer column.*

______ 1. Inflows of money or other assets resulting from sales of goods or service

______ 2. An expression of the relationship in which assets equal liabilities plus owner's equity

______ 3. A business obligation or debt

______ 4. Property owned by a business

______ 5. Owner's financial interest in the business

______ 6. Those to whom money is owed

______ 7. Amount remaining when total revenue is more than total expenses

______ 8. Amounts owed by charge account customers

a. Accounts Receivable
b. Assets
c. Creditors
d. Revenue
e. Owner's equity
f. Liability
g. Net income
h. Fundamental accounting equation

Part C Completion

In the answer column, supply the missing word or words needed to complete each of the following statements.

______ 1. When supplies are first purchased for use in operations, they are considered a type of ______.

______ 2. Regardless of the number and variety of transactions, liabilities plus owner's equity always equal ______.

______ 3. When expenses are paid, the owner's equity is ______.

______ 4. Accounts receivable result when goods are sold or services are performed on ______.

______ 5. The basic reason for starting a business is the possibility of making a ______.

______ 6. When property values and financial interest increase or decrease, the sum of the items on both sides of the equation always remains ______.

______ 7. The purchase of new equipment on account creates a debt that is called a(n) ______.

______ 8. Accountants must ______ each business transaction before they can intelligently record, report, and interpret it.

Demonstration Problem

The account balances for Debra Hill, CPA, for the month of January 2010 are shown below in random order.

Rent Expense	$ 4,000	Advertising Expense	$ 2,500
Fees Earned	69,120	Office Equipment	25,560
Accounts Payable	14,912	D. Hill, Drawing	7,578
Salaries Expense	11,890	Accounts Receivable	14,900
Cash	91,138	D. Hill, Capital 1/1	?

Instructions

1. Determine the balance for **Debra Hill, Capital,** on January 1, 2010.
2. Prepare an income statement, a statement of owner's equity, and a balance sheet as of January 31, 2010.
3. List the expenses on the income statement in alphabetical order.

SOLUTION

Determine the balance for Debra Hill Capital, on January 1, 2010.
Let Debra Hill, Capital = X. Solving for X:

Assets						= Liabilities +		Owner's Equity						
Cash	+	Accts. Rec.	+	Office Equip.	=	Accounts Payable	+	D. Hill, Capital	−	Drawing	+	Revenue	−	Expenses
91,138	+	14,900	+	25,560	=	14,912	+	X	−	7,578	+	69,120	−	18,390
				131,598	=	58,064	+	X						
		131,598	−	58,064	=	X								
				73,534	=	X								

Debra Hill, Capital, January 1, 2010 = **$73,534**

Total Expenses:

Rent Expense	$ 4,000
Salaries Expense	11,890
Advertising Expense	2,500
	$18,390

Debra Hill, CPA
Income Statement
Month Ended January 31, 2010

Revenue		
Fees Earned		69 1 2 0 00
Expenses		
Rent Expense	4 0 0 0 00	
Salaries Expense	11 8 9 0 00	
Advertising Expense	2 5 0 0 00	
Total Expenses		18 3 9 0 00
Net Income		50 7 3 0 00

Debra Hill, CPA
Statement of Owner's Equity
Month Ended January 31, 2010

Debra Hill, Capital, January 1, 2010		73 5 3 4 00
Net Income	50 7 3 0 00	
Less Withdrawals	7 5 7 8 00	
Increase in Capital		43 1 5 2 00
Debra Hill, Capital, January 31, 2010		116 6 8 6 00

SOLUTION (continued)

Debra Hill, CPA

Balance Sheet

January 31, 2010

Assets		Liabilities	
Cash	91 138 00	Accounts Payable	14 912 00
Accounts Receivable	14 900 00	Owner's Equity	
Office Equipment	25 560 00	Debra Hill, Capital	116 686 00
Total Assets	131 598 00	Total Liabilities and Owner's Equity	131 598 00

WORKING PAPERS

Chapter 2, objective 1

Name ______________________________

EXERCISE 2.1

1. Invested Cash = 100,000
2. Owner's equity
3. Carolyn Wells
4. + 100,000
5. Property +100,000 = Financial interest = $100,000

EXERCISE 2.2

Assets	103,500.00
Liabilities	3,500.00
Owner's Equity	100,000.00

EXERCISE 2.3

	Assets	=	Liabilities	+	Owner's Equity
1.		=		+	
2.		=		+	
3.		=		+	
4.		=		+	
5.		=		+	

EXERCISE 2.4

Transaction	Assets	=	Liabilities	+	Owner's Equity
1.	+	=		+	+
2.		=		+	
3.		=		+	
4.		=		+	
5.		=		+	
6.		=		+	
7.		=		+	
8.		=		+	
9.		=		+	
10.		=		+	

Name ______________________________

EXERCISE 2.5

	Assets			= Liabilities	+ Owner's Equity		
	Cash	+ Accounts Receivable	+ Equipment	= Accounts Payable	+ Amos Roberts Capital	+ Revenue	− Expenses
1.							
2.							
3.							
4.							
5.							
6.							
7.							
8.							
Totals		+	+	=	+	+	−

EXERCISE 2.6

____

Revenue

____

Expenses

____

EXERCISE 2.7

1. ______________________________
2. ______________________________
3. ______________________________
4. ______________________________
5. ______________________________
6. ______________________________
7. ______________________________

Name

EXERCISE 2.8

Revenue

Expenses

EXERCISE 2.9

Name

EXERCISE 2.10

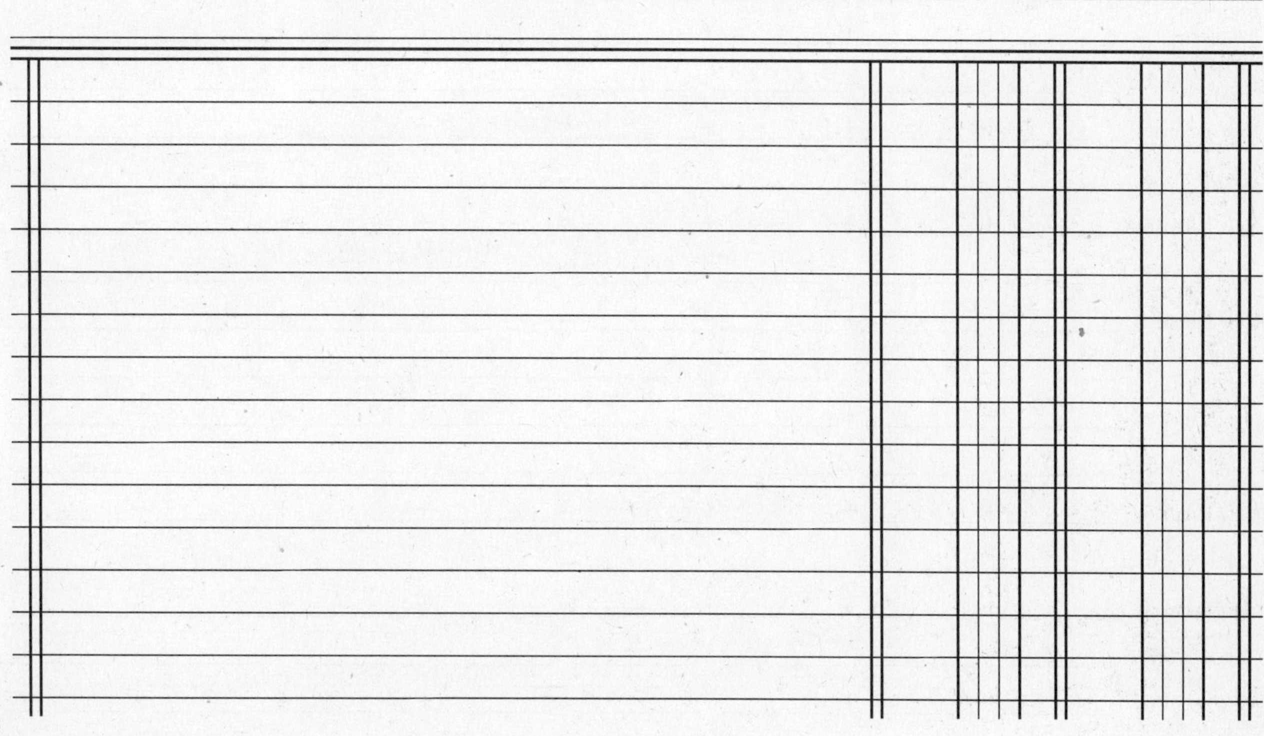

Name ______________________________

PROBLEM 2.1A or 2.1B

	Assets				= Liabilities +	Owner's Equity		
	Cash	+ Accounts Receivable	+	+	= Accounts Payable	+ Capital	+ Revenue	− Expenses
Beginning Balances								
1.								
New Balances								
2.								
New Balances								
3.								
New Balances								
4.								
New Balances								
5.								
New Balances								
6.								
New Balances								
7.								
New Balances								
8.								
New Balances								
9.								
New Balances								
10.								
New Balances								

Analyze: ____

Name Ms

PROBLEM 2.2A or 2.2B

Sub Title Revenue

	Assets				=	Liabilities	+	Owner's Equity
	Cash	+ Accounts Receivable	+ Supplies	+ Equipment	=	Accounts Payable	+	Owner's Capital
1.	+18,000							+18,000
2.	−8,000			+8,000				
3.				+3,000		+3,000		
4.	−1,500					−1,500		
5.	+3,000							+3,000
6.	+2,160							+2,160
7.		+1,560						+1,560
Rent 8.	−1,300							−1,300
9.	+1,100	−1,100						
10.	−1,550		+1,550					
11.	−2,000							−2,000
Totals	9,910	+ 460	+ 1,550	+ 11,000	=	1,500	+	21,420

Analyze: ____

Name

PROBLEM 2.3A or 2.3B

Name

PROBLEM 2.3A or 2.3B (continued)

Analyze:

PROBLEM 2.4A or 2.4B

Analyze:

Name ______________________

CRITICAL THINKING PROBLEM 2.1

Determine the balance for **Kawonza Carter**, April 30, 2010.

Assets			= Liabilities +	Owner's Equity			
Cash	+ Accounts Receivable	+ Machinery	= Accounts Payable	+ K. Carter Capital	− K. Carter Drawing	+ Revenue	− Expenses
$13,000 +	$5,600 +	$17,000 =	$6,400 +	?	− $2,400	+ $19,000	− $10,000

Let Kawonza Carter, Capital = X.

Solving for X:

Kawonza Carter, Capital, April 1, 2010, = ______

Advertising Expense	$ 1,800
Maintenance Expense	2,200
Salaries Expense	6,000
Total Expenses	

Name

CRITICAL THINKING PROBLEM 2.1 (continued)

Analyze:

Name

CRITICAL THINKING PROBLEM 2.2

Chapter 2 Practice Test Answer Key

Part A True-False

1. F
2. T
3. F
4. T
5. F
6. T
7. T
8. T
9. F
10. T

Part B Matching

1. d
2. h
3. f
4. b
5. e
6. c
7. g
8. a

Part C Completion

1. asset or property
2. assets
3. reduced or decreased
4. credit or on account
5. profit
6. equal
7. accounts payable or liability
8. analyze

CHAPTER 3

Analyzing Business Transactions Using T Accounts

STUDY GUIDE

STUDY GUIDE

Understanding the Chapter

Objectives

1. Set up T accounts for assets, liabilities, and owner's equity. **2.** Analyze business transactions and enter them in the accounts. **3.** Determine the balance of an account. **4.** Set up T accounts for revenue and expenses. **5.** Prepare a trial balance from T accounts. **6.** Prepare an income statement, a statement of owner's equity, and a balance sheet. **7.** Develop a chart of accounts. **8.** Define the accounting terms new to this chapter.

Reading Assignment

Read Chapter 3 in the textbook. Complete the textbook Section Self Review as you finish reading each section of the chapter, and the Comprehensive Self Review at the end of the chapter. Refer to the Chapter 3 Glossary or to the Glossary at the end of the book to find definitions for terms that are not familiar to you.

Activities

- ❑ **Thinking Critically** — Answer the *Thinking Critically* questions for Johnson & Johnson and Managerial Implications.
- ❑ **Discussion Questions** — Answer each assigned discussion question in Chapter 3.
- ❑ **Exercises** — Complete each assigned exercise in Chapter 3. Use the forms provided in this SGWP. The objectives covered by an exercise are given after the exercise number. If you need help with an exercise, review the portion of the chapter related to the objective(s) covered.
- ❑ **Problems A/B** — Complete each assigned problem in Chapter 3. Use the forms provided in this SGWP. The objectives covered by a problem are given after the problem number. If you need help with a problem, review the portion of the chapter related to the objective(s) covered.
- ❑ **Critical Thinking Problems** — Complete the critical thinking problems as assigned. Use the forms provided in this SGWP.
- ❑ **Business Connections** — Complete the Business Connections activities as assigned to gain a deeper understanding of Chapter 3 concepts.

Practice Tests

Complete the Practice Tests, which cover the main points in your reading assignment. Compare your answers with those in the Practice Test Answer Key for Chapter 3 at the end of this chapter. If you have answered any questions incorrectly, review the related section of the text.

STUDY GUIDE

Part A True-False *For each of the following statements, circle T in the answer column if the answer is true or F if the answer is false.*

T F 1. The receipt of cash is recorded by a debit entry to the **Cash** account.

T F 2. A reduction in the equity of the owners is recorded by making a debit entry in the **Owner's Drawing** account.

T F 3. An entry on the left side of any account is called a debit.

T F 4. Revenue accounts are increased by credits.

T F 5. An increase in the owner's investment is recorded by crediting the owner's capital account.

T F 6. Decreases in liabilities are credited to the liability account.

T F 7. A cash payment by a business is recorded as a debit entry in the **Cash** account.

T F 8. Increases in liabilities are recorded on the debit side of an account.

T F 9. The owner's beginning investment is entered as a debit in the owner's capital account.

T F 10. Decreases in assets are recorded on the left side of an account.

T F 11. Increases in assets are recorded on the debit side of an account.

T F 12. The T account allows increases and decreases to be separated and recorded on different sides.

T F 13. Accountants keep a separate record for each asset, liability, and owner's equity item.

T F 14. Increases in expense accounts are recorded by credit entries.

T F 15. The **Accounts Payable** account is decreased by a debit entry.

STUDY GUIDE

Part B Matching *For each numbered item, choose the matching item from the box and write the identifying letter in the answer column.*

a. Account
b. Double-entry system
c. Credit
d. Permanent accounts
e. Temporary accounts
f. Expense
g. Revenue
h. Chart of accounts
i. Debit

_______ **1.** A separate written record that is kept for each asset, liability, and owner's equity item.

_______ **2.** A subdivision of owner's equity that is used to record various types of income of a business.

_______ **3.** Accounts whose balances are transferred to a summary account at the end of the accounting period.

_______ **4.** A system for arranging accounts in logical order.

_______ **5.** An entry on the right side of an account.

_______ **6.** An entry on the left side of an account.

_______ **7.** Accounts whose balances are carried forward to start a new period.

_______ **8.** The system of accounting that requires equality of the entries on each side of the equation.

_______ **9.** An operating cost that decreases owner's equity.

Part C Completion *In the answer column, supply the missing word or words needed to complete each of the following statements.*

_______________ **1.** A(n) ______ is the total of several entries on either side of an account that is entered in small pencil.

_______________ **2.** A(n) ______ is an error where the decimal point is misplaced.

_______________ **3.** A(n) ______ is an error where the digits of a number are switched.

_______________ **4.** The ______ is a statement prepared to test the accuracy of the figures recorded in the accounts.

_______________ **5.** The ______ of an account is where increases in the account are recorded and where the balance is recorded.

Demonstration Problem

Nina Turner is an investment broker who operates her own business, Turner Investment Counseling.

Instructions

1. Analyze the transactions for the month of January 2010, and record each in the appropriate T accounts. Use plus and minus signs to show increases and decreases. Identify each entry in the T accounts by writing the number of the transaction next to the entry.
2. Determine the balance for each T account. Prepare a trial balance.

Transactions

1. Nina Turner invested $50,000 in cash to start the business.
2. Turner Investment Counseling purchased office furniture for $9,000 on account.
3. Paid $3,000 for one month's rent.
4. Sold an investment portfolio to the Dotson Family and received fees of $50,000.
5. Purchased a computer for $4,000, paying $2,000 in cash and putting the balance on account for 60 days.
6. Paid $8,400 for employee salaries.
7. Purchased office equipment for $7,500 with credit terms of 60 days.
8. Sold an investment portfolio to the Carter Family and will receive commission fees of $21,000 in 30 days.
9. Issued a check for $3,750 for partial payment of the amount for office equipment.
10. Nina Turner withdrew $5,000 in cash for personal use.
11. Issued a check for $1,040 to pay the utility bill.

SOLUTION

Cash

(1)	+ 50,000	(3)	− 3,000
(4)	+ 50,000	(5)	− 2,000
		(6)	− 8,400
		(9)	− 3,750
	100,000	(10)	− 5,000
		(11)	− 1,040
Bal.	76,810		23,190

Accounts Receivable

(8)	+ 21,000		

Office Furniture

(2)	+ 9,000		

Office Equipment

(5)	+ 4,000		
(7)	+ 7,500		
Bal.	11,500		

Accounts Payable

(9)	− 3,750	(2)	+ 9,000
		(5)	+ 2,000
		(7)	+ 7,500
		Bal.	14,750

Nina Turner, Capital

		(1)	+ 50,000

Nina Turner, Drawing

(10)	+ 5,000		

Fees Income

		(4)	+ 50,000
		(8)	+ 21,000
		Bal.	71,000

Rent Expense

(3)	+ 3,000		

Salaries Expense

(6)	+ 8,400		

Utilities Expense

(11)	+ 1040		

SOLUTION (continued)

Turner Investment Counseling

Trial Balance

January 31, 2010

ACCOUNT NAME	DEBIT	CREDIT
Cash	76,810.00	
Accounts Receivable	2,100.00	
Office Furniture	9,000.00	
Office Equipment	11,500.00	
Accounts Payable		14,750.00
Nina Turner, Capital		50,000.00
Nina Turner, Drawing	5,000.00	
Fees Income		71,000.00
Rent Expense	3,000.00	
Salaries Expense	8,400.00	
Utilities Expense	1,040.00	
Totals	135,750.00	135,750.00

WORKING PAPERS

Name ______________________________

EXERCISE 3.1

EXERCISE 3.2

EXERCISE 3.3

1. ______________________________
2. ______________________________
3. ______________________________
4. ______________________________
5. ______________________________
6. ______________________________
7. ______________________________
8. ______________________________

Name ______________________

EXERCISE 3.4

1. ______________________
2. ______________________
3. ______________________
4. ______________________
5. ______________________

EXERCISE 3.5

EXERCISE 3.6

ACCOUNT NAME	DEBIT	CREDIT

Name

EXERCISE 3.6 (continued)

EXERCISE 3.7

Name

EXERCISE 3.7 (continued)

EXERCISE 3.8

Name

PROBLEM 3.1A or 3.1B

1. Cash

2. Equipment

3. Accounts payable

4.

5.

6.

7.

8.

Analyze:

PROBLEM 3.2A or 3.2B

1.

2.

3.

4.

5.

6.

7.

8.

Analyze:

Name

PROBLEM 3.3A or 3.3B

1.

2.

3.

4.

5.

6.

7.

8.

9.

10.

11.

12.

Name

PROBLEM 3.4A or 3.4B

Analyze:

Name

PROBLEM 3.5A or 3.5B

ACCOUNT NAME	DEBIT	CREDIT

Name

PROBLEM 3.5A or 3.5B (continued)

Analyze:

Name

CRITICAL THINKING PROBLEM 3.1

Name

CRITICAL THINKING PROBLEM 3.1 (continued)

ACCOUNT NAME	DEBIT	CREDIT

Name

CRITICAL THINKING PROBLEM 3.1 (continued)

Analyze:

Name

CRITICAL THINKING PROBLEM 3.2

Name

CRITICAL THINKING PROBLEM 3.2 (continued)

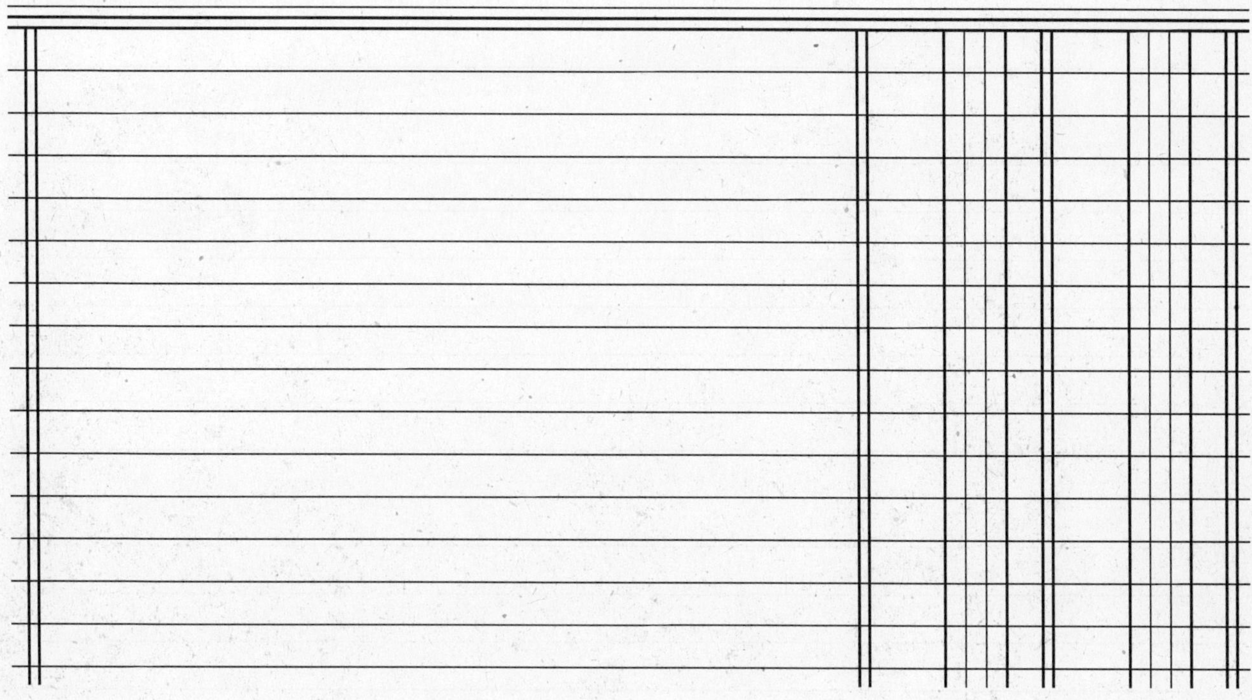

Name

CRITICAL THINKING PROBLEM 3.2 (continued)

Chapter 3 Practice Test Answer Key

Part A True-False

1. T
2. T
3. T
4. T
5. T
6. F
7. F
8. F
9. F
10. F
11. T
12. T
13. T
14. F
15. T

Part B Matching

1. a
2. g
3. e
4. h
5. c
6. i
7. d
8. b
9. f

Part C Completion

1. footing
2. slide
3. transposition
4. trial balance
5. normal balance

CHAPTER 4

The General Journal and the General Ledger

STUDY GUIDE

Understanding the Chapter

Objectives

1. Record transactions in the general journal. **2.** Prepare compound journal entries. **3.** Post journal entries to general ledger accounts. **4.** Correct errors made in the journal or ledger. **5.** Define the accounting terms new to this chapter.

Reading Assignment

Read Chapter 4 in the textbook. Complete the textbook Section Self Review as you finish reading each section of the chapter, and the Comprehensive Self Review at the end of the chapter. Refer to the Chapter 4 Glossary or to the Glossary at the end of the book to find definitions for terms that are not familiar to you.

Activities

- ❑ **Thinking Critically** — Answer the *Thinking Critically* questions for Willamette Valley Vineyards and Managerial Implications.
- ❑ **Discussion Questions** — Answer each assigned discussion question in Chapter 4.
- ❑ **Exercises** — Complete each assigned exercise in Chapter 4. Use the forms provided in this SGWP. The objectives covered by an exercise are given after the exercise number. If you need help with an exercise, review the portion of the chapter related to the objective(s) covered.
- ❑ **Problems A/B** — Complete each assigned problem in Chapter 4. Use the forms provided in this SGWP. The objectives covered by a problem are given after the problem number. If you need help with a problem, review the portion of the chapter related to the objective(s) covered.
- ❑ **Critical Thinking Problems** — Complete the critical thinking problems as assigned. Use the forms provided in this SGWP.
- ❑ **Business Connections** — Complete the Business Connections activities as assigned to gain a deeper understanding of Chapter 4 concepts.

Practice Tests

Complete the Practice Tests, which cover the main points in your reading assignment. Compare your answers with those in the Practice Test Answer Key for Chapter 4 at the end of this chapter. If you have answered any questions incorrectly, review the related section of the text.

STUDY GUIDE

Part A Matching *For each numbered item, choose the matching term from the box and write the identifying letter in the answer column.*

a. journal
b. source documents
c. posting
d. general ledger
e. T accounts
f. journalizing
g. correcting entry
h. compound entry
i. balance ledger form
j. audit trail

_______ **1.** A chain of references that makes it possible to trace information about transactions through an accounting system.

_______ **2.** Invoices and other business forms that contain the original data about transactions.

_______ **3.** The process of recording transactions in the journal.

_______ **4.** Record of original entry.

_______ **5.** An entry that is made when there is an error in data that has been journalized and posted.

_______ **6.** The process of transferring information from the journal to the ledger.

_______ **7.** Used to analyze transactions but not used to maintain financial records.

_______ **8.** A permanent, classified record of all accounts used by a business.

_______ **9.** A journal entry that consists of more than one debit or more than one credit.

_______ **10.** A ledger account form that always shows the current balance of an account.

Part B Completion *In the answer column, supply the missing word or words needed to complete each of the following statements.*

_______________ **1.** On the balance ledger form the first money column is used to record ______ amounts.

_______________ **2.** On the balance ledger form the second money column is used to record ______ amounts.

_______________ **3.** Descriptions in the general journal should be complete but ______.

_______________ **4.** Notations that allow the data in journals and ledgers to be easily traced are called ______.

_______________ **5.** All the accounts together constitute a(n) ______, or a record of final entry.

_______________ **6.** If an error is discovered in a journal before the entry is ______, the error can be neatly crossed out and the correct data written above it.

_______________ **7.** The pages in the ledger are usually organized so that the ______ come first.

_______________ **8.** The accountant enters transactions in the general journal in ______ order.

_______________ **9.** The ______ is always entered at the top of the Date column.

_______________ **10.** The accountant always records the ______ items first in the Description column of the journal.

Demonstration Problem

On January 1, 2010, Amy Carter opened her consulting office and began business as Carter Consulting Services. Selected transactions for the first month of operations follow.

Instructions

1. Journalize the transactions on page 1 of a general journal. Write the year at the top of the Date column; include an explanation for each entry.
2. Post to the general ledger accounts.
3. Prepare a trial balance.

DATE	TRANSACTIONS
January 1	Amy Carter invested $80,000 cash in the business.
2	Issued Check 101 for $4,000 to pay the January rent.
5	Purchased office equipment for $25,000 from Davis Office Supply, Invoice 7045; issued Check 102 for $5,000 down payment with the balance due in 30 days.
12	Wrote a lease contract for Helen Kennedy for $4,000 cash.
15	Performed consulting services for a client, Sims Davis Supply Company, for $18,000 to be received in 30 days.
28	Issued Check 103 for $10,000 for payment to Sims Davis Office Supply.
29	Issued Check 104 for $5,000 to Amy Carter for personal use.
31	Received $9,000 from Sims Supply Company for partial payment of their account.

SOLUTION

GENERAL JOURNAL

PAGE 1

DATE		DESCRIPTION	POST. REF.	DEBIT	CREDIT
2010					
Jan.	1	Cash	101	80,000.00	
		Amy Carter, Capital	301		80,000.00
		Investment to start business			
	2	Rent Expense	514	4,000.00	
		Cash	101		4,000.00
		Issued Check 101 for January rent			
	5	Office Equipment	131	25,000.00	
		Cash	101		5,000.00
		Accounts Payable	202		20,000.00
		Issued Check 102 for office equipment,			
		balance due in 30 days.			
	12	Cash	101	4,000.00	
		Fees Income	401		4,000.00
		Performed services for cash.			
	15	Accounts Receivable	111	18,000.00	
		Fees Income	401		18,000.00
		Performed services on account.			
	28	Accounts Payable	202	10,000.00	
		Cash	101		10,000.00
		Paid Invoice 4507, Check 103			
	29	Amy Carter, Drawing	302	5,000.00	
		Cash	101		5,000.00
		Issued Check 104 to owner for personal use.			
	31	Cash	101	9,000.00	
		Accounts Receivable	111		9,000.00
		Received partial payment			
		from Sims Supply Company			

SOLUTION (continued)

GENERAL LEDGER

ACCOUNT **Cash** ACCOUNT NO. **101**

DATE		DESCRIPTION	POST. REF.	DEBIT	CREDIT	BALANCE DEBIT	BALANCE CREDIT
2010							
Jan.	**1**		**J1**	**80,000.00**		**80,000.00**	
	2		**J1**		**4,000.00**	**76,000.00**	
	5		**J1**		**5,000.00**	**71,000.00**	
	12		**J1**	**4,000.00**		**75,000.00**	
	28		**J1**		**10,000.00**	**65,000.00**	
	29		**J1**		**5,000.00**	**60,000.00**	
	31		**J1**	**9,000.00**		**69,000.00**	

ACCOUNT **Accounts Receivable** ACCOUNT NO. **111**

DATE		DESCRIPTION	POST. REF.	DEBIT	CREDIT	BALANCE DEBIT	BALANCE CREDIT
2010							
Jan.	**15**		**J1**	**18,000.00**		**18,000.00**	
	31		**J1**		**9,000.00**	**9,000.00**	

ACCOUNT **Office Equipment** ACCOUNT NO. **131**

DATE		DESCRIPTION	POST. REF.	DEBIT	CREDIT	BALANCE DEBIT	BALANCE CREDIT
2010							
Jan.	**5**		**J1**	**25,000.00**		**25,000.00**	

ACCOUNT **Accounts Payable** ACCOUNT NO. **202**

DATE		DESCRIPTION	POST. REF.	DEBIT	CREDIT	BALANCE DEBIT	BALANCE CREDIT
2010							
Jan.	**5**		**J1**		**20,000.00**		**20,000.00**
	28		**J1**	**10,000.00**			**10,000.00**

ACCOUNT **Amy Carter, Capital** ACCOUNT NO. **301**

DATE		DESCRIPTION	POST. REF.	DEBIT	CREDIT	BALANCE DEBIT	BALANCE CREDIT
2010							
Jan.	**1**		**J1**		**80,000.00**		**80,000.00**

SOLUTION (continued)

ACCOUNT **Amy Carter, Drawing** ACCOUNT NO. **302**

DATE		DESCRIPTION	POST. REF.	DEBIT	CREDIT	BALANCE DEBIT	BALANCE CREDIT
2007							
Jan.	29		J1	5,000.00		5,000.00	

ACCOUNT **Fees Income** ACCOUNT NO. **401**

DATE		DESCRIPTION	POST. REF.	DEBIT	CREDIT	BALANCE DEBIT	BALANCE CREDIT
2010							
Jan.	12		J1		4,000.00		4,000.00
	15		J1		18,000.00		22,000.00

ACCOUNT **Rent Expense** ACCOUNT NO. **514**

DATE		DESCRIPTION	POST. REF.	DEBIT	CREDIT	BALANCE DEBIT	BALANCE CREDIT
2010							
Jan.	2		J1	4,000.00		4,000.00	

Carter Consulting Services

Trial Balance

January 31, 2010

ACCOUNT NAME	DEBIT	CREDIT
Cash	69,000.00	
Accounts Receivable	9,000.00	
Office Equipment	25,000.00	
Accounts Payable		10,000.00
Amy Carter, Capital		80,000.00
Amy Carter, Drawing	5,000.00	
Fees Income		22,000.00
Rent Expense	4,000.00	
Totals	112,000.00	112,000.00

WORKING PAPERS

Name ______________________

EXERCISE 4.1

GENERAL JOURNAL

PAGE ________

DATE		DESCRIPTION	POST. REF.	DEBIT	CREDIT

Name ____________________

EXERCISE 4.1 (continued)

GENERAL JOURNAL

PAGE ______

	DATE		DESCRIPTION	POST. REF.	DEBIT	CREDIT	
1							1
2							2
3							3
4							4
5							5
6							6
7							7
8							8
9							9

EXERCISE 4.2

	Debit	Credit		Debit	Credit		Debit	Credit
1.			**5.**			**8.**		
2.			**6.**			**9.**		
3.			**7.**			**10.**		
4.								

EXERCISE 4.3

GENERAL LEDGER

ACCOUNT ____________________ ACCOUNT NO. ______

DATE		DESCRIPTION	POST. REF.	DEBIT	CREDIT	BALANCE	
						DEBIT	CREDIT

Name ______________________

EXERCISE 4.3 (continued)

GENERAL LEDGER

ACCOUNT ______________________ ACCOUNT NO. ________

DATE		DESCRIPTION	POST. REF.	DEBIT	CREDIT	BALANCE	
						DEBIT	CREDIT

ACCOUNT ______________________ ACCOUNT NO. ________

DATE		DESCRIPTION	POST. REF.	DEBIT	CREDIT	BALANCE	
						DEBIT	CREDIT

ACCOUNT ______________________ ACCOUNT NO. ________

DATE		DESCRIPTION	POST. REF.	DEBIT	CREDIT	BALANCE	
						DEBIT	CREDIT

ACCOUNT ______________________ ACCOUNT NO. ________

DATE		DESCRIPTION	POST. REF.	DEBIT	CREDIT	BALANCE	
						DEBIT	CREDIT

ACCOUNT ______________________ ACCOUNT NO. ________

DATE		DESCRIPTION	POST. REF.	DEBIT	CREDIT	BALANCE	
						DEBIT	CREDIT

Name ______________________

EXERCISE 4.3 (continued)

GENERAL LEDGER

ACCOUNT ______________________ ACCOUNT NO. ________

DATE		DESCRIPTION	POST. REF.	DEBIT	CREDIT	BALANCE DEBIT	BALANCE CREDIT

ACCOUNT ______________________ ACCOUNT NO. ________

DATE		DESCRIPTION	POST. REF.	DEBIT	CREDIT	BALANCE DEBIT	BALANCE CREDIT

ACCOUNT ______________________ ACCOUNT NO. ________

DATE		DESCRIPTION	POST. REF.	DEBIT	CREDIT	BALANCE DEBIT	BALANCE CREDIT

ACCOUNT ______________________ ACCOUNT NO. ________

DATE		DESCRIPTION	POST. REF.	DEBIT	CREDIT	BALANCE DEBIT	BALANCE CREDIT

ACCOUNT ______________________ ACCOUNT NO. ________

DATE		DESCRIPTION	POST. REF.	DEBIT	CREDIT	BALANCE DEBIT	BALANCE CREDIT

ACCOUNT ______________________ ACCOUNT NO. ________

DATE		DESCRIPTION	POST. REF.	DEBIT	CREDIT	BALANCE DEBIT	BALANCE CREDIT

Name ________________________________

EXERCISE 4.4

GENERAL JOURNAL

PAGE ________

	DATE		DESCRIPTION	POST. REF.	DEBIT	CREDIT	
1							1
2							2
3							3
4							4
5							5
6							6
7							7
8							8
9							9
10							10
11							11
12							12
13							13
14							14
15							15
16							16
17							17
18							18
19							19
20							20
21							21
22							22
23							23
24							24
25							25
26							26
27							27
28							28
29							29
30							30
31							31
32							32
33							33
34							34
35							35
36							36
37							37

Name

EXERCISE 4.5

GENERAL JOURNAL PAGE

	DATE		DESCRIPTION	POST. REF.	DEBIT	CREDIT	
1							1
2							2
3							3
4							4
5							5
6							6

EXERCISE 4.6

GENERAL JOURNAL PAGE

	DATE		DESCRIPTION	POST. REF.	DEBIT	CREDIT	
1							1
2							2
3							3
4							4
5							5
6							6

EXTRA FORM

GENERAL JOURNAL PAGE

	DATE		DESCRIPTION	POST. REF.	DEBIT	CREDIT	
1							1
2							2
3							3
4							4
5							5
6							6
7							7
8							8
9							9
10							10
11							11
12							12
13							13

Name ______________________

PROBLEM 4.1A or 4.1B

GENERAL JOURNAL

PAGE ________

DATE	DESCRIPTION	POST. REF.	DEBIT	CREDIT

Name ______________________

PROBLEM 4.1A or 4.1B (continued)

GENERAL JOURNAL PAGE ______

DATE	DESCRIPTION	POST. REF.	DEBIT	CREDIT

Analyze: ______________________

Name ______________________

PROBLEM 4.2A or 4.2B

GENERAL JOURNAL

PAGE ________

DATE		DESCRIPTION	POST. REF.	DEBIT	CREDIT

Name

PROBLEM 4.2A or 4.2B (continued)

GENERAL JOURNAL

PAGE

DATE		DESCRIPTION	POST. REF.	DEBIT	CREDIT

Name ______________________

PROBLEM 4.2A or 4.2B (continued)

GENERAL LEDGER

ACCOUNT ______________________ ACCOUNT NO. __________

DATE	DESCRIPTION	POST. REF.	DEBIT	CREDIT	BALANCE	
					DEBIT	CREDIT

ACCOUNT ______________________ ACCOUNT NO. __________

DATE	DESCRIPTION	POST. REF.	DEBIT	CREDIT	BALANCE	
					DEBIT	CREDIT

ACCOUNT ______________________ ACCOUNT NO. __________

DATE	DESCRIPTION	POST. REF.	DEBIT	CREDIT	BALANCE	
					DEBIT	CREDIT

ACCOUNT ______________________ ACCOUNT NO. __________

DATE	DESCRIPTION	POST. REF.	DEBIT	CREDIT	BALANCE	
					DEBIT	CREDIT

Name ____________________

PROBLEM 4.2A or 4.2B (continued)

GENERAL LEDGER

ACCOUNT ____________________ ACCOUNT NO. ________

DATE		DESCRIPTION	POST. REF.	DEBIT	CREDIT	BALANCE	
						DEBIT	CREDIT

ACCOUNT ____________________ ACCOUNT NO. ________

DATE		DESCRIPTION	POST. REF.	DEBIT	CREDIT	BALANCE	
						DEBIT	CREDIT

ACCOUNT ____________________ ACCOUNT NO. ________

DATE		DESCRIPTION	POST. REF.	DEBIT	CREDIT	BALANCE	
						DEBIT	CREDIT

ACCOUNT ____________________ ACCOUNT NO. ________

DATE		DESCRIPTION	POST. REF.	DEBIT	CREDIT	BALANCE	
						DEBIT	CREDIT

ACCOUNT ____________________ ACCOUNT NO. ________

DATE		DESCRIPTION	POST. REF.	DEBIT	CREDIT	BALANCE	
						DEBIT	CREDIT

Name ____________________

PROBLEM 4.2A or 4.2B (continued)

GENERAL LEDGER

ACCOUNT ____________________ ACCOUNT NO. ________

DATE	DESCRIPTION	POST. REF.	DEBIT	CREDIT	BALANCE	
					DEBIT	CREDIT

ACCOUNT ____________________ ACCOUNT NO. ________

DATE	DESCRIPTION	POST. REF.	DEBIT	CREDIT	BALANCE	
					DEBIT	CREDIT

ACCOUNT ____________________ ACCOUNT NO. ________

DATE	DESCRIPTION	POST. REF.	DEBIT	CREDIT	BALANCE	
					DEBIT	CREDIT

ACCOUNT ____________________ ACCOUNT NO. ________

DATE	DESCRIPTION	POST. REF.	DEBIT	CREDIT	BALANCE	
					DEBIT	CREDIT

ACCOUNT ____________________ ACCOUNT NO. ________

DATE	DESCRIPTION	POST. REF.	DEBIT	CREDIT	BALANCE	
					DEBIT	CREDIT

Analyze: ____________________

#7 on Homework

Name ______________________

PROBLEM 4.3A or 4.3B

____

____

____

____

____

____

Analyze: ______________________

____

PROBLEM 4.4A or 4.4B

GENERAL JOURNAL PAGE ______

	DATE		DESCRIPTION	POST. REF.	DEBIT	CREDIT	
1							1
2							2
3							3
4							4
5							5
6							6
7							7
8							8
9							9
10							10
11							11
12							12
13							13
14							14
15							15
16							16
17							17
18							18
19							19
20							20
21							21
22							22
23							23
24							24
25							25
26							26

Name ______________________

PROBLEM 4.4A or 4.4B (continued)

GENERAL LEDGER

ACCOUNT ______________________ ACCOUNT NO. ________

DATE		DESCRIPTION	POST. REF.	DEBIT	CREDIT	BALANCE DEBIT	BALANCE CREDIT

ACCOUNT ______________________ ACCOUNT NO. ________

DATE		DESCRIPTION	POST. REF.	DEBIT	CREDIT	BALANCE DEBIT	BALANCE CREDIT

ACCOUNT ______________________ ACCOUNT NO. ________

DATE		DESCRIPTION	POST. REF.	DEBIT	CREDIT	BALANCE DEBIT	BALANCE CREDIT

ACCOUNT ______________________ ACCOUNT NO. ________

DATE		DESCRIPTION	POST. REF.	DEBIT	CREDIT	BALANCE DEBIT	BALANCE CREDIT

ACCOUNT ______________________ ACCOUNT NO. ________

DATE		DESCRIPTION	POST. REF.	DEBIT	CREDIT	BALANCE DEBIT	BALANCE CREDIT

Name ______________________

PROBLEM 4.4A or 4.4B (continued)

GENERAL LEDGER

ACCOUNT ______________________ ACCOUNT NO. ________

DATE		DESCRIPTION	POST. REF.	DEBIT	CREDIT	BALANCE DEBIT	BALANCE CREDIT

ACCOUNT ______________________ ACCOUNT NO. ________

DATE		DESCRIPTION	POST. REF.	DEBIT	CREDIT	BALANCE DEBIT	BALANCE CREDIT

ACCOUNT ______________________ ACCOUNT NO. ________

DATE		DESCRIPTION	POST. REF.	DEBIT	CREDIT	BALANCE DEBIT	BALANCE CREDIT

ACCOUNT ______________________ ACCOUNT NO. ________

DATE		DESCRIPTION	POST. REF.	DEBIT	CREDIT	BALANCE DEBIT	BALANCE CREDIT

Analyze: ____

____

EXTRA FORM

GENERAL LEDGER

ACCOUNT ______________________ ACCOUNT NO. ________

DATE		DESCRIPTION	POST. REF.	DEBIT	CREDIT	BALANCE DEBIT	BALANCE CREDIT

Name

CRITICAL THINKING PROBLEM 4.1

GENERAL JOURNAL

PAGE

DATE	DESCRIPTION	POST. REF.	DEBIT	CREDIT

Name ______________________

CRITICAL THINKING PROBLEM 4.1 (continued)

GENERAL JOURNAL

PAGE ________

DATE		DESCRIPTION	POST. REF.	DEBIT	CREDIT

Name ____________________

CRITICAL THINKING PROBLEM 4.1 (continued)

GENERAL JOURNAL

PAGE ______

	DATE		DESCRIPTION	POST. REF.	DEBIT	CREDIT	
1							1
2							2
3							3
4							4
5							5
6							6
7							7
8							8
9							9
10							10
11							11
12							12
13							13
14							14

GENERAL LEDGER

ACCOUNT ____________________ ACCOUNT NO. ______

DATE		DESCRIPTION	POST. REF.	DEBIT	CREDIT	BALANCE	
						DEBIT	CREDIT

Name

CRITICAL THINKING PROBLEM 4.1 (continued)

GENERAL LEDGER

ACCOUNT ____________________ ACCOUNT NO. ________

DATE	DESCRIPTION	POST. REF.	DEBIT	CREDIT	BALANCE DEBIT	BALANCE CREDIT

ACCOUNT ____________________ ACCOUNT NO. ________

DATE	DESCRIPTION	POST. REF.	DEBIT	CREDIT	BALANCE DEBIT	BALANCE CREDIT

ACCOUNT ____________________ ACCOUNT NO. ________

DATE	DESCRIPTION	POST. REF.	DEBIT	CREDIT	BALANCE DEBIT	BALANCE CREDIT

ACCOUNT ____________________ ACCOUNT NO. ________

DATE	DESCRIPTION	POST. REF.	DEBIT	CREDIT	BALANCE DEBIT	BALANCE CREDIT

ACCOUNT ____________________ ACCOUNT NO. ________

DATE	DESCRIPTION	POST. REF.	DEBIT	CREDIT	BALANCE DEBIT	BALANCE CREDIT

Name ______________________

CRITICAL THINKING PROBLEM 4.1 (continued)

GENERAL LEDGER

ACCOUNT ______________________ ACCOUNT NO. ________

DATE		DESCRIPTION	POST. REF.	DEBIT	CREDIT	BALANCE DEBIT	BALANCE CREDIT

ACCOUNT ______________________ ACCOUNT NO. ________

DATE		DESCRIPTION	POST. REF.	DEBIT	CREDIT	BALANCE DEBIT	BALANCE CREDIT

ACCOUNT ______________________ ACCOUNT NO. ________

DATE		DESCRIPTION	POST. REF.	DEBIT	CREDIT	BALANCE DEBIT	BALANCE CREDIT

ACCOUNT ______________________ ACCOUNT NO. ________

DATE		DESCRIPTION	POST. REF.	DEBIT	CREDIT	BALANCE DEBIT	BALANCE CREDIT

ACCOUNT ______________________ ACCOUNT NO. ________

DATE		DESCRIPTION	POST. REF.	DEBIT	CREDIT	BALANCE DEBIT	BALANCE CREDIT

Name ____________________

CRITICAL THINKING PROBLEM 4.1 (continued)

GENERAL LEDGER

ACCOUNT ____________________ ACCOUNT NO. ________

DATE		DESCRIPTION	POST. REF.	DEBIT	CREDIT	BALANCE	
						DEBIT	CREDIT

ACCOUNT ____________________ ACCOUNT NO. ________

DATE		DESCRIPTION	POST. REF.	DEBIT	CREDIT	BALANCE	
						DEBIT	CREDIT

ACCOUNT ____________________ ACCOUNT NO. ________

DATE		DESCRIPTION	POST. REF.	DEBIT	CREDIT	BALANCE	
						DEBIT	CREDIT

EXTRA FORMS

GENERAL LEDGER

ACCOUNT ____________________ ACCOUNT NO. ________

DATE		DESCRIPTION	POST. REF.	DEBIT	CREDIT	BALANCE	
						DEBIT	CREDIT

ACCOUNT ____________________ ACCOUNT NO. ________

DATE		DESCRIPTION	POST. REF.	DEBIT	CREDIT	BALANCE	
						DEBIT	CREDIT

Name

CRITICAL THINKING PROBLEM 4.1 (continued)

ACCOUNT NAME	DEBIT	CREDIT

Name

CRITICAL THINKING PROBLEM 4.1 (continued)

Analyze:

Name

CRITICAL THINKING PROBLEM 4.2

Name

CRITICAL THINKING PROBLEM 4.2 (continued)

Chapter 4 Practice Test Answer Key

Part A Matching

1. j
2. b
3. f
4. a
5. g
6. c
7. e
8. d
9. h
10. i

Part B Completion

1. debit
2. credit
3. brief or concise
4. posting references
5. ledger
6. posted
7. assets or balance sheet accounts
8. chronological or date
9. year
10. debit

CHAPTER 5 Adjustments and the Worksheet

STUDY GUIDE

Understanding the Chapter

Objectives — **1.** Complete a trial balance on a worksheet. **2.** Prepare adjustments for unrecorded business transactions. **3.** Complete the worksheet. **4.** Prepare an income statement, statement of owner's equity, and balance sheet from the completed worksheet. **5.** Journalize and post the adjusting entries. **6.** Define the accounting terms new to this chapter.

Reading Assignment — Read Chapter 5 in the textbook. Complete the textbook Section Self Review as you finish reading each section of the chapter, and the Comprehensive Self Review at the end of the chapter. Refer to the Chapter 5 Glossary or to the Glossary at the end of the book to find definitions for terms that are not familiar to you.

Activities

- ❑ **Thinking Critically** — Answer the *Thinking Critically* questions for Boeing and Managerial Implications.
- ❑ **Discussion Questions** — Answer each assigned discussion question in Chapter 5.
- ❑ **Exercises** — Complete each assigned exercise in Chapter 5. Use the forms provided in this SGWP. The objectives covered by an exercise are given after the exercise number. If you need help with an exercise, review the portion of the chapter related to the objective(s) covered.
- ❑ **Problems A/B** — Complete each assigned problem in Chapter 5. Use the forms provided in this SGWP. The objectives covered by a problem are given after the problem number. If you need help with a problem, review the portion of the chapter related to the objective(s) covered.
- ❑ **Critical Thinking Problems** — Complete the critical thinking problems as assigned. Use the forms provided in this SGWP.
- ❑ **Business Connections** — Complete the Business Connections activities as assigned to gain a deeper understanding of Chapter 5 concepts.

Practice Tests

Complete the Practice Tests, which cover the main points in your reading assignment. Compare your answers with those in the Practice Test Answer Key for Chapter 5 at the end of this chapter. If you have answered any questions incorrectly, review the related section of the text.

Part A True-False *For each of the following statements, circle T in the answer column if the statement is true or F if the statement is false.*

T F **1.** Liability account balances from the trial balance are normally transferred to the Balance Sheet credit column of the worksheet.

T F **2.** Asset account balances from the trial balance are normally transferred to the Income Statement Debit column of the worksheet.

T F **3.** The first two money columns of the worksheet contain a trial balance of the general ledger accounts.

T F **4.** Accountants use a worksheet as a means of organizing their figures quickly.

T F **5.** The ledger must be in balance before financial statements are prepared.

T F **6.** The Income Statement columns and Balance Sheet columns provide the figures for preparing the financial statements.

T F **7.** On a worksheet, the difference between the Debit and Credit Column totals in the Income Statement section must equal the difference between the Debit and Credit column totals in the Balance Sheet section.

T F **8.** After the net income (or net loss) is computed in the Income Statement section of the worksheet, this amount is transferred to the Balance Sheet section of the worksheet.

T F **9.** When the Balance Sheet columns of the worksheet are first added, the total of the Debit column should equal the total of the Credit column.

T F **10.** The balances of the expense accounts are normally transferred to the Income Statement Debit column of the worksheet.

Part B Matching *For each numbered item, choose the matching term from the box and write the identifying letter in the answer column.*

a. Worksheet
b. Trial balance
c. Debit balance
d. Fundamental accounting equation
e. Credit balance
f. In balance

________ **1.** Assets = Liabilities + Owner's Equity

________ **2.** A way to test the accuracy of the figures recorded in the general ledger

________ **3.** The term used for an account with an excess of debits over credits

________ **4.** The term used when the total of the debit amounts in the general ledger and the total of the credit amounts are equal

________ **5.** The term used when referring to an account in which there is an excess of credits over debits

________ **6.** A form used to organize the amounts needed to prepare the financial statements

Demonstration Problem

The general ledger accounts listed on the worksheet for the Green Space Design Company on January 31, 2010, show the results of the first month of operation.

Instructions

1. Record the following adjustments in the Adjustments section of the worksheet using the information below.
   - **a.** Supplies used during the month, $4,425.
   - **b.** The amount in the **Prepaid Rent** account represents a payment made on January 1 for the rent for 12 months.
   - **c.** The equipment, purchased in January, has an estimated useful life of 10 years with no salvage value. The firm uses the straight-line method of depreciation.
2. Complete the worksheet.
3. Journalize and post the adjusting entries. Use journal page number 2.

SOLUTION

Green Space Design Company

Worksheet

Month Ended January 31, 2010

ACCOUNT NAME	TRIAL BALANCE		ADJUSTMENTS		ADJUSTED TRIAL BALANCE		INCOME STATEMENT		BALANCE SHEET	
	DEBIT	CREDIT	DEBIT	CREDIT	DEBIT	CREDIT	DEBIT	CREDIT	DEBIT	CREDIT
Cash	37,350.00				37,350.00				37,350.00	
Accounts Receivable	50,700.00				50,700.00				50,900.00	
Supplies	8,700.00			(a) 4,425.00	4,275.00				4,275.00	
Prepaid Rent	126,000.00			(b)10,500.00	115,500.00				115,500.00	
Equipment	126,000.00				126,000.00				126,000.00	
Accum. Depr.—Equipment				(c) 1,050.00		1,050.00				1,050.00
Accounts Payable		80,400.00				80,400.00				80,400.00
Curtis Buham, Capital		147,600.00				147,600.00				147,600.00
Curtis Buham, Drawing	9,000.00				9,000.00				9,000.00	
Fees Income		226,515.00				226,515.00		226,515.00		
Advertising Expense	11,400.00				11,400.00		11,400.00			
Insurance Expense	12,000.00				12,000.00		12,000.00			
Salaries Expense	67,500.00				67,500.00		67,500.00			
Supplies Expense			(a) 4,425.00		4,425.00		4,425.00			
Rent Expense			(b)10,500.00		10,500.00		10,500.00			
Telephone Expense	2,625.00				2,625.00		2,625.00			
Utilities Expense	3,240.00				3,240.00		3,240.00			
Depr. Expense—Equipment			(c) 1,050.00		1,050.00		1,050.00			
Totals	454,515.00	454,515.00	15,975.00	15,975.00	455,565.00	455,565.00	112,740.00	226,515.00	342,825.00	229,050.00
Net Income							113,775.00			113,775.00
							226,515.00	226,515.00	342,825.00	342,825.00

SOLUTION (continued)

GENERAL JOURNAL PAGE 2

DATE		DESCRIPTION	POST. REF.	DEBIT	CREDIT
		Adjusting Entries			
2010					
Jan.	31	Supplies Expense	518	4,425.00	
		Supplies	121		4,425.00
	31	Rent Expense	519	10,500.00	
		Prepaid Rent	131		10,500.00
	31	Depreciation Expense—Equipment	524	1,050.00	
		Accumulated Depreciation—Equipment	142		1,050.00

GENERAL LEDGER (PARTIAL)

ACCOUNT **Supplies** ACCOUNT NO. **121**

DATE		DESCRIPTION	POST. REF.	DEBIT	CREDIT	BALANCE DEBIT	BALANCE CREDIT
2010							
Jan.	3		J1	8,700.00		8,700.00	
	31	Adjusting	J2		4,425.00	4,275.00	

ACCOUNT **Prepaid Rent** ACCOUNT NO. **131**

DATE		DESCRIPTION	POST. REF.	DEBIT	CREDIT	BALANCE DEBIT	BALANCE CREDIT
2010							
Jan.	2		J1	126,000.00		126,000.00	
	31	Adjusting	J2		10,500.00	115,500.00	

ACCOUNT **Accumulated Depreciation—Equipment** ACCOUNT NO. **142**

DATE		DESCRIPTION	POST. REF.	DEBIT	CREDIT	BALANCE DEBIT	BALANCE CREDIT
2010							
Jan.	31	Adjusting	J2		1,050.00		1,050.00

SOLUTION (continued)

GENERAL LEDGER (PARTIAL)

ACCOUNT Supplies Expense ACCOUNT NO. 518

DATE		DESCRIPTION	POST. REF.	DEBIT	CREDIT	BALANCE DEBIT	BALANCE CREDIT
2010							
Jan.	31	Adjusting	J2	4 4 2 5 00		4 4 2 5 00	

ACCOUNT Rent Expense ACCOUNT NO. 519

DATE		DESCRIPTION	POST. REF.	DEBIT	CREDIT	BALANCE DEBIT	BALANCE CREDIT
2010							
Jan.	31	Adjusting	J2	10 5 0 0 00		10 5 0 0 00	

ACCOUNT Depreciation Expense—Equipment ACCOUNT NO. 524

DATE		DESCRIPTION	POST. REF.	DEBIT	CREDIT	BALANCE DEBIT	BALANCE CREDIT
2010							
Jan.	31	Adjusting	J2	1 0 5 0 00		1 0 5 0 00	

WORKING PAPERS

Name ______________________

EXERCISE 5.1

1. ______________________

2. ______________________

3. ______________________

EXERCISE 5.2

1. ______________________

2. ______________________

Name ____________________

EXERCISE 5.3

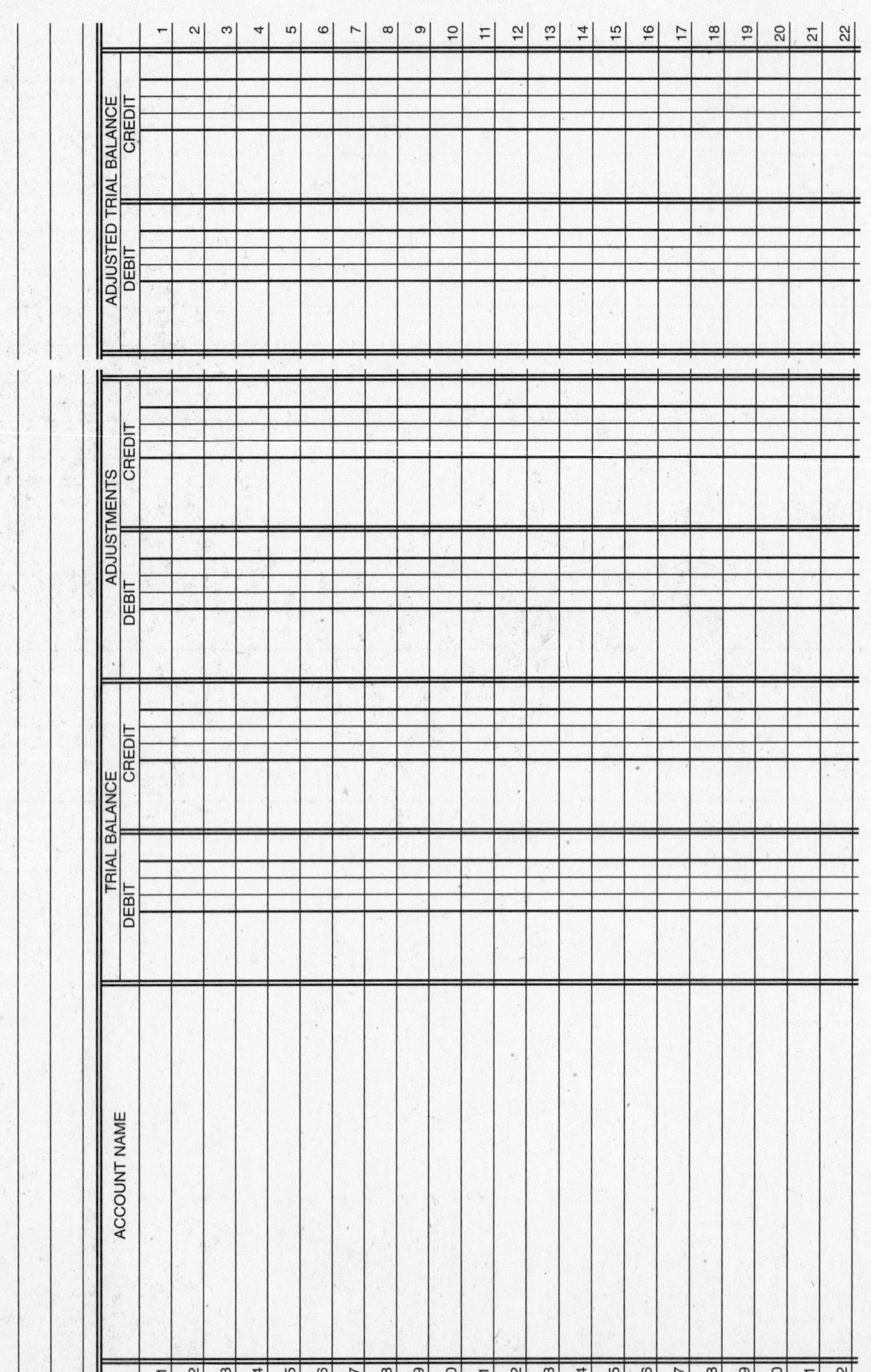

Name

EXERCISE 5.4

Name ______________________

EXERCISE 5.5

GENERAL JOURNAL

PAGE ______

	DATE		DESCRIPTION	POST. REF.	DEBIT	CREDIT	
1							1
2							2
3							3
4							4
5							5
6							6
7							7
8							8
9							9
10							10
11							11

GENERAL LEDGER

ACCOUNT **Supplies** ACCOUNT NO. **121**

DATE		DESCRIPTION	POST. REF.	DEBIT	CREDIT	BALANCE	
						DEBIT	CREDIT

ACCOUNT **Prepaid Insurance** ACCOUNT NO. **131**

DATE		DESCRIPTION	POST. REF.	DEBIT	CREDIT	BALANCE	
						DEBIT	CREDIT

ACCOUNT **Accumulated Depreciation—Equipment** ACCOUNT NO. **142**

DATE		DESCRIPTION	POST. REF.	DEBIT	CREDIT	BALANCE	
						DEBIT	CREDIT

Name ______________________

EXERCISE 5.5 (continued)

GENERAL LEDGER

ACCOUNT **Depreciation Expense—Equipment** ACCOUNT NO. **517**

DATE		DESCRIPTION	POST. REF.	DEBIT	CREDIT	BALANCE DEBIT	BALANCE CREDIT

ACCOUNT **Insurance Expense** ACCOUNT NO. **521**

DATE		DESCRIPTION	POST. REF.	DEBIT	CREDIT	BALANCE DEBIT	BALANCE CREDIT

ACCOUNT **Supplies Expense** ACCOUNT NO. **523**

DATE		DESCRIPTION	POST. REF.	DEBIT	CREDIT	BALANCE DEBIT	BALANCE CREDIT

EXTRA FORMS

ACCOUNT ______________________ ACCOUNT NO. ________

DATE		DESCRIPTION	POST. REF.	DEBIT	CREDIT	BALANCE DEBIT	BALANCE CREDIT

ACCOUNT ______________________ ACCOUNT NO. ________

DATE		DESCRIPTION	POST. REF.	DEBIT	CREDIT	BALANCE DEBIT	BALANCE CREDIT

Name

PROBLEM 5.1A or 5.1B

	ACCOUNT NAME	TRIAL BALANCE DEBIT	TRIAL BALANCE CREDIT	ADJUSTMENTS DEBIT	ADJUSTMENTS CREDIT
1					
2					
3					
4					
5					
6					
7					
8					
9					
10					
11					
12					
13					
14					
15					
16					
17					
18					
19					
20					
21					
22					
23					
24					
25					
26					
27					
28					
29					
30					
31					
32					

Name

PROBLEM 5.1A or 5.1B (continued)

ADJUSTED TRIAL BALANCE		INCOME STATEMENT		BALANCE SHEET		
DEBIT	CREDIT	DEBIT	CREDIT	DEBIT	CREDIT	
						1
						2
						3
						4
						5
						6
						7
						8
						9
						10
						11
						12
						13
						14
						15
						16
						17
						18
						19
						20
						21
						22
						23
						24
						25
						26
						27
						28
						29
						30
						31
						32

Analyze:

Name

PROBLEM 5.2A or 5.2B

	ACCOUNT NAME	TRIAL BALANCE		ADJUSTMENTS	
		DEBIT	CREDIT	DEBIT	CREDIT
1					
2					
3					
4					
5					
6					
7					
8					
9					
10					
11					
12					
13					
14					
15					
16					
17					
18					
19					
20					
21					
22					
23					
24					
25					
26					
27					
28					
29					
30					
31					
32					

Name

PROBLEM 5.2A or 5.2B (continued)

ADJUSTED TRIAL BALANCE		INCOME STATEMENT		BALANCE SHEET		
DEBIT	CREDIT	DEBIT	CREDIT	DEBIT	CREDIT	
						1
						2
						3
						4
						5
						6
						7
						8
						9
						10
						11
						12
						13
						14
						15
						16
						17
						18
						19
						20
						21
						22
						23
						24
						25
						26
						27
						28
						29
						30
						31
						32

Analyze:

Name ______________________

PROBLEM 5.3A or 5.3B

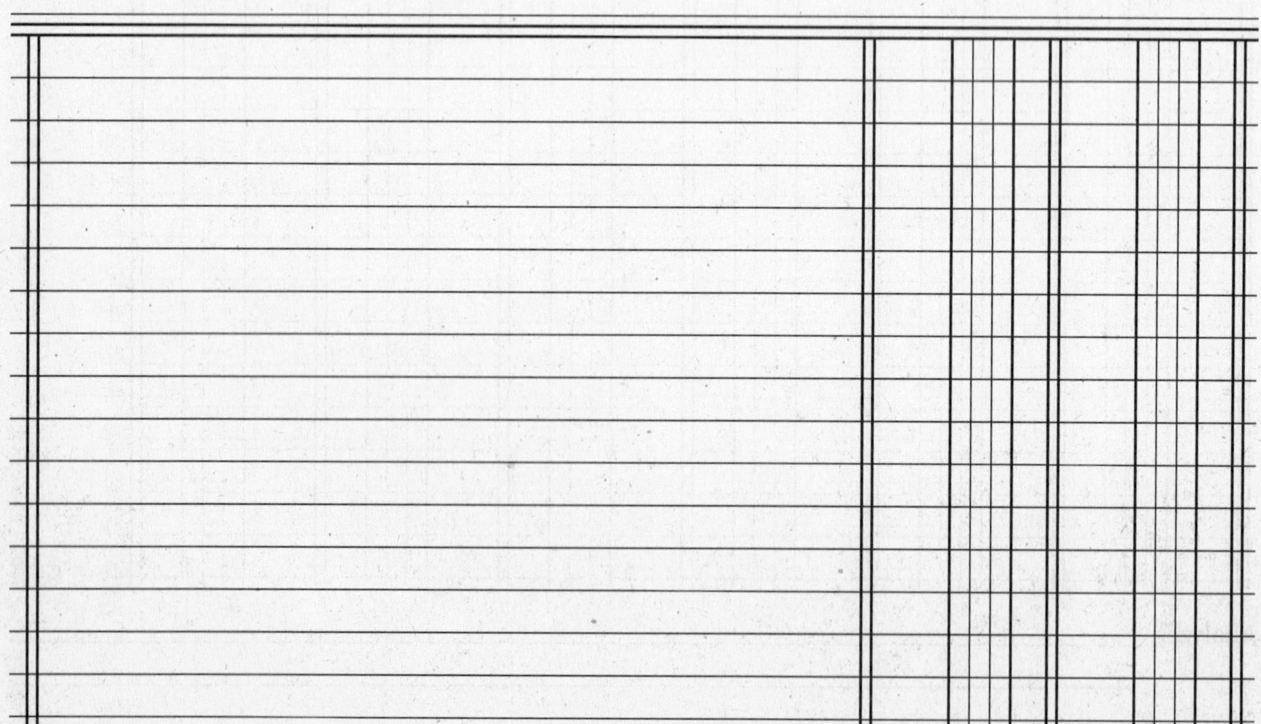

Name

PROBLEM 5.3A or 5.3B (continued)

Analyze:

Name ______________________

PROBLEM 5.4A or 5.4B

	ACCOUNT NAME	TRIAL BALANCE		ADJUSTMENTS	
		DEBIT	CREDIT	DEBIT	CREDIT
1					
2					
3					
4					
5					
6					
7					
8					
9					
10					
11					
12					
13					
14					
15					
16					
17					
18					
19					
20					
21					
22					
23					
24					
25					
26					
27					
28					
29					
30					
31					
32					

Name

PROBLEM 5.4A or 5.4B (continued)

ADJUSTED TRIAL BALANCE		INCOME STATEMENT		BALANCE SHEET		
DEBIT	CREDIT	DEBIT	CREDIT	DEBIT	CREDIT	
						1
						2
						3
						4
						5
						6
						7
						8
						9
						10
						11
						12
						13
						14
						15
						16
						17
						18
						19
						20
						21
						22
						23
						24
						25
						26
						27
						28
						29
						30
						31
						32

Name

PROBLEM 5.4A or 5.4B (continued)

Name

PROBLEM 5.4A or 5.4B (continued)

Name ______________________

PROBLEM 5.4A or 5.4B (continued)

GENERAL JOURNAL

PAGE ______

	DATE	DESCRIPTION	POST. REF.	DEBIT	CREDIT	
1						1
2						2
3						3
4						4
5						5
6						6
7						7
8						8
9						9
10						10
11						11
12						12
13						13
14						14

GENERAL LEDGER

ACCOUNT ______________________ ACCOUNT NO. ______

DATE	DESCRIPTION	POST. REF.	DEBIT	CREDIT	BALANCE	
					DEBIT	CREDIT

ACCOUNT ______________________ ACCOUNT NO. ______

DATE	DESCRIPTION	POST. REF.	DEBIT	CREDIT	BALANCE	
					DEBIT	CREDIT

ACCOUNT ______________________ ACCOUNT NO. ______

DATE	DESCRIPTION	POST. REF.	DEBIT	CREDIT	BALANCE	
					DEBIT	CREDIT

Name ____________________

PROBLEM 5.4A or 5.4B (continued)

GENERAL LEDGER

ACCOUNT ____________________ ACCOUNT NO. ________

DATE		DESCRIPTION	POST. REF.	DEBIT	CREDIT	BALANCE DEBIT	BALANCE CREDIT

ACCOUNT ____________________ ACCOUNT NO. ________

DATE		DESCRIPTION	POST. REF.	DEBIT	CREDIT	BALANCE DEBIT	BALANCE CREDIT

ACCOUNT ____________________ ACCOUNT NO. ________

DATE		DESCRIPTION	POST. REF.	DEBIT	CREDIT	BALANCE DEBIT	BALANCE CREDIT

ACCOUNT ____________________ ACCOUNT NO. ________

DATE		DESCRIPTION	POST. REF.	DEBIT	CREDIT	BALANCE DEBIT	BALANCE CREDIT

ACCOUNT ____________________ ACCOUNT NO. ________

DATE		DESCRIPTION	POST. REF.	DEBIT	CREDIT	BALANCE DEBIT	BALANCE CREDIT

Analyze: ____________________

Name ______________________

CRITICAL THINKING PROBLEM 5.1

	ACCOUNT NAME	TRIAL BALANCE		ADJUSTMENTS	
		DEBIT	CREDIT	DEBIT	CREDIT
1					
2					
3					
4					
5					
6					
7					
8					
9					
10					
11					
12					
13					
14					
15					
16					
17					
18					
19					
20					
21					
22					
23					
24					
25					
26					
27					
28					
29					
30					
31					
32					

Name

CRITICAL THINKING PROBLEM 5.1 (continued)

	ADJUSTED TRIAL BALANCE		INCOME STATEMENT		BALANCE SHEET		
	DEBIT	CREDIT	DEBIT	CREDIT	DEBIT	CREDIT	
							1
							2
							3
							4
							5
							6
							7
							8
							9
							10
							11
							12
							13
							14
							15
							16
							17
							18
							19
							20
							21
							22
							23
							24
							25
							26
							27
							28
							29
							30
							31
							32

Name

CRITICAL THINKING PROBLEM 5.1 (continued)

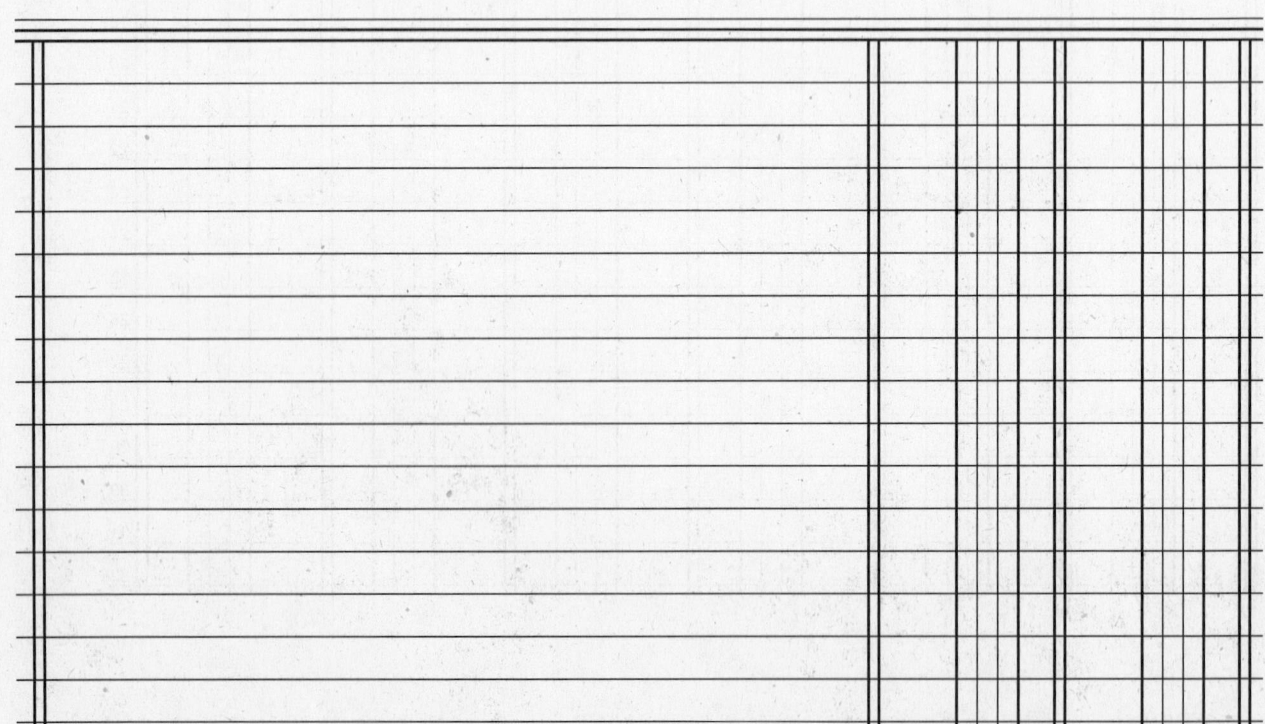

Name

CRITICAL THINKING PROBLEM 5.1 (continued)

Name ______________________________

CRITICAL THINKING PROBLEM 5.1 (continued)

GENERAL JOURNAL PAGE ______

	DATE		DESCRIPTION	POST. REF.	DEBIT	CREDIT	
1							1
2							2
3							3
4							4
5							5
6							6
7							7
8							8
9							9
10							10
11							11

GENERAL LEDGER

ACCOUNT ______________________ ACCOUNT NO. ______

DATE		DESCRIPTION	POST. REF.	DEBIT	CREDIT	BALANCE	
						DEBIT	CREDIT

ACCOUNT ______________________ ACCOUNT NO. ______

DATE		DESCRIPTION	POST. REF.	DEBIT	CREDIT	BALANCE	
						DEBIT	CREDIT

ACCOUNT ______________________ ACCOUNT NO. ______

DATE		DESCRIPTION	POST. REF.	DEBIT	CREDIT	BALANCE	
						DEBIT	CREDIT

Name ______________________

CRITICAL THINKING PROBLEM 5.1 (continued)

GENERAL LEDGER

ACCOUNT ______________________ ACCOUNT NO. ______

DATE		DESCRIPTION	POST. REF.	DEBIT	CREDIT	BALANCE DEBIT	BALANCE CREDIT

ACCOUNT ______________________ ACCOUNT NO. ______

DATE		DESCRIPTION	POST. REF.	DEBIT	CREDIT	BALANCE DEBIT	BALANCE CREDIT

ACCOUNT ______________________ ACCOUNT NO. ______

DATE		DESCRIPTION	POST. REF.	DEBIT	CREDIT	BALANCE DEBIT	BALANCE CREDIT

Analyze: ______________________

____

EXTRA FORMS

ACCOUNT ______________________ ACCOUNT NO. ______

DATE		DESCRIPTION	POST. REF.	DEBIT	CREDIT	BALANCE DEBIT	BALANCE CREDIT

ACCOUNT ______________________ ACCOUNT NO. ______

DATE		DESCRIPTION	POST. REF.	DEBIT	CREDIT	BALANCE DEBIT	BALANCE CREDIT

Name

CRITICAL THINKING PROBLEM 5.2

TO:

FROM:

DATE:

SUBJECT:

Chapter 5 Practice Test Answer Key

Part A True-False

1. T	6. T
2. F	7. T
3. T	8. T
4. T	9. F
5. T	10. T

Part B Matching

1. d	4. f
2. b	5. e
3. c	6. a

CHAPTER 6

Closing Entries and the Postclosing Trial Balance

STUDY GUIDE

Understanding the Chapter

Objectives

1. Journalize and post closing entries. **2.** Prepare a postclosing trial balance. **3.** Interpret financial statements. **4.** Review the steps in the accounting cycle. **5.** Define the accounting terms new to this chapter.

Reading Assignment

Read Chapter 6 in the textbook. Complete the textbook Section Self Review as you finish reading each section of the chapter, and the Comprehensive Self Review at the end of the chapter. Refer to the Chapter 6 Glossary or to the Glossary at the end of the book to find definitions for terms that are not familiar to you.

Activities

- ❑ **Thinking Critically** — Answer the *Thinking Critically* questions for Carnival Corporation and Managerial Implications.
- ❑ **Discussion Questions** — Answer each assigned discussion question in Chapter 6.
- ❑ **Exercises** — Complete each assigned exercise in Chapter 6. Use the forms provided in this SGWP. The objectives covered by an exercise are given after the exercise number. If you need help with an exercise, review the portion of the chapter related to the objective(s) covered.
- ❑ **Problems A/B** — Complete each assigned problem in Chapter 6. Use the forms provided in this SGWP. The objectives covered by a problem are given after the problem number. If you need help with a problem, review the portion of the chapter related to the objective(s) covered.
- ❑ **Critical Thinking Problems** — Complete the critical thinking problems as assigned. Use the forms provided in this SGWP.
- ❑ **Business Connections** — Complete the Business Connections activities as assigned to gain a deeper understanding of Chapter 6 concepts.

Practice Tests

Complete the Practice Tests, which cover the main points in your reading assignment. Compare your answers with those in the Practice Test Answer Key for Chapter 6 at the end of this chapter. If you have answered any questions incorrectly, review the related section of the text.

Part A True-False *For each of the following statements, circle T in the answer column if the statement is true or F if the statement is false.*

T F 1. Closing entries reduce the balance of revenue and asset accounts to zero so that they are ready to receive data for the next period.

T F 2. If an adjustment is not made for supplies used, the net income for the period will be understated.

T F 3. Adjusting entries create a permanent record of any changes in account balances that are shown on the worksheet.

T F 4. The Income Summary is a financial statement prepared at the end of each accounting period.

T F 5. The balance of the **Income Summary** account—net income or net loss—is transferred to the owner's capital account.

T F 6. All asset accounts are closed into the **Income Summary** account.

T F 7. To close a revenue account, the accountant debits that account and credits the **Income Summary** account.

T F 8. The total of all expenses appears on the credit side of the **Income Summary** account.

T F 9. The postclosing trial balance will show figures for asset, liability, owner's equity, revenue, and expense accounts.

T F 10. The general ledger is a continuing record.

Part B Matching *For each numbered item, choose the matching term from the box and write the identifying letter in the answer column.*

a. Closing the accounting records
b. Closing entries
c. Closed account
d. Postclosing trial balance
e. Income Summary

_______ 1. The last step in the end-of-period procedure, which shows the accountant that it is safe to proceed with entries for the new period.

_______ 2. Special account in the general ledger used for combining data about revenue and expenses.

_______ 3. Term used when referring to an account after its balance has been transferred out.

_______ 4. Journal entries used to transfer the balances of the revenue and expense accounts to the summary accounts as part of the end-of-period procedures.

_______ 5. The procedure of journalizing and posting the results of operations at the end of an accounting period.

Demonstration Problem

The Income Statement and Balance Sheet sections of the worksheet for Thomas Keller for the period ended December 31, 2010 are shown below.

Instructions

1. Journalize the closing entries on page 24 of a general journal.
2. Determine the new balance for Capital once the closing entries have been posted.

Thomas Keller

Worksheet

Month Ended December 31, 2010

	ACCOUNT NAME	INCOME STATEMENT		BALANCE SHEET	
		DEBIT	CREDIT	DEBIT	CREDIT
1	Cash			48,000.00	
2	Accounts Receivable			3,000.00	
3	Supplies			6,000.00	
4	Prepaid Rent			4,500.00	
5	Equipment			30,000.00	
6	Accumulated Depreciation—Equipment				720.00
7	Accounts Payable				7,500.00
8	Thomas Keller, Capital				54,750.00
9	Thomas Keller, Drawing			3,000.00	
10	Fees Income		45,000.00		
11	Salaries Expense	7,200.00			
12	Utilities Expense	1,050.00			
13	Supplies Expense	2,400.00			
14	Advertising Expense	2,100.00			
15	Depreciation Expense—Equipment	720.00			
16	Totals	13,470.00	45,000.00	94,500.00	62,970.00
17	Net Income	31,530.00			31,530.00
18		45,000.00	45,000.00	94,500.00	94,500.00
19					

SOLUTION

GENERAL JOURNAL PAGE 24

DATE		DESCRIPTION	POST. REF.	DEBIT	CREDIT
		Closing Entries			
2010					
Dec.	31	Fees Income	401	45,000.00	
		Income Summary	399		45,000.00
	31	Income Summary	399	13,470.00	
		Salaries Expense	511		7,200.00
		Utilities Expense	514		1,050.00
		Supplies Expense	517		2,400.00
		Advertising Expense	522		2,100.00
		Depreciation Expense—Equipment	523		720.00
	31	Income Summary	399	31,530.00	
		Thomas Keller, Capital	301		31,530.00
	31	Thomas Keller, Capital	301	3,000.00	
		Thomas Keller, Drawing	302		3,000.00

New Capital Balance:		
Thomas Keller, Capital, December 1, 2010		$54,750.00
Add: Net Income	31,530.00	
Less Withdrawals for December	3,000.00	
Increase in Capital		28,530.00
Thomas Keller, Capital, December 31, 2010		$83,280.00

WORKING PAPERS

Name ______________________________

EXERCISE 6.1

GENERAL JOURNAL

PAGE ________

	DATE		DESCRIPTION	POST. REF.	DEBIT	CREDIT	
1							1
2							2
3							3
4							4
5							5
6							6
7							7
8							8
9							9
10							10
11							11
12							12
13							13
14							14
15							15
16							16
17							17
18							18
19							19
20							20
21							21

EXERCISE 6.2

1. ______________________________ **5.** ______________________________

2. ______________________________ **6.** ______________________________

3. ______________________________ **7.** ______________________________

4. ______________________________

Name ______________________

EXERCISE 6.3

1. ______________________
2. ______________________
3. ______________________
4. ______________________
5. ______________________
6. ______________________
7. ______________________
8. ______________________
9. ______________________

EXERCISE 6.4

1. ________	6. ________	11. ________
2. ________	7. ________	12. ________
3. ________	8. ________	13. ________
4. ________	9. ________	14. ________
5. ________	10. ________	15. ________

EXERCISE 6.5

1. Total revenue for the period is ________.

2. Total expenses for the period are ________.

3. Net income for the period is ________.

4. Owner's withdrawals for the period are ________.

Name

EXERCISE 6.6

GENERAL JOURNAL

PAGE

DATE	DESCRIPTION	POST. REF.	DEBIT	CREDIT

Name

EXERCISE 6.6 (continued)

GENERAL LEDGER

ACCOUNT Elizabeth Chavez, Capital ACCOUNT NO. 301

DATE		DESCRIPTION	POST. REF.	DEBIT	CREDIT	BALANCE DEBIT	BALANCE CREDIT
2010							
Mar.	31	Balance	✔				117,600.00

ACCOUNT Elizabeth Chavez, Drawing ACCOUNT NO. 302

DATE		DESCRIPTION	POST. REF.	DEBIT	CREDIT	BALANCE DEBIT	BALANCE CREDIT
2010							
Mar.	31	Balance	✔			6,000.00	

ACCOUNT Income Summary ACCOUNT NO. 399

DATE		DESCRIPTION	POST. REF.	DEBIT	CREDIT	BALANCE DEBIT	BALANCE CREDIT

ACCOUNT Fees Income ACCOUNT NO. 401

DATE		DESCRIPTION	POST. REF.	DEBIT	CREDIT	BALANCE DEBIT	BALANCE CREDIT
2010							
Mar.	31	Balance	✔				276,000.00

ACCOUNT Depreciation Expense—Equipment ACCOUNT NO. 510

DATE		DESCRIPTION	POST. REF.	DEBIT	CREDIT	BALANCE DEBIT	BALANCE CREDIT
2010							
Mar.	31	Balance	✔			10,080.00	

Name ______________________

EXERCISE 6.6 (continued)

GENERAL LEDGER

ACCOUNT Insurance Expense — ACCOUNT NO. 511

DATE		DESCRIPTION	POST. REF.	DEBIT	CREDIT	BALANCE DEBIT	BALANCE CREDIT
2010							
Mar.	31	Balance	✔			9,600.00	

ACCOUNT Rent Expense — ACCOUNT NO. 514

DATE		DESCRIPTION	POST. REF.	DEBIT	CREDIT	BALANCE DEBIT	BALANCE CREDIT
2010							
Mar.	31	Balance	✔			28,800.00	

ACCOUNT Salaries Expense — ACCOUNT NO. 517

DATE		DESCRIPTION	POST. REF.	DEBIT	CREDIT	BALANCE DEBIT	BALANCE CREDIT
2010							
Mar.	31	Balance	✔			141,600.00	

ACCOUNT Supplies Expense — ACCOUNT NO. 518

DATE		DESCRIPTION	POST. REF.	DEBIT	CREDIT	BALANCE DEBIT	BALANCE CREDIT
2010							
Mar.	31	Balance	✔			3,900.00	

ACCOUNT Telephone Expense — ACCOUNT NO. 519

DATE		DESCRIPTION	POST. REF.	DEBIT	CREDIT	BALANCE DEBIT	BALANCE CREDIT
2010							
Mar.	31	Balance	✔			5,400.00	

Name

EXERCISE 6.6 (continued)

GENERAL LEDGER

ACCOUNT Utilities Expense ACCOUNT NO. 523

DATE		DESCRIPTION	POST. REF.	DEBIT	CREDIT	BALANCE DEBIT	BALANCE CREDIT
2010							
Mar.	31	Balance	✓			7,200.00	

EXTRA FORMS

ACCOUNT ACCOUNT NO.

DATE	DESCRIPTION	POST. REF.	DEBIT	CREDIT	BALANCE DEBIT	BALANCE CREDIT

ACCOUNT ACCOUNT NO.

DATE	DESCRIPTION	POST. REF.	DEBIT	CREDIT	BALANCE DEBIT	BALANCE CREDIT

ACCOUNT ACCOUNT NO.

DATE	DESCRIPTION	POST. REF.	DEBIT	CREDIT	BALANCE DEBIT	BALANCE CREDIT

Name ____________________

EXERCISE 6.7

GENERAL JOURNAL

PAGE ______

	DATE		DESCRIPTION	POST. REF.	DEBIT	CREDIT	
1							1
2							2
3							3
4							4
5							5
6							6
7							7
8							8

EXERCISE 6.8

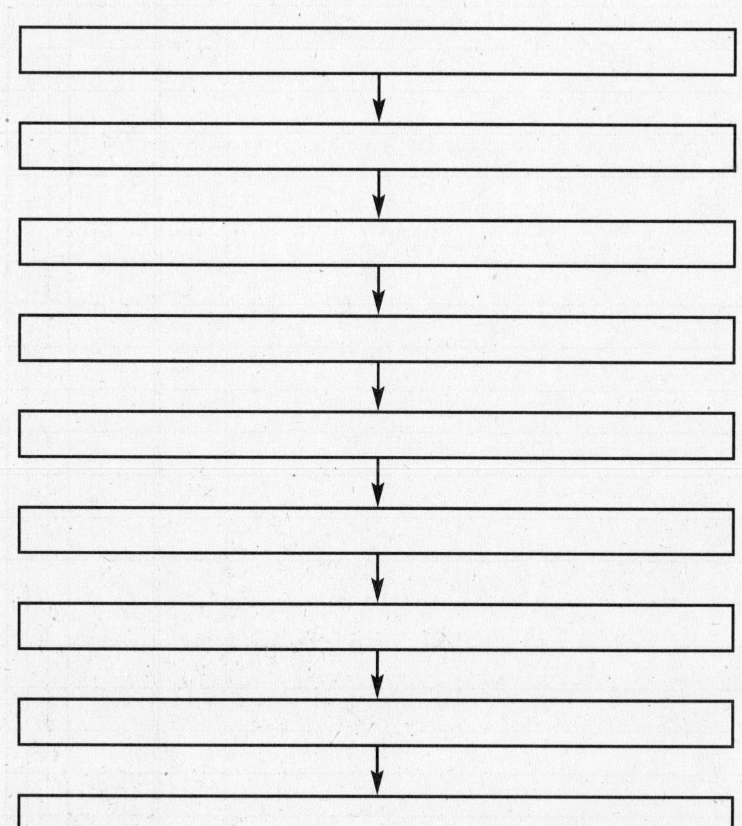

Name ______________________

PROBLEM 6.1A or 6.1B

GENERAL JOURNAL PAGE ______

DATE		DESCRIPTION	POST. REF.	DEBIT	CREDIT

GENERAL JOURNAL PAGE ______

DATE		DESCRIPTION	POST. REF.	DEBIT	CREDIT

Analyze: ______________________

Name ____________________

PROBLEM 6.2A or 6.2B

GENERAL JOURNAL PAGE ______

	DATE	DESCRIPTION	POST. REF.	DEBIT	CREDIT	
1						1
2						2
3						3
4						4
5						5
6						6
7						7
8						8
9						9
10						10
11						11

GENERAL JOURNAL PAGE ______

	DATE	DESCRIPTION	POST. REF.	DEBIT	CREDIT	
1						1
2						2
3						3
4						4
5						5
6						6
7						7
8						8
9						9
10						10
11						11
12						12
13						13
14						14
15						15
16						16
17						17
18						18

Name

PROBLEM 6.2A or 6.2B (continued)

GENERAL LEDGER

ACCOUNT **Supplies** ACCOUNT NO. **121**

DATE		DESCRIPTION	POST. REF.	DEBIT	CREDIT	BALANCE DEBIT	BALANCE CREDIT

ACCOUNT **Prepaid Advertising** ACCOUNT NO. **131**

DATE		DESCRIPTION	POST. REF.	DEBIT	CREDIT	BALANCE DEBIT	BALANCE CREDIT

ACCOUNT **Accumulated Depreciation—Equipment** ACCOUNT NO. **142**

DATE		DESCRIPTION	POST. REF.	DEBIT	CREDIT	BALANCE DEBIT	BALANCE CREDIT

ACCOUNT **Capital** ACCOUNT NO. **301**

DATE		DESCRIPTION	POST. REF.	DEBIT	CREDIT	BALANCE DEBIT	BALANCE CREDIT

ACCOUNT **Drawing** ACCOUNT NO. **302**

DATE		DESCRIPTION	POST. REF.	DEBIT	CREDIT	BALANCE DEBIT	BALANCE CREDIT

Name

PROBLEM 6.2A or 6.2B (continued)

GENERAL LEDGER

ACCOUNT Income Summary ACCOUNT NO. 399

DATE		DESCRIPTION	POST. REF.	DEBIT	CREDIT	BALANCE DEBIT	BALANCE CREDIT

ACCOUNT Fees Income ACCOUNT NO. 401

DATE		DESCRIPTION	POST. REF.	DEBIT	CREDIT	BALANCE DEBIT	BALANCE CREDIT

GENERAL LEDGER

ACCOUNT Salaries Expense ACCOUNT NO. 511

DATE		DESCRIPTION	POST. REF.	DEBIT	CREDIT	BALANCE DEBIT	BALANCE CREDIT

ACCOUNT Utilities Expense ACCOUNT NO. 514

DATE		DESCRIPTION	POST. REF.	DEBIT	CREDIT	BALANCE DEBIT	BALANCE CREDIT

ACCOUNT Supplies Expense ACCOUNT NO. 517

DATE		DESCRIPTION	POST. REF.	DEBIT	CREDIT	BALANCE DEBIT	BALANCE CREDIT

Name

PROBLEM 6.2A or 6.2B (continued)

ACCOUNT **Depreciation Expense—Equipment** ACCOUNT NO. **523**

DATE	DESCRIPTION	POST. REF.	DEBIT	CREDIT	BALANCE DEBIT	BALANCE CREDIT

ACCOUNT **Advertising Expense** ACCOUNT NO. **526**

DATE	DESCRIPTION	POST. REF.	DEBIT	CREDIT	BALANCE DEBIT	BALANCE CREDIT

ACCOUNT NAME	DEBIT	CREDIT

Analyze:

Name ______________________

PROBLEM 6.3A or 6.3B

GENERAL JOURNAL — PAGE ______

DATE	DESCRIPTION	POST. REF.	DEBIT	CREDIT

Name

PROBLEM 6.3A or 6.3B (continued)

GENERAL LEDGER

ACCOUNT Capital ACCOUNT NO. 301

DATE		DESCRIPTION	POST. REF.	DEBIT	CREDIT	BALANCE DEBIT	BALANCE CREDIT

ACCOUNT Drawing ACCOUNT NO. 302

DATE		DESCRIPTION	POST. REF.	DEBIT	CREDIT	BALANCE DEBIT	BALANCE CREDIT

ACCOUNT Income Summary ACCOUNT NO. 399

DATE		DESCRIPTION	POST. REF.	DEBIT	CREDIT	BALANCE DEBIT	BALANCE CREDIT

ACCOUNT Fees Income ACCOUNT NO. 401

DATE		DESCRIPTION	POST. REF.	DEBIT	CREDIT	BALANCE DEBIT	BALANCE CREDIT

Name

PROBLEM 6.3A or 6.3B (continued)

GENERAL LEDGER

ACCOUNT **Advertising Expense** ACCOUNT NO. **511**

DATE		DESCRIPTION	POST. REF.	DEBIT	CREDIT	BALANCE	
						DEBIT	CREDIT

ACCOUNT **Depreciation Expense—Equipment** ACCOUNT NO. **514**

DATE		DESCRIPTION	POST. REF.	DEBIT	CREDIT	BALANCE	
						DEBIT	CREDIT

ACCOUNT **Rent Expense** ACCOUNT NO. **517**

DATE		DESCRIPTION	POST. REF.	DEBIT	CREDIT	BALANCE	
						DEBIT	CREDIT

ACCOUNT **Salaries Expense** ACCOUNT NO. **519**

DATE		DESCRIPTION	POST. REF.	DEBIT	CREDIT	BALANCE	
						DEBIT	CREDIT

ACCOUNT **Utilities Expense** ACCOUNT NO. **523**

DATE		DESCRIPTION	POST. REF.	DEBIT	CREDIT	BALANCE	
						DEBIT	CREDIT

Analyze:

Name ____________________

PROBLEM 6.3A or 6.3B (continued)

GENERAL LEDGER

ACCOUNT ____________________ ACCOUNT NO. ________

DATE		DESCRIPTION	POST. REF.	DEBIT	CREDIT	BALANCE	
						DEBIT	CREDIT

ACCOUNT ____________________ ACCOUNT NO. ________

DATE		DESCRIPTION	POST. REF.	DEBIT	CREDIT	BALANCE	
						DEBIT	CREDIT

ACCOUNT ____________________ ACCOUNT NO. ________

DATE		DESCRIPTION	POST. REF.	DEBIT	CREDIT	BALANCE	
						DEBIT	CREDIT

ACCOUNT ____________________ ACCOUNT NO. ________

DATE		DESCRIPTION	POST. REF.	DEBIT	CREDIT	BALANCE	
						DEBIT	CREDIT

ACCOUNT ____________________ ACCOUNT NO. ________

DATE		DESCRIPTION	POST. REF.	DEBIT	CREDIT	BALANCE	
						DEBIT	CREDIT

Name ______________________

PROBLEM 6.3A or 6.3B (continued)

GENERAL LEDGER

ACCOUNT ______________________ ACCOUNT NO. ______

DATE		DESCRIPTION	POST. REF.	DEBIT	CREDIT	BALANCE DEBIT	BALANCE CREDIT

ACCOUNT ______________________ ACCOUNT NO. ______

DATE		DESCRIPTION	POST. REF.	DEBIT	CREDIT	BALANCE DEBIT	BALANCE CREDIT

ACCOUNT ______________________ ACCOUNT NO. ______

DATE		DESCRIPTION	POST. REF.	DEBIT	CREDIT	BALANCE DEBIT	BALANCE CREDIT

ACCOUNT ______________________ ACCOUNT NO. ______

DATE		DESCRIPTION	POST. REF.	DEBIT	CREDIT	BALANCE DEBIT	BALANCE CREDIT

ACCOUNT ______________________ ACCOUNT NO. ______

DATE		DESCRIPTION	POST. REF.	DEBIT	CREDIT	BALANCE DEBIT	BALANCE CREDIT

Name ______________________

PROBLEM 6.4A or 6.4B

	ACCOUNT NAME	TRIAL BALANCE		ADJUSTMENTS	
		DEBIT	CREDIT	DEBIT	CREDIT
1					
2					
3					
4					
5					
6					
7					
8					
9					
10					
11					
12					
13					
14					
15					
16					
17					
18					
19					
20					
21					
22					
23					
24					
25					
26					
27					
28					
29					
30					
31					
32					

Name

PROBLEM 6.4A or 6.4B (continued)

ADJUSTED TRIAL BALANCE		INCOME STATEMENT		BALANCE SHEET	
DEBIT	CREDIT	DEBIT	CREDIT	DEBIT	CREDIT

Name

PROBLEM 6.4A or 6.4B (continued)

GENERAL JOURNAL PAGE

DATE		DESCRIPTION	POST. REF.	DEBIT	CREDIT

GENERAL JOURNAL PAGE

DATE		DESCRIPTION	POST. REF.	DEBIT	CREDIT

Name

PROBLEM 6.4A or 6.4B (continued)

GENERAL LEDGER

ACCOUNT **Supplies** ACCOUNT NO. **121**

DATE		DESCRIPTION	POST. REF.	DEBIT	CREDIT	BALANCE DEBIT	BALANCE CREDIT

ACCOUNT **Prepaid Advertising** ACCOUNT NO. **131**

DATE		DESCRIPTION	POST. REF.	DEBIT	CREDIT	BALANCE DEBIT	BALANCE CREDIT

ACCOUNT **Accumulated Depreciation—** ACCOUNT NO. **142**

DATE		DESCRIPTION	POST. REF.	DEBIT	CREDIT	BALANCE DEBIT	BALANCE CREDIT

ACCOUNT **Capital** ACCOUNT NO. **301**

DATE		DESCRIPTION	POST. REF.	DEBIT	CREDIT	BALANCE DEBIT	BALANCE CREDIT

ACCOUNT **Drawing** ACCOUNT NO. **302**

DATE		DESCRIPTION	POST. REF.	DEBIT	CREDIT	BALANCE DEBIT	BALANCE CREDIT

Name ____________________

PROBLEM 6.4A or 6.4B (continued)

GENERAL LEDGER

ACCOUNT **Income Summary** ACCOUNT NO. **399**

DATE	DESCRIPTION	POST. REF.	DEBIT	CREDIT	BALANCE DEBIT	BALANCE CREDIT

ACCOUNT **Fees Income** ACCOUNT NO. **401**

DATE	DESCRIPTION	POST. REF.	DEBIT	CREDIT	BALANCE DEBIT	BALANCE CREDIT

GENERAL LEDGER

ACCOUNT **Salaries Expense** ACCOUNT NO. **511**

DATE	DESCRIPTION	POST. REF.	DEBIT	CREDIT	BALANCE DEBIT	BALANCE CREDIT

ACCOUNT **Utilities Expense** ACCOUNT NO. **514**

DATE	DESCRIPTION	POST. REF.	DEBIT	CREDIT	BALANCE DEBIT	BALANCE CREDIT

ACCOUNT **Supplies Expense** ACCOUNT NO. **517**

DATE	DESCRIPTION	POST. REF.	DEBIT	CREDIT	BALANCE DEBIT	BALANCE CREDIT

Name ______________________

PROBLEM 6.4A or 6.4B (continued)

ACCOUNT **Depreciation Expense—** ACCOUNT NO. **523**

DATE		DESCRIPTION	POST. REF.	DEBIT	CREDIT	BALANCE DEBIT	BALANCE CREDIT

ACCOUNT **Advertising Expense** ACCOUNT NO. **526**

DATE		DESCRIPTION	POST. REF.	DEBIT	CREDIT	BALANCE DEBIT	BALANCE CREDIT

ACCOUNT NAME	DEBIT	CREDIT

Analyze: ______________________

Name ______________________________

CRITICAL THINKING PROBLEM 6.1

The Style Shop

Worksheet

Month Ended December 31, 2010

ACCOUNT NAME	TRIAL BALANCE		ADJUSTMENTS	
	DEBIT	CREDIT	DEBIT	CREDIT
Cash	81,600.00			
Accounts Receivable	18,000.00			
Supplies	14,400.00			(a) 7,200.00
Prepaid Insurance	21,600.00			(b) 4,800.00
Machinery	168,000.00			
Accumulated Depreciation—Machinery				(c) 2,400.00
Accounts Payable		27,000.00		
Sarah Palmer, Capital		149,160.00		
Sarah Palmer, Drawing	12,000.00			
Fees Income		165,000.00		
Supplies Expense			(a) 7,200.00	
Insurance Expense			(b) 4,800.00	
Salaries Expense	22,200.00			
Depreciation Expense—Machinery			(c) 2,400.00	
Utilities Expense	3,360.00			
Totals	341,160.00	341,160.00	14,400.00	14,400.00
Net Income				

Name

CRITICAL THINKING PROBLEM 6.1 (continued)

ADJUSTED TRIAL BALANCE		INCOME STATEMENT		BALANCE SHEET	
DEBIT	CREDIT	DEBIT	CREDIT	DEBIT	CREDIT

Name

CRITICAL THINKING PROBLEM 6.1 (continued)

Name

CRITICAL THINKING PROBLEM 6.1 (continued)

GENERAL JOURNAL

PAGE

	DATE		DESCRIPTION	POST. REF.	DEBIT	CREDIT	
1							1
2							2
3							3
4							4
5							5
6							6
7							7
8							8
9							9
10							10
11							11
12							12
13							13
14							14
15							15
16							16

Name ____________________

CRITICAL THINKING PROBLEM 6.1 (continued)

GENERAL JOURNAL PAGE ______

DATE	DESCRIPTION	POST. REF.	DEBIT	CREDIT

ACCOUNT NAME	DEBIT	CREDIT

Analyze: ____________________

Name

CRITICAL THINKING PROBLEM 6.2

1.

2.

GENERAL JOURNAL

PAGE

	DATE		DESCRIPTION	POST. REF.	DEBIT	CREDIT	
1							1
2							2
3							3
4							4
5							5
6							6

3.

Name

CRITICAL THINKING PROBLEM 6.2 (continued)

Chapter 6 Practice Test Answer Key

Part A True-False

1. F
2. F
3. T
4. F
5. T
6. F
7. T
8. F
9. F
10. T

Part B Matching

1. d
2. e
3. c
4. b
5. a

MINI-PRACTICE SET 1

Name

Service Bu
Accounting

MINI-PR

GENERAL JOURNAL

PAGE

	DATE		DESCRIPTION	POST. REF.	DEBIT	CREDIT	
1							1
2							2
3							3
4							4
5							5
6							6
7							7
8							8
9							9
10							10
11							11
12							12
13							13
14							14
15							15
16							16
17							17
18							18
19							19
20							20
21							21
22							22
23							23
24							24
25							25
26							26
27							27
28							28
29							29
30							30
31							31
32							32
33							33
34							34

ACTICE SET 1 (continued)

Name ______________________

GENERAL JOURNAL

PAGE ______

DATE		DESCRIPTION	POST. REF.	DEBIT	CREDIT

 Name __________

GENERAL JOURNAL

PAGE ______

DATE		DESCRIPTION	POST. REF.	DEBIT	CREDIT

Name ____________________

GENERAL JOURNAL

PAGE ______

DATE		DESCRIPTION	POST. REF.	DEBIT	CREDIT

 Name

GENERAL LEDGER

ACCOUNT ______ ACCOUNT NO. ______

DATE		DESCRIPTION	POST. REF.	DEBIT	CREDIT	BALANCE	
						DEBIT	CREDIT

ACCOUNT ______ ACCOUNT NO. ______

DATE		DESCRIPTION	POST. REF.	DEBIT	CREDIT	BALANCE	
						DEBIT	CREDIT

 Name ______________________

GENERAL LEDGER

ACCOUNT ______________________ ACCOUNT NO. ________

DATE	DESCRIPTION	POST. REF.	DEBIT	CREDIT	BALANCE	
					DEBIT	CREDIT

ACCOUNT ______________________ ACCOUNT NO. ________

DATE	DESCRIPTION	POST. REF.	DEBIT	CREDIT	BALANCE	
					DEBIT	CREDIT

ACCOUNT ______________________ ACCOUNT NO. ________

DATE	DESCRIPTION	POST. REF.	DEBIT	CREDIT	BALANCE	
					DEBIT	CREDIT

ACCOUNT ______________________ ACCOUNT NO. ________

DATE	DESCRIPTION	POST. REF.	DEBIT	CREDIT	BALANCE	
					DEBIT	CREDIT

ACCOUNT ______________________ ACCOUNT NO. ________

DATE	DESCRIPTION	POST. REF.	DEBIT	CREDIT	BALANCE	
					DEBIT	CREDIT

 Name

GENERAL LEDGER

ACCOUNT ______ ACCOUNT NO. ______

DATE		DESCRIPTION	POST. REF.	DEBIT	CREDIT	BALANCE DEBIT	BALANCE CREDIT

ACCOUNT ______ ACCOUNT NO. ______

DATE		DESCRIPTION	POST. REF.	DEBIT	CREDIT	BALANCE DEBIT	BALANCE CREDIT

ACCOUNT ______ ACCOUNT NO. ______

DATE		DESCRIPTION	POST. REF.	DEBIT	CREDIT	BALANCE DEBIT	BALANCE CREDIT

ACCOUNT ______ ACCOUNT NO. ______

DATE		DESCRIPTION	POST. REF.	DEBIT	CREDIT	BALANCE DEBIT	BALANCE CREDIT

 Name

GENERAL LEDGER

ACCOUNT ACCOUNT NO.

DATE		DESCRIPTION	POST. REF.	DEBIT	CREDIT	BALANCE	
						DEBIT	CREDIT

ACCOUNT ACCOUNT NO.

DATE		DESCRIPTION	POST. REF.	DEBIT	CREDIT	BALANCE	
						DEBIT	CREDIT

ACCOUNT ACCOUNT NO.

DATE		DESCRIPTION	POST. REF.	DEBIT	CREDIT	BALANCE	
						DEBIT	CREDIT

ACCOUNT ACCOUNT NO.

DATE		DESCRIPTION	POST. REF.	DEBIT	CREDIT	BALANCE	
						DEBIT	CREDIT

ACCOUNT ACCOUNT NO.

DATE		DESCRIPTION	POST. REF.	DEBIT	CREDIT	BALANCE	
						DEBIT	CREDIT

 Name ______

GENERAL LEDGER

ACCOUNT ______ ACCOUNT NO. ______

DATE		DESCRIPTION	POST. REF.	DEBIT	CREDIT	BALANCE DEBIT	BALANCE CREDIT

ACCOUNT ______ ACCOUNT NO. ______

DATE		DESCRIPTION	POST. REF.	DEBIT	CREDIT	BALANCE DEBIT	BALANCE CREDIT

ACCOUNT ______ ACCOUNT NO. ______

DATE		DESCRIPTION	POST. REF.	DEBIT	CREDIT	BALANCE DEBIT	BALANCE CREDIT

ACCOUNT ______ ACCOUNT NO. ______

DATE		DESCRIPTION	POST. REF.	DEBIT	CREDIT	BALANCE DEBIT	BALANCE CREDIT

ACCOUNT ______ ACCOUNT NO. ______

DATE		DESCRIPTION	POST. REF.	DEBIT	CREDIT	BALANCE DEBIT	BALANCE CREDIT

Name ______________________________

	ACCOUNT NAME	TRIAL BALANCE		ADJUSTMENTS	
		DEBIT	CREDIT	DEBIT	CREDIT
1					
2					
3					
4					
5					
6					
7					
8					
9					
10					
11					
12					
13					
14					
15					
16					
17					
18					
19					
20					
21					
22					
23					
24					
25					
26					
27					
28					
29					
30					
31					
32					
33					
34					
35					
36					
37					

 Name

ADJUSTED TRIAL BALANCE		INCOME STATEMENT		BALANCE SHEET	
DEBIT	CREDIT	DEBIT	CREDIT	DEBIT	CREDIT

Name

 Name

ACCOUNT NAME	DEBIT	CREDIT

 Name

Analyze:

CHAPTER 7

Accounting for Sales and Accounts Receivable

STUDY GUIDE

Understanding the Chapter

Objectives

1. Record credit sales in a sales journal. **2.** Post from the sales journal to the general ledger accounts. **3.** Post from the sales journal to the customers' accounts in the accounts receivable subsidiary ledger. **4.** Record sales returns and allowances in the general journal. **5.** Post sales returns and allowances. **6.** Prepare a schedule of accounts receivable. **7.** Compute trade discounts. **8.** Record credit card sales in appropriate journals. **9.** Prepare the state sales tax return. **10.** Define the accounting terms new to this chapter.

Reading Assignment

Read Chapter 7 in the textbook. Complete the textbook Section Self Review as you finish reading each section of the chapter, and the Comprehensive Self Review at the end of the chapter. Refer to the Chapter 7 Glossary or to the Glossary at the end of the book to find definitions for terms that are not familiar to you.

Activities

- ❑ **Thinking Critically** — Answer the *Thinking Critically* questions for Lands' End and Managerial Implications.
- ❑ **Discussion Questions** — Answer each assigned discussion question in Chapter 7.
- ❑ **Exercises** — Complete each assigned exercise in Chapter 7. Use the forms provided in this SGWP. The objectives covered by an exercise are given after the exercise number. If you need help with an exercise, review the portion of the chapter related to the objective(s) covered.
- ❑ **Problems A/B** — Complete each assigned problem in Chapter 7. Use the forms provided in this SGWP. The objectives covered by a problem are given after the problem number. If you need help with a problem, review the portion of the chapter related to the objective(s) covered.
- ❑ **Critical Thinking Problems** — Complete the critical thinking problems 7.1 and 7.2 as assigned. Use the forms provided in this SGWP.
- ❑ **Business Connections** — Complete the Business Connections activities as assigned to gain a deeper understanding of Chapter 7 concepts.

Practice Tests

Complete the Practice Tests, which cover the main points in your reading assignment. Compare your answers with those in the Practice Test Answer Key for Chapter 7 at the end of this chapter. If you have answered any questions incorrectly, review the related section of the text.

Part A True-False *For each of the following statements, circle T in the answer column if the statement is true and F if the statement is false.*

T F **1.** A credit sale made on a credit card issued by a credit card company is accounted for in the same manner as a credit sale made on a bank credit card.

T F **2.** The accountant must keep an individual record of dealings with each customer to answer questions received from managers and salespeople of the company, from the customers themselves, and from banks and credit bureaus.

T F **3.** As proof of accuracy, the total of all customers' accounts in the accounts receivable ledger is compared with the balance of the **Accounts Receivable** account in the general ledger.

T F **4.** The **Accounts Receivable** account in the general ledger is known as a control account because it contains a summary of all activities involving accounts receivable.

T F **5.** When the balance-form ledger sheet is used in the accounts receivable ledger, the accountant figures the running balance of each account after each posting during the month.

T F **6.** The basic procedure for posting totals from the sales journal to the general ledger is not affected by the use of an accounts receivable ledger.

T F **7.** The amount of each credit sale is posted daily to the customer's account in the accounts receivable ledger.

T F **8.** The accounts receivable ledger is called a subsidiary ledger because it is only a part of the general ledger.

T F **9.** The **Accounts Receivable** account in the general ledger must be individually debited for each credit sale as it is made.

T F **10.** When a customer returns goods on which sales tax was charged, the firm gives credit for the price of goods but not the sales tax.

T F **11.** The amount of a sales allowance is debited to the Sales account because the revenue from sales has been reduced.

T F **12.** The larger the volume of credit sales, the more desirable it is to use a special sales journal.

T F **13.** The use of a special sales journal enables more than one person to work on the journals of a business at the same time.

T F **14.** The Sales Slip Number column in the sales journal shows where to look when more information is needed.

T F **15.** The use of a special sales journal makes posting individual sales transactions to accounts in the general ledger unnecessary.

T F **16.** The columns and headings in the sales journal eliminate the need for a description of each entity.

T F **17.** The special sales journal is used for recording both cash sales and sales on credit.

T F **18.** The Sales account may be credited for a sale made for cash or on account.

T F **19.** Sales on credit require debits to **Accounts Payable.**

T F **20.** Special journals are needed when the transactions of a business include groups of repetitive entries.

STUDY GUIDE

Part B Matching *For each numbered item, choose the matching term from the box and write the identifying letter in the answer column.*

a. Trade discount
b. Sales return or allowance
c. Business credit card
d. Sales tax payable
e. Open-account credit
f. Sales journal
g. Bank credit cards

_______ **1.** A reduction in price, based on volume purchased, given by wholesalers to retailers who buy goods for resale.

_______ **2.** The type of credit usually given by a business on the basis of the personal knowledge of the customer.

_______ **3.** Identification cards given by some businesses to their customers who have established credit.

_______ **4.** Identification cards used by some banks to individuals for use in making credit card purchases at participating businesses.

_______ **5.** A special journal for recording only the credit sales of a company.

_______ **6.** A liability account for recording a tax levied by some states on certain retail sales.

_______ **7.** A reduction in the amount charged to a customer who has received defective goods or services.

Part C Exercise *Answer each question about the accounts receivable subsidiary ledger account shown below.*

ACCOUNTS RECEIVABLE SUBSIDIARY LEDGER

NAME **Charles O'Brien** TERMS ________

ADDRESS **1891 Windsor Drive, Dallas, TX 75623-6998**

DATE		DESCRIPTION	POST. REF.	DEBIT	CREDIT	BALANCE DEBIT	BALANCE CREDIT
2010							
Jan.	1	Balance	✔			400 00	
	4	Sales Slip 101	S1	60 00		460 00	
	7	Sales Slip 167	S1	90 00		550 00	
	17		J1		75 00	475 00	

1. Where did the $400 entry come from?

____

____

2. How could you find a complete description of the $60 charge on January 4?

____

____

3. What was the probable reason for the $75.00 entry? How can you find out for sure?

____

____

STUDY GUIDE

Demonstration Problem

Beach Auto Supply sells tires and auto supplies to retail stores. The firm offers a trade discount of 40 percent on tires and 20 percent on auto supplies. Transactions involving credit sales and sales returns and allowances for the month of April 2010 follow, along with the general ledger accounts used to record these transactions. Account balances shown are for the beginning of April 2010.

Instructions

1. Open the general ledger accounts; enter the balance for **Accounts Receivable.**
   - 111 Accounts Receivable $61,020
   - 401 Sales
   - 451 Sales Returns and Allowances
2. Set up the accounts receivable subsidiary ledger. Open an account for each credit customer and enter the balances as of April 1, 2010. All customers have terms of n/45.

Bob's Auto Mart	$14,790
Auto Warehouse	
Jazzy Wheels and Window Tint Center	$42,000
Mike's Car Care Center	$4,230
City Auto Accessories Express	

3. Record the transactions on page 6 of a sales journal and on page 16 of the general journal. (Be sure to enter each sale at its net price.)
4. Post individual entries from the sales journal and the general journal to the appropriate ledger accounts.
5. Total and rule the sales journal as of April 30, 2010.
6. Post from the sales journal to the appropriate general ledger accounts.
7. Prepare a schedule of accounts receivable for April 30, 2010.
8. Compare the total of the schedule of accounts receivable to the balance of the **Accounts Receivable** account. The two should be equal.

DATE	TRANSACTIONS
April 1	Sold tires to Auto Warehouse; issued invoice 6701 with a list price of $40,000.
5	Sold auto supplies to Mike's Car Care Center; issued invoice 6702 with a list price of $55,200.
9	Sold auto supplies to Jazzy Wheels and Window Tint Center; issued invoice 6703 with a list price of $19,800.
14	Sold tires to Bob's Auto Mart, issued invoice 6704 with a list price of $49,200.
18	Accepted a return of all auto supplies damaged in shipment to Jazzy Wheels and Window Tint Center; issued Credit Memorandum 251. The original sale was made on Invoice 6703 on April 9.
22	Sold auto supplies to Auto Warehouse; issued Invoice 6705 with a list price of $93,480.
29	Sold tires to Mike's Car Care Center; issued Invoice 6706 with a list price of $82,230.
30	Sold tires to City Auto Accessories Express; issued Invoice 6707 with a list price of $43,230.

SOLUTION

SALES JOURNAL

PAGE 6

DATE		INVOICE NO.	CUSTOMER'S NAME	POST. REF.	ACCOUNTS RECEIVABLE/ DR. SALES CR.
2010					
April	1	6701	Auto Warehouse	✔	24,000.00
	5	6702	Mike's Car Care Center	✔	44,160.00
	9	6703	Jazzy Wheels and Window Tint Center	✔	15,840.00
	14	6704	Bob's Auto Mart	✔	29,520.00
	22	6705	Auto Warehouse	✔	74,784.00
	29	6706	Mike's Car Care Center	✔	49,338.00
	30	6707	City Auto Accessories Express	✔	25,938.00
					263,580.00
					(111/401)

GENERAL JOURNAL

PAGE 16

DATE		DESCRIPTION	POST. REF.	DEBIT	CREDIT
2010					
April	18	Sales Returns and Allowances	451	15,840.00	
		Accounts Rec./Jazzy Wheels	111 / ✔		15,840.00
		and Window Tint Center			
		Accepted return of damaged supplies,			
		Credit Memo 251; original sale			
		made on Invoice 6703 of April 9			

GENERAL LEDGER

ACCOUNT Accounts Receivable ACCOUNT NO. 111

DATE		DESCRIPTION	POST. REF.	DEBIT	CREDIT	BALANCE DEBIT	BALANCE CREDIT
2010							
April	1	Balance	✔			61,020.00	
	18		J16		15,840.00	45,180.00	
	30		S6	263,580.00		308,760.00	

SOLUTION (continued)

GENERAL LEDGER

ACCOUNT **Sales** ACCOUNT NO. **401**

DATE		DESCRIPTION	POST. REF.	DEBIT	CREDIT	BALANCE DEBIT	BALANCE CREDIT
2010							
April	30		S6		263,580.00		263,580.00

ACCOUNT **Sales Returns and Allowances** ACCOUNT NO. **451**

DATE		DESCRIPTION	POST. REF.	DEBIT	CREDIT	BALANCE DEBIT	BALANCE CREDIT
2010							
April	18		J16	15,840.00		15,840.00	

ACCOUNTS RECEIVABLE SUBSIDIARY LEDGER

NAME **Auto Warehouse** TERMS **n/45**

DATE		DESCRIPTION	POST. REF.	DEBIT	CREDIT	BALANCE DEBIT	BALANCE CREDIT
2010							
April	1		S6	24,000.00		24,000.00	
	22		S6	74,784.00		98,784.00	

NAME **Bob's Auto Mart** TERMS **n/45**

DATE		DESCRIPTION	POST. REF.	DEBIT	CREDIT	BALANCE DEBIT	BALANCE CREDIT
2010							
April	1	Balance	✔			14,790.00	
	14		S6	29,520.00		44,310.00	

NAME **City Auto Accessories Express** TERMS **n/45**

DATE		DESCRIPTION	POST. REF.	DEBIT	CREDIT	BALANCE DEBIT	BALANCE CREDIT
2010							
April	30		S6	25,938.00		25,938.00	

SOLUTION (continued)

ACCOUNTS RECEIVABLE SUBSIDIARY LEDGER

NAME Jazzy Wheels and Window Tint Center TERMS n/45

DATE		DESCRIPTION	POST. REF.	DEBIT	CREDIT	BALANCE DEBIT	BALANCE CREDIT
2010							
April	1	Balance	✔			42,000.00	
	9		S6	15,840.00		57,840.00	
	18		J16		15,840.00	42,000.00	

NAME Mike's Car Care Center TERMS n/45

DATE		DESCRIPTION	POST. REF.	DEBIT	CREDIT	BALANCE DEBIT	BALANCE CREDIT
2010							
April	1		✔			4,230.00	
	5		S6	44,160.00		48,390.00	
	29		S6	49,338.00		97,728.00	

Beach Auto Supply
Schedule of Accounts Receivable
April 30, 2010

Auto Warehouse	98,784.00
Bob's Auto Mart	44,310.00
City Auto Accessories Express	25,938.00
Jazzy Wheels and Window Tint Center	42,000.00
Mike's Car Care Center	97,728.00
Total	308,760.00

WORKING PAPERS

Name ______________________

EXERCISE 7.1

1. ______________________
2. ______________________
3. ______________________
4. ______________________
5. ______________________
6. ______________________
7. ______________________
8. ______________________

EXERCISE 7.2

	Dr.	Cr.		Dr.	Cr.
1.			4.		
2.			5.		
3.			6.		

EXERCISE 7.3

SALES JOURNAL

PAGE ______

	DATE		SALES SLIP NO.	CUSTOMER'S NAME	POST. REF.	ACCOUNTS RECEIVABLE DEBIT	SALES TAX PAYABLE CREDIT	SALES CREDIT	
1									1
2									2
3									3
4									4
5									5

Name ______________________

EXERCISE 7.4

GENERAL JOURNAL PAGE ______

	DATE	DESCRIPTION	POST. REF.	DEBIT	CREDIT	
1						1
2						2
3						3
4						4
5						5
6						6
7						7
8						8
9						9
10						10
11						11
12						12
13						13
14						14
15						15

EXERCISE 7.5

1. ______________________

2. ______________________

3. ______________________

4. ______________________

EXERCISE 7.6

1. ______________________

2. ______________________

3. ______________________

Name ____________________

EXERCISE 7.7

1. ____________________
2. ____________________
3. ____________________

EXERCISE 7.8

GENERAL JOURNAL PAGE ______

	DATE	DESCRIPTION	POST. REF.	DEBIT	CREDIT	
1						1
2						2
3						3
4						4
5						5

EXERCISE 7.9

Balance of Accounts Receivable: ______

Name ______________________

EXERCISE 7.10

GENERAL LEDGER

ACCOUNT ______________________ ACCOUNT NO. __________

DATE		DESCRIPTION	POST. REF.	DEBIT	CREDIT	BALANCE DEBIT	BALANCE CREDIT

ACCOUNT ______________________ ACCOUNT NO. __________

DATE		DESCRIPTION	POST. REF.	DEBIT	CREDIT	BALANCE DEBIT	BALANCE CREDIT

ACCOUNT ______________________ ACCOUNT NO. __________

DATE		DESCRIPTION	POST. REF.	DEBIT	CREDIT	BALANCE DEBIT	BALANCE CREDIT

ACCOUNTS RECEIVABLE SUBSIDIARY LEDGER

NAME ______________________ TERMS __________

DATE		DESCRIPTION	POST. REF.	DEBIT	CREDIT	BALANCE

NAME ______________________ TERMS __________

DATE		DESCRIPTION	POST. REF.	DEBIT	CREDIT	BALANCE

Name ______________________

PROBLEM 7.1A or 7.1B

SALES JOURNAL

PAGE ________

	DATE		SALES SLIP NO.	CUSTOMER'S NAME	POST. REF.	ACCOUNTS RECEIVABLE DEBIT	SALES TAX PAYABLE CREDIT	SALES CREDIT	
1									1
2									2
3									3
4									4
5									5
6									6
7									7
8									8
9									9
10									10
11									11
12									12

GENERAL LEDGER

ACCOUNT ______________________ ACCOUNT NO. ________

DATE		DESCRIPTION	POST. REF.	DEBIT	CREDIT	BALANCE	
						DEBIT	CREDIT

ACCOUNT ______________________ ACCOUNT NO. ________

DATE		DESCRIPTION	POST. REF.	DEBIT	CREDIT	BALANCE	
						DEBIT	CREDIT

ACCOUNT ______________________ ACCOUNT NO. ________

DATE		DESCRIPTION	POST. REF.	DEBIT	CREDIT	BALANCE	
						DEBIT	CREDIT

Analyze: ____

____

Name

PROBLEM 7.2A or 7.2B

SALES JOURNAL

PAGE

DATE		SALES SLIP NO.	CUSTOMER'S NAME	POST. REF.	ACCOUNTS RECEIVABLE DEBIT	SALES TAX PAYABLE CREDIT	SALES CREDIT

GENERAL JOURNAL

PAGE

DATE		DESCRIPTION	POST. REF.	DEBIT	CREDIT

Name ________________

PROBLEM 7.2A or 7.2B (continued)

GENERAL LEDGER

ACCOUNT ________________ ACCOUNT NO. ________

DATE	DESCRIPTION	POST. REF.	DEBIT	CREDIT	BALANCE	
					DEBIT	CREDIT

ACCOUNT ________________ ACCOUNT NO. ________

DATE	DESCRIPTION	POST. REF.	DEBIT	CREDIT	BALANCE	
					DEBIT	CREDIT

ACCOUNT ________________ ACCOUNT NO. ________

DATE	DESCRIPTION	POST. REF.	DEBIT	CREDIT	BALANCE	
					DEBIT	CREDIT

ACCOUNT ________________ ACCOUNT NO. ________

DATE	DESCRIPTION	POST. REF.	DEBIT	CREDIT	BALANCE	
					DEBIT	CREDIT

Name ______________________

PROBLEM 7.2A or 7.2B (continued)

Analyze:

PROBLEM 7.3A or 7.3B

SALES JOURNAL

PAGE ______

	DATE	SALES SLIP NO.	CUSTOMER'S NAME	POST. REF.	ACCOUNTS RECEIVABLE DEBIT	SALES TAX PAYABLE CREDIT	SALES CREDIT	
1								1
2								2
3								3
4								4
5								5
6								6
7								7
8								8
9								9
10								10
11								11
12								12

Name ____________________

PROBLEM 7.3A or 7.3B (continued)

GENERAL JOURNAL

PAGE ______

	DATE		DESCRIPTION	POST. REF.	DEBIT	CREDIT	
1							1
2							2
3							3
4							4
5							5
6							6
7							7
8							8
9							9
10							10
11							11
12							12
13							13
14							14
15							15

GENERAL LEDGER

ACCOUNT ____________________ ACCOUNT NO. ______

DATE		DESCRIPTION	POST. REF.	DEBIT	CREDIT	BALANCE	
						DEBIT	CREDIT

ACCOUNT ____________________ ACCOUNT NO. ______

DATE		DESCRIPTION	POST. REF.	DEBIT	CREDIT	BALANCE	
						DEBIT	CREDIT

Name ____________________

PROBLEM 7.3A or 7.3B (continued)

GENERAL LEDGER

ACCOUNT ____________________ ACCOUNT NO. ________

DATE	DESCRIPTION	POST. REF.	DEBIT	CREDIT	BALANCE	
					DEBIT	CREDIT

ACCOUNT ____________________ ACCOUNT NO. ________

DATE	DESCRIPTION	POST. REF.	DEBIT	CREDIT	BALANCE	
					DEBIT	CREDIT

ACCOUNTS RECEIVABLE SUBSIDIARY LEDGER

NAME ____________________ TERMS ________

DATE	DESCRIPTION	POST. REF.	DEBIT	CREDIT	BALANCE

NAME ____________________ TERMS ________

DATE	DESCRIPTION	POST. REF.	DEBIT	CREDIT	BALANCE

NAME ____________________ TERMS ________

DATE	DESCRIPTION	POST. REF.	DEBIT	CREDIT	BALANCE

Name ______________________________

PROBLEM 7.3A or 7.3B (continued)

ACCOUNTS RECEIVABLE SUBSIDIARY LEDGER

NAME ______________________________ TERMS __________

DATE		DESCRIPTION	POST. REF.	DEBIT	CREDIT	BALANCE

NAME ______________________________ TERMS __________

DATE		DESCRIPTION	POST. REF.	DEBIT	CREDIT	BALANCE

NAME ______________________________ TERMS __________

DATE		DESCRIPTION	POST. REF.	DEBIT	CREDIT	BALANCE

NAME ______________________________ TERMS __________

DATE		DESCRIPTION	POST. REF.	DEBIT	CREDIT	BALANCE

NAME ______________________________ TERMS __________

DATE		DESCRIPTION	POST. REF.	DEBIT	CREDIT	BALANCE

NAME ______________________________ TERMS __________

DATE		DESCRIPTION	POST. REF.	DEBIT	CREDIT	BALANCE

Name

PROBLEM 7.3A or 7.3B (continued)

Balance of Accounts Receivable account:

Analyze:

PROBLEM 7.4A or 7.4B

SALES JOURNAL

PAGE

	DATE		SALES SLIP NO.	CUSTOMER'S NAME	POST. REF.	ACCOUNTS RECEIVABLE DR./ SALES CR.	
1							1
2							2
3							3
4							4
5							5
6							6
7							7
8							8
9							9
10							10
11							11
12							12

Name ______________________

PROBLEM 7.4A or 7.4B (continued)

GENERAL JOURNAL

PAGE ______

DATE		DESCRIPTION	POST. REF.	DEBIT	CREDIT

GENERAL LEDGER

ACCOUNT ______________________ ACCOUNT NO. ______

DATE		DESCRIPTION	POST. REF.	DEBIT	CREDIT	BALANCE	
						DEBIT	CREDIT

ACCOUNT ______________________ ACCOUNT NO. ______

DATE		DESCRIPTION	POST. REF.	DEBIT	CREDIT	BALANCE	
						DEBIT	CREDIT

ACCOUNT ______________________ ACCOUNT NO. ______

DATE		DESCRIPTION	POST. REF.	DEBIT	CREDIT	BALANCE	
						DEBIT	CREDIT

Name

PROBLEM 7.4A or 7.4B (continued)

ACCOUNTS RECEIVABLE SUBSIDIARY LEDGER

NAME ____________________ TERMS ________

DATE		DESCRIPTION	POST. REF.	DEBIT	CREDIT	BALANCE

NAME ____________________ TERMS ________

DATE		DESCRIPTION	POST. REF.	DEBIT	CREDIT	BALANCE

NAME ____________________ TERMS ________

DATE		DESCRIPTION	POST. REF.	DEBIT	CREDIT	BALANCE

NAME ____________________ TERMS ________

DATE		DESCRIPTION	POST. REF.	DEBIT	CREDIT	BALANCE

NAME ____________________ TERMS ________

DATE		DESCRIPTION	POST. REF.	DEBIT	CREDIT	BALANCE

Name ____________________

PROBLEM 7.4A or 7.4B (continued)

ACCOUNTS RECEIVABLE SUBSIDIARY LEDGER

NAME ____________________ TERMS ________

DATE		DESCRIPTION	POST. REF.	DEBIT	CREDIT	BALANCE

Balance of Accounts Receivable account: ________

Analyze: ____________________

CRITICAL THINKING PROBLEM 7.1

SALES JOURNAL

PAGE ________

	DATE		SALES SLIP NO.	CUSTOMER'S NAME	POST. REF.	ACCOUNTS RECEIVABLE DR./ SALES CR.	
1							1
2							2
3							3
4							4
5							5
6							6
7							7
8							8
9							9
10							10
11							11

Name

CRITICAL THINKING PROBLEM 7.1 (continued)

GENERAL JOURNAL

PAGE

	DATE		DESCRIPTION	POST. REF.	DEBIT	CREDIT	
1							1
2							2
3							3
4							4
5							5
6							6
7							7

GENERAL LEDGER

ACCOUNT ACCOUNT NO.

DATE		DESCRIPTION	POST. REF.	DEBIT	CREDIT	BALANCE DEBIT	BALANCE CREDIT

ACCOUNT ACCOUNT NO.

DATE		DESCRIPTION	POST. REF.	DEBIT	CREDIT	BALANCE DEBIT	BALANCE CREDIT

ACCOUNT ACCOUNT NO.

DATE		DESCRIPTION	POST. REF.	DEBIT	CREDIT	BALANCE DEBIT	BALANCE CREDIT

Name

CRITICAL THINKING PROBLEM 7.1 (continued)

ACCOUNTS RECEIVABLE LEDGER

NAME TERMS

DATE		DESCRIPTION	POST. REF.	DEBIT	CREDIT	BALANCE

NAME TERMS

DATE		DESCRIPTION	POST. REF.	DEBIT	CREDIT	BALANCE

NAME TERMS

DATE		DESCRIPTION	POST. REF.	DEBIT	CREDIT	BALANCE

NAME TERMS

DATE		DESCRIPTION	POST. REF.	DEBIT	CREDIT	BALANCE

NAME TERMS

DATE		DESCRIPTION	POST. REF.	DEBIT	CREDIT	BALANCE

Name ______________________

CRITICAL THINKING PROBLEM 7.1 (continued)

ACCOUNTS RECEIVABLE SUBSIDIARY LEDGER

NAME ______________________ TERMS ______________

DATE		DESCRIPTION	POST. REF.	DEBIT	CREDIT	BALANCE

Balance of Accounts Receivable account: __________

Analyze: ______________________________

Name ______________________

CRITICAL THINKING PROBLEM 7.2

1. ______________________

2. ______________________

3. ______________________

4. ______________________

Chapter 7 Practice Test Answer Key

Part A True-False

1.	F	11.	F
2.	T	12.	T
3.	T	13.	T
4.	T	14.	T
5.	T	15.	F
6.	T	16.	T
7.	T	17.	F
8.	F	18.	T
9.	F	19.	F
10.	F	20.	T

Part B Matching

1. a
2. e
3. c
4. g
5. f
6. d
7. b

Part C Exercises

1. The balance was carried over from December 2009.
2. By referring to a copy of Sales Slip 101.
3. It was most likely a sales return or allowance. Refer to the January 17 entry on page 1 of the general journal.

CHAPTER 8

Accounting for Purchases and Accounts Payable

STUDY GUIDE

STUDY GUIDE

Understanding the Chapter

Objectives — **1.** Record purchases of merchandise on credit in a three-column purchases journal. **2.** Post from the three-column purchases journal to the general ledger accounts. **3.** Post credit purchases from the purchases journal to the accounts payable subsidiary ledger. **4.** Record purchases returns and allowances in the general journal and post them to the accounts payable subsidiary ledger. **5.** Prepare a schedule of accounts payable. **6.** Compute the net delivered cost of purchases. **7.** Demonstrate a knowledge of the procedures for effective internal control of purchases. **8.** Define the accounting terms new to this chapter.

Reading Assignment — Read Chapter 8 in the textbook. Complete the textbook Section Self Review as you finish reading each section of the chapter, and the Comprehensive Self Review at the end of the chapter. Refer to the Chapter 8 Glossary or to the Glossary at the end of the book to find definitions for terms that are not familiar to you.

Activities

- ❑ **Thinking Critically** — Answer the *Thinking Critically* questions for Pier 1 Imports and Managerial Implications.
- ❑ **Discussion Questions** — Answer each assigned discussion question in Chapter 8.
- ❑ **Exercises** — Complete each assigned exercise in Chapter 8. Use the forms provided in this SGWP. The objectives covered by an exercise are given after the exercise number. If you need help with an exercise, review the portion of the chapter related to the objective(s) covered.
- ❑ **Problems A/B** — Complete each assigned problem in Chapter 8. Use the forms provided in this SGWP. The objectives covered by a problem are given after the problem number. If you need help with a problem, review the portion of the chapter related to the objective(s) covered.
- ❑ **Critical Thinking Problems** — Complete the critical thinking problems as assigned. Use the forms provided in this SGWP.
- ❑ **Business Connections** — Complete the Business Connections activities as assigned to gain a deeper understanding of Chapter 8 concepts.

Practice Tests

Complete the Practice Tests, which cover the main points in your reading assignment. Compare your answers with those in the Practice Test Answer Key for Chapter 8 at the end of this chapter. If you have answered any questions incorrectly, review the related section of the text.

STUDY GUIDE

Part A True-False *For each of the following statements, circle T in the answer column if the statement is true or F if the statement is false.*

T F **1.** At the end of the month, the total of the payments made to creditors is debited to the **Accounts Payable** account.

T F **2.** The use of the balance ledger form makes each creditor's balance readily available.

T F **3.** Within the accounts payable ledger, the accounts for creditors are arranged alphabetically or by account number.

T F **4.** After all postings for a period are completed, the total of the individual balances in the accounts payable ledger should be equal to the balance of the **Accounts Payable** control account in the general ledger.

T F **5.** As soon as it is recorded in the **Purchases** journal, the amount of a purchase is posted as a credit to the supplier's account in the accounts payable ledger.

T F **6.** A payment is first recorded in the cash payments journal and then debited immediately to the supplier's account in the accounts payable ledger.

T F **7.** The procedure for posting totals from the purchases journal remains the same, whether or not an accounts payable ledger is used.

T F **8.** Freight In becomes part of the cost of purchases shown in the Cost of Goods Sold section of the income statement.

T F **9.** A receiving report is prepared to show the quantity of goods received and their condition.

T F **10.** The special purchases journal is used to record all transactions in which merchandise or equipment is purchased on credit.

T F **11.** When properly designed, a purchases journal makes posting to the general ledger unnecessary.

T F **12.** The provision in the purchases journal of special columns for the invoice number, the invoice date, and the credit terms is intended to ensure payment of the bill when it is due.

T F **13.** An account called **Purchases** is charged with the cost of the merchandise as it is sold.

T F **14.** One of the basic advantages of the purchases journal is that the posting to **Accounts Receivable** is simplified.

T F **15.** Each purchase of merchandise on credit should be recorded in the purchases journal as it occurs during the month.

T F **16.** The balance of each creditor's account in the accounts payable ledger is not computed until the end of the accounting period.

T F **17.** At the end of the month, the total of the Accounts Payable column in the purchases journal is debited to the **Accounts Payable** control account.

T F **18.** Payments made to creditors are recorded in the cash payments journal.

T F **19.** Purchases Returns and Allowances is a contra-revenue account.

T F **20.** Returns of merchandise to suppliers are recorded in the general journal.

Part B Exercise *Answer each of the following in the space provided. Make your answers complete but as brief as possible.*

A firm uses a multicolumn purchases journal with the following money columns: Accounts Payable Credit, Purchases Debit, and Freight In Debit

1. Where is the **Freight In** account shown on the income statement?

2. Where would you record the purchase of office equipment on open account credit terms?

3. The figures of which column are used to update the accounts payable ledger?

4. If the buyer pays freight charges directly to the carrier on a purchase of merchandise, where is the freight transaction recorded?

5. Which columns are totaled and summary posted to the general ledger?

6. How is the accuracy of the totals verified at the end of the month?

7. How is the **Purchases** account classified?

Demonstration Problem

Orange Office Supply is a retail business that sells office equipment, furniture, and office supplies. Its credit purchases and purchases returns and allowances for the month of October 2010 follow. The general ledger accounts used to record these transactions are given below.

Instructions

1. Open the general ledger accounts and enter the balance of Accounts Payable for October 1, 2010.
2. Using the list of creditors that follows, open the accounts in the accounts payable subsidiary ledger and enter the account balances for October 1, 2010.
3. Record the transactions in a purchases journal, page 12, and a general journal, page 30.
4. Post individual entries from the purchases journal to the accounts payable subsidiary ledger, then post from the general journal to the general ledger and accounts payable subsidiary ledger.
5. Total, prove, and rule the purchases journal as of October 31, 2010.
6. Post the column totals from the purchases journal to the appropriate general ledger accounts.
7. Compute the net delivered cost of the firm's purchases for the month.
8. Prepare a schedule of accounts payable for October 31, 2010.
9. Check the total of the schedule of accounts payable against the balance of the **Accounts Payable** account in the general ledger. The two amounts should be equal.

GENERAL LEDGER ACCOUNTS

205 Accounts Payable	$18,900 Cr.
501 Purchases	
502 Freight In	
503 Purchases Returns and Allowances	

CREDITORS

Name	Terms	Balance
Banuelos Office Supplies	n/30	
Dallas Office Supply	n/60	$2,320
Davis Office Products	n/30	
Metroplex Office Center	2/10, n/30	5,670
Tran Copy and Paper	1/10, n/30	10,910

DATE	TRANSACTIONS
October 4	Purchased desks for $9,160 plus a freight charge of $280 from Davis Office Products, Invoice 3124 dated September 30, terms payable in 30 days.
9	Purchased computers for $7,250 from Banuelos Office Supplies, Invoice 7129 dated October 4, net due and payable in 30 days.
11	Received Credit Memo 165 for $600 from Davis Office Products as an allowance for slightly damaged but usable desks purchased on Invoice 3124 of September 30.
16	Purchased file cabinets for $2,720 plus a freight charge of $124 from Dallas Office Supply, Invoice 9088 dated October 11, terms of 60 days.
21	Purchased electronic calculators for $2,200 from Banuelos Office Supplies, Invoice 2765 dated October 16, net due and payable in 30 days.
24	Purchased laser printer paper for $3,350 plus a freight charge of $320 from Tran Copy and Paper on Invoice 4891 dated October 19, terms of 1/10, n/30.
29	Received Credit Memo 629 for $440 from Banuelos Office Supplies for defective calculators that were returned. The calculators were originally purchased on Invoice 2765 of October 16.
31	Purchased office chairs for $4,200 plus a freight charge of $156 from Metroplex Office Center, Invoice 966 dated October 26, terms of 2/10, n/30.

SOLUTION

PURCHASES JOURNAL

PAGE 12

DATE		CUSTOMER'S NAME	INVOICE NUMBER	INVOICE DATE	TERMS	POST. REF.	ACCOUNTS PAYABLE CREDIT	PURCHASES DEBIT	FREIGHT IN DEBIT
2010									
Oct.	4	Davis Office Products	3124	9/30	n/30		9440 00	9160 00	280 00
	9	Banuelos Office Supplies	7129	10/4	n/30		7250 00	7250 00	
	16	Dallas Office Supply	9088	10/11	n/60		2844 00	2720 00	124 00
	21	Banuelos Office Supplies	2765	10/16	n/30		2200 00	2200 00	
	24	Tran Copy & Paper							
		Company	4891	10/19	1/10, n/30		3670 00	3350 00	320 00
	31	Metroplex Office Center	966	10/26	2/10, n/30		4356 00	4200 00	156 00
	31						29760 00	28880 00	880 00

GENERAL JOURNAL

PAGE 30

DATE		DESCRIPTION	POST. REF.	DEBIT	CREDIT
2010					
Oct.	11	Accounts Payable/Davis Office Products	205 ✓	600 00	
		Purchases Returns and Allowances	503		600 00
		Received Credit Memo 165 for			
		damaged merchandise; original			
		purchase was made on Invoice 3124,			
		September 30, 2010			
	29	Accounts Payable/Banuelos Office Supplies	205 ✓	440 00	
		Purchases Returns & Allowances	503		440 00
		Received Credit Memo 629 for damaged			
		merchandise that was returned;			
		original purchase was made on			
		Invoice 2765, October 16.			

SOLUTION (continued)

GENERAL LEDGER

ACCOUNT **Accounts Payable** ACCOUNT NO. **205**

DATE		DESCRIPTION	POST. REF.	DEBIT	CREDIT	BALANCE DEBIT	BALANCE CREDIT
2010							
Oct.	1	Balance	✔				18,900.00
	11		J30	600.00			18,300.00
	29		J30	440.00			17,860.00
	31		P12		29,760.00		47,620.00

ACCOUNT **Purchases** ACCOUNT NO. **501**

DATE		DESCRIPTION	POST. REF.	DEBIT	CREDIT	BALANCE DEBIT	BALANCE CREDIT
2010							
Oct.	31		P12	28,880.00		28,880.00	

ACCOUNT **Freight In** ACCOUNT NO. **502**

DATE		DESCRIPTION	POST. REF.	DEBIT	CREDIT	BALANCE DEBIT	BALANCE CREDIT
2010							
Oct.	31		P12	880.00		880.00	

ACCOUNT **Purchases Returns and Allowances** ACCOUNT NO. **503**

DATE		DESCRIPTION	POST. REF.	DEBIT	CREDIT	BALANCE DEBIT	BALANCE CREDIT
2010							
Oct.	11		J30		600.00		600.00
	29		J30		440.00		1,040.00

Purchases	**$28,880**
Freight In	**880**
Delivered Cost of Purchases	**$29,760**
Less Purchases Returns and Allowances	**1,040**
Net Delivered Cost of Purchases	**$28,720**

SOLUTION (continued)

ACCOUNTS PAYABLE SUBSIDIARY LEDGER

NAME **Banuelos Office Supplies** TERMS **n/30**

DATE		DESCRIPTION	POST. REF.	DEBIT	CREDIT	BALANCE
2010						
Oct.	9	Invoice 7129, 10/4/10	P12		7,250.00	7,250.00
	21	Invoice 2765, 10/16/10	P12		2,200.00	9,450.00
	29	CM 629	J30	440.00		9,010.00

NAME **Dallas Office Supply** TERMS **n/60**

DATE		DESCRIPTION	POST. REF.	DEBIT	CREDIT	BALANCE
2010						
Oct.	1	Balance	✔			2,320.00
	16	Invoice 9088, 10/11/10	P12		2,844.00	5,164.00

NAME **Davis Office Products** TERMS **n/30**

DATE		DESCRIPTION	POST. REF.	DEBIT	CREDIT	BALANCE
2010						
Oct.	4	Invoice 3124, 9/30/10	P12		9,440.00	9,440.00
	11	CM 165	J30	600.00		8,840.00

NAME **Metroplex Office Center** TERMS **2/10, n/30**

DATE		DESCRIPTION	POST. REF.	DEBIT	CREDIT	BALANCE
2010						
Oct.	1	Balance	✔			5,670.00
	31	Invoice 966, 10/26/10	P12		4,356.00	10,026.00

NAME **Tran Copy and Paper Company** TERMS **1/10, n/30**

DATE		DESCRIPTION	POST. REF.	DEBIT	CREDIT	BALANCE
2010						
Oct.	1	Balance	✔			10,910.00
	24	Invoice 4891, 10/19/10	P12		3,670.00	14,580.00

SOLUTION (continued)

Orange Office Supply
Schedule of Accounts Payable
October 31, 2010

Banuelos Office Supplies	9 0 1 0 00
Dallas Office Supply	5 1 6 4 00
Davis Office Products	8 8 4 0 00
Metroplex Office Center	10 0 2 6 00
Tran Copy and Paper Company	14 5 8 0 00
Total	47 6 2 0 00

WORKING PAPERS

Name ______________________

EXERCISE 8.1

1. ______________________
2. ______________________
3. ______________________
4. ______________________
5. ______________________
6. ______________________

EXERCISE 8.2

	Dr.	Cr.		Dr.	Cr.
1.			4.		
2.			5.		
3.			6.		

EXERCISE 8.3

PURCHASES JOURNAL

PAGE ______

DATE		PURCHASED FROM	INVOICE NUMBER	INVOICE DATE	TERMS	POST. REF.	ACCOUNTS PAYABLE CREDIT	PURCHASES DEBIT	FREIGHT IN DEBIT

EXERCISE 8.4

GENERAL JOURNAL

PAGE ______

	DATE		DESCRIPTION	POST. REF.	DEBIT	CREDIT	
1							1
2							2
3							3
4							4
5							5
6							6
7							7
8							8
9							9
10							10

Name ______________________

EXERCISE 8.5

GENERAL JOURNAL PAGE ______

	DATE		DESCRIPTION	POST. REF.	DEBIT	CREDIT	
1							1
2							2
3							3
4							4
5							5
6							6
7							7

EXERCISE 8.6

____

____

____

____

____

____

EXERCISE 8.7

a. ______________________

____

b. ______________________

____

c. ______________________

d. ______________________

____

EXERCISE 8.8

a. ______________________

b. ______________________

c. ______________________

d. ______________________

Name ______________________

PROBLEM 8.1A or 8.1B

PURCHASES JOURNAL

PAGE ________

DATE	PURCHASED FROM	INVOICE NUMBER	INVOICE DATE	TERMS	POST. REF.	ACCOUNTS PAYABLE CREDIT	PURCHASES DEBIT	FREIGHT IN DEBIT

GENERAL JOURNAL

PAGE ________

DATE	DESCRIPTION	POST. REF.	DEBIT	CREDIT

Name ______________________________

PROBLEM 8.1A or 8.1B (continued)

GENERAL LEDGER

ACCOUNT ______________________________ ACCOUNT NO. ________

DATE		DESCRIPTION	POST. REF.	DEBIT	CREDIT	BALANCE	
						DEBIT	CREDIT

ACCOUNT ______________________________ ACCOUNT NO. ________

DATE		DESCRIPTION	POST. REF.	DEBIT	CREDIT	BALANCE	
						DEBIT	CREDIT

ACCOUNT ______________________________ ACCOUNT NO. ________

DATE		DESCRIPTION	POST. REF.	DEBIT	CREDIT	BALANCE	
						DEBIT	CREDIT

ACCOUNT ______________________________ ACCOUNT NO. ________

DATE		DESCRIPTION	POST. REF.	DEBIT	CREDIT	BALANCE	
						DEBIT	CREDIT

Analyze: ______________________________

Name ______________________

PROBLEM 8.2A or 8.2B

ACCOUNTS PAYABLE SUBSIDIARY LEDGER

NAME ______________________ TERMS ______

DATE		DESCRIPTION	POST. REF.	DEBIT	CREDIT	BALANCE

NAME ______________________ TERMS ______

DATE		DESCRIPTION	POST. REF.	DEBIT	CREDIT	BALANCE

NAME ______________________ TERMS ______

DATE		DESCRIPTION	POST. REF.	DEBIT	CREDIT	BALANCE

NAME ______________________ TERMS ______

DATE		DESCRIPTION	POST. REF.	DEBIT	CREDIT	BALANCE

NAME ______________________ TERMS ______

DATE		DESCRIPTION	POST. REF.	DEBIT	CREDIT	BALANCE

Name

PROBLEM 8.2A or 8.2B (continued)

Analyze:

EXTRA FORM

Name

PROBLEM 8.3A or 8.3B

PURCHASES JOURNAL

PAGE

DATE		PURCHASED FROM	INVOICE NUMBER	INVOICE DATE	TERMS	POST. REF.	ACCOUNTS PAYABLE CREDIT	PURCHASES DEBIT	FREIGHT IN DEBIT

GENERAL JOURNAL

PAGE

	DATE		DESCRIPTION	POST. REF.	DEBIT	CREDIT	
1							1
2							2
3							3
4							4
5							5
6							6
7							7
8							8
9							9
10							10
11							11
12							12
13							13
14							14
15							15

Name

PROBLEM 8.3A or 8.3B (continued)

GENERAL LEDGER

ACCOUNT ______ ACCOUNT NO. ______

DATE		DESCRIPTION	POST. REF.	DEBIT	CREDIT	BALANCE	
						DEBIT	CREDIT

ACCOUNT ______ ACCOUNT NO. ______

DATE		DESCRIPTION	POST. REF.	DEBIT	CREDIT	BALANCE	
						DEBIT	CREDIT

ACCOUNT ______ ACCOUNT NO. ______

DATE		DESCRIPTION	POST. REF.	DEBIT	CREDIT	BALANCE	
						DEBIT	CREDIT

ACCOUNT ______ ACCOUNT NO. ______

DATE		DESCRIPTION	POST. REF.	DEBIT	CREDIT	BALANCE	
						DEBIT	CREDIT

Name ______________________

PROBLEM 8.3A or 8.3B (continued)

ACCOUNTS PAYABLE SUBSIDIARY LEDGER

NAME ______________________ TERMS ________

DATE		DESCRIPTION	POST. REF.	DEBIT	CREDIT	BALANCE

NAME ______________________ TERMS ________

DATE		DESCRIPTION	POST. REF.	DEBIT	CREDIT	BALANCE

NAME ______________________ TERMS ________

DATE		DESCRIPTION	POST. REF.	DEBIT	CREDIT	BALANCE

NAME ______________________ TERMS ________

DATE		DESCRIPTION	POST. REF.	DEBIT	CREDIT	BALANCE

NAME ______________________ TERMS ________

DATE		DESCRIPTION	POST. REF.	DEBIT	CREDIT	BALANCE

Name

PROBLEM 8.3A or 8.3B (continued)

Analyze:

EXTRA FORMS

NAME TERMS

DATE		DESCRIPTION	POST. REF.	DEBIT	CREDIT	BALANCE

NAME TERMS

DATE		DESCRIPTION	POST. REF.	DEBIT	CREDIT	BALANCE

Name ______________________

PROBLEM 8.4A or 8.4B

PURCHASES JOURNAL

PAGE ______

DATE	PURCHASED FROM	INVOICE NUMBER	INVOICE DATE	TERMS	POST. REF.	ACCOUNTS PAYABLE CREDIT	PURCHASES DEBIT	FREIGHT IN DEBIT

GENERAL JOURNAL

PAGE ______

DATE	DESCRIPTION	POST. REF.	DEBIT	CREDIT

Name ____________________

PROBLEM 8.4A or 8.4B (continued)

GENERAL LEDGER

ACCOUNT ____________________ ACCOUNT NO. ________

DATE		DESCRIPTION	POST. REF.	DEBIT	CREDIT	BALANCE DEBIT	BALANCE CREDIT

ACCOUNT ____________________ ACCOUNT NO. ________

DATE		DESCRIPTION	POST. REF.	DEBIT	CREDIT	BALANCE DEBIT	BALANCE CREDIT

ACCOUNT ____________________ ACCOUNT NO. ________

DATE		DESCRIPTION	POST. REF.	DEBIT	CREDIT	BALANCE DEBIT	BALANCE CREDIT

ACCOUNT ____________________ ACCOUNT NO. ________

DATE		DESCRIPTION	POST. REF.	DEBIT	CREDIT	BALANCE DEBIT	BALANCE CREDIT

Net Delivered Cost of Purchases

Name

PROBLEM 8.4A or 8.4B (continued)

ACCOUNTS PAYABLE SUBSIDIARY LEDGER

NAME TERMS

DATE		DESCRIPTION	POST. REF.	DEBIT	CREDIT	BALANCE

NAME TERMS

DATE		DESCRIPTION	POST. REF.	DEBIT	CREDIT	BALANCE

NAME TERMS

DATE		DESCRIPTION	POST. REF.	DEBIT	CREDIT	BALANCE

NAME TERMS

DATE		DESCRIPTION	POST. REF.	DEBIT	CREDIT	BALANCE

NAME TERMS

DATE		DESCRIPTION	POST. REF.	DEBIT	CREDIT	BALANCE

Name ______________________

PROBLEM 8.4A or 8.4B (continued)

Analyze:

EXTRA FORM

Name

CRITICAL THINKING PROBLEM 8.1

PURCHASES JOURNAL

PAGE

DATE		PURCHASED FROM	INVOICE NUMBER	INVOICE DATE	TERMS	POST. REF.	ACCOUNTS PAYABLE CREDIT	PURCHASES DEBIT	FREIGHT IN DEBIT

SALES JOURNAL

PAGE

DATE		SALES SLIP NO.	CUSTOMER'S NAME	POST. REF.	ACCOUNTS RECEIVABLE DEBIT	SALES TAX PAYABLE CREDIT	SALES CREDIT

Name ______________________

CRITICAL THINKING PROBLEM 8.1 (continued)

ACCOUNTS PAYABLE SUBSIDIARY LEDGER

NAME ______________________ TERMS __________

DATE		DESCRIPTION	POST. REF.	DEBIT	CREDIT	BALANCE

NAME ______________________ TERMS __________

DATE		DESCRIPTION	POST. REF.	DEBIT	CREDIT	BALANCE

NAME ______________________ TERMS __________

DATE		DESCRIPTION	POST. REF.	DEBIT	CREDIT	BALANCE

NAME ______________________ TERMS __________

DATE		DESCRIPTION	POST. REF.	DEBIT	CREDIT	BALANCE

NAME ______________________ TERMS __________

DATE		DESCRIPTION	POST. REF.	DEBIT	CREDIT	BALANCE

NAME ______________________ TERMS __________

DATE		DESCRIPTION	POST. REF.	DEBIT	CREDIT	BALANCE

Name ____________________

CRITICAL THINKING PROBLEM 8.1 (continued)

ACCOUNTS PAYABLE SUBSIDIARY LEDGER

NAME ____________________ TERMS ________

DATE		DESCRIPTION	POST. REF.	DEBIT	CREDIT	BALANCE

NAME ____________________ TERMS ________

DATE		DESCRIPTION	POST. REF.	DEBIT	CREDIT	BALANCE

ACCOUNTS RECEIVABLE SUBSIDIARY LEDGER

NAME ____________________ TERMS ________

DATE		DESCRIPTION	POST. REF.	DEBIT	CREDIT	BALANCE

NAME ____________________ TERMS ________

DATE		DESCRIPTION	POST. REF.	DEBIT	CREDIT	BALANCE

NAME ____________________ TERMS ________

DATE		DESCRIPTION	POST. REF.	DEBIT	CREDIT	BALANCE

Name

CRITICAL THINKING PROBLEM 8.1 (continued)

ACCOUNTS RECEIVABLE SUBSIDIARY LEDGER

NAME ______ TERMS ______

DATE		DESCRIPTION	POST. REF.	DEBIT	CREDIT	BALANCE

NAME ______ TERMS ______

DATE		DESCRIPTION	POST. REF.	DEBIT	CREDIT	BALANCE

NAME ______ TERMS ______

DATE		DESCRIPTION	POST. REF.	DEBIT	CREDIT	BALANCE

NAME ______ TERMS ______

DATE		DESCRIPTION	POST. REF.	DEBIT	CREDIT	BALANCE

NAME ______ TERMS ______

DATE		DESCRIPTION	POST. REF.	DEBIT	CREDIT	BALANCE

NAME ______ TERMS ______

DATE		DESCRIPTION	POST. REF.	DEBIT	CREDIT	BALANCE

Name

CRITICAL THINKING PROBLEM 8.1 (continued)

ACCOUNTS RECEIVABLE SUBSIDIARY LEDGER

NAME TERMS

DATE		DESCRIPTION	POST. REF.	DEBIT	CREDIT	BALANCE

NAME TERMS

DATE		DESCRIPTION	POST. REF.	DEBIT	CREDIT	BALANCE

GENERAL LEDGER

ACCOUNT ACCOUNT NO.

DATE		DESCRIPTION	POST. REF.	DEBIT	CREDIT	BALANCE DEBIT	BALANCE CREDIT

ACCOUNT ACCOUNT NO.

DATE		DESCRIPTION	POST. REF.	DEBIT	CREDIT	BALANCE DEBIT	BALANCE CREDIT

ACCOUNT ACCOUNT NO.

DATE		DESCRIPTION	POST. REF.	DEBIT	CREDIT	BALANCE DEBIT	BALANCE CREDIT

ACCOUNT ACCOUNT NO.

DATE		DESCRIPTION	POST. REF.	DEBIT	CREDIT	BALANCE DEBIT	BALANCE CREDIT

Name

CRITICAL THINKING PROBLEM 8.1 (continued)

GENERAL LEDGER

ACCOUNT ______ ACCOUNT NO. ______

DATE		DESCRIPTION	POST. REF.	DEBIT	CREDIT	BALANCE DEBIT	BALANCE CREDIT

ACCOUNT ______ ACCOUNT NO. ______

DATE		DESCRIPTION	POST. REF.	DEBIT	CREDIT	BALANCE DEBIT	BALANCE CREDIT

Name

CRITICAL THINKING PROBLEM 8.1 (continued)

Analyze:

Name

CRITICAL THINKING PROBLEM 8.2

Chapter 8 Practice Test Answer Key

Part A True-False

1.	**T**	**11.**	**F**
2.	**T**	**12.**	**T**
3.	**T**	**13.**	**F**
4.	**T**	**14.**	**F**
5.	**T**	**15.**	**T**
6.	**T**	**16.**	**F**
7.	**T**	**17.**	**F**
8.	**T**	**18.**	**T**
9.	**T**	**19.**	**F**
10.	**F**	**20.**	**T**

Part B Exercises

1. In the Cost of Goods Sold Section.
2. The General Journal.
3. The Accounts Payable Column.
4. It is not recorded in the purchases journal at all; it is entered in the cash payments journal.
5. All Columns.
6. Accounts Payable Credit = Purchases Debit + Freight In Debit.
7. An Expense.

CHAPTER 9 Cash Receipts, Cash Payments, and Banking Procedures

STUDY GUIDE

Understanding the Chapter

Objectives

1. Record cash receipts in a cash receipts journal. **2.** Account for cash short or over. **3.** Post from the cash receipts journal to subsidiary and general ledgers. **4.** Record cash payments in a cash payments journal. **5.** Post from the cash payments journal to subsidiary and general ledgers. **6.** Demonstrate a knowledge of procedures for a petty cash fund. **7.** Demonstrate a knowledge of internal control routines for cash. **8.** Write a check, endorse checks, prepare a bank deposit slip, and maintain a checkbook balance. **9.** Reconcile the monthly bank statement. **10.** Record any adjusting entries required from the bank reconciliation. **11.** Define accounting terms new to this chapter.

Reading Assignment

Read Chapter 9 in the textbook. Complete the Section Self Review as you finish reading each section of the chapter, and the Comprehensive Self Review at the end of the chapter. Refer to the Chapter 9 Glossary or to the Glossary at the end of the book to find definitions for terms that are not familiar to you.

Activities

- ❑ **Thinking Critically** — Answer the *Thinking Critically* questions for H&R Block and Managerial Implications
- ❑ **Discussion Questions** — Answer each assigned review question in Chapter 9.
- ❑ **Exercises** — Complete each assigned exercise in Chapter 9. Use the forms provided in this SGWP. The objectives covered by an exercise are given after the exercise number. If you need help with an exercise, review the portion of the chapter related to the objective(s) covered.
- ❑ **Problems A/B** — Complete each assigned problem in Chapter 9. Use the forms provided in this SGWP. The objectives covered by a problem are given after the problem number. If you need help with a problem review the portion of the chapter related to the objective(s) covered.
- ❑ **Critical Thinking Problems** — Complete the critical thinking problems as assigned. Use the forms provided in this SGWP.
- ❑ **Business Connections** — Complete the Business Connections activities as assigned to gain a deeper understanding of Chapter 9 concepts.

Practice Tests

Complete the Practice Tests, which cover the main points in your reading assignment. Compare your answers with those in the Practice Test Answer Key for Chapter 9 at the end of this chapter. If you have answered any questions incorrectly, review the related section of the text.

STUDY GUIDE

Part A True-False *For each of the following statements, circle T in the answer column if the statement is true or F if the statement is false.*

T F **1.** The money represented by deposited checks becomes available for use as soon as the deposit is made.

T F **2.** Checks made payable to cash or to bearer need not be endorsed when deposited.

T F **3.** Checks can be identified on a deposit slip by the use of the American Bankers Association transit numbers.

T F **4.** Only checks are listed on the deposit slip.

T F **5.** Cash received by mail should be deposited by the same person who accepts and lists it.

T F **6.** **Cash Short or Over** is a general ledger account that normally has a credit balance because cash tends to be short more often than over.

T F **7.** The **Sales Tax Payable** account represents a liability of the business.

T F **8.** The title of a special journal makes it possible to omit much of the explanation that would be needed in a general journal entry.

T F **9.** A cash investment by the owner in a business should be recorded in the cash receipts journal.

T F **10.** Account numbers are recorded below the totals of each column as each summary posting from the cash payments journal is completed.

T F **11.** The Other Accounts Debit column of a cash payments journal is used to record the debits that are to be posted individually.

T F **12.** The abbreviation "CP5" in the Posting Reference column of a ledger account indicates that the posting was made from the cash payments journal on the fifth day of the month.

T F **13.** When posting from the cash payments journal at the end of the month, the accountant posts the total cash payments as a single credit to cash.

T F **14.** The check to replenish the petty cash fund is written for an amount sufficient to restore the fund to its established balance.

T F **15.** The petty cash analysis sheet is a memorandum record of petty cash payments rather than a record of original entry.

T F **16.** Each petty cash payment is entered separately in the cash payments journal.

T F **17.** An adequate system of internal control over cash will provide for safeguarding both incoming and outgoing funds.

T F **18.** Correct internal control procedures require that the approval for paying all bills, writing all checks, and signing all checks should be the responsibility of the same person.

T F **19.** Except for petty cash payments, all payments should be made by check.

T F **20.** Internal controls are not necessary if payments are made by check.

T F **21.** The best form of endorsement for business purposes is the restrictive endorsement, which limits the use of the check to a stated purpose.

Part B Matching *For each numbered item, choose the matching term from the box and write the identifying letter in the answer column.*

a.	NSF Check
b.	Deposit in Transit
c.	Outstanding checks
d.	Bank reconciliation
e.	Bank statement
f.	Stub
g.	Payee
h.	Drawer
i.	Deposit slip
j.	Promissory note
k.	Summary posting
l.	Internal control

_______ **1.** The process by which a single amount is posted instead of each entry being posted separately.

_______ **2.** A system designed to safeguard assets and to help ensure the accuracy and reliability of accounting records.

_______ **3.** A written promise to pay a specific amount at a specific time.

_______ **4.** Receipts that have been deposited and entered in the firm's accounting records but have not yet been entered on the bank's records.

_______ **5.** A form received from the bank showing all transactions recorded in the depositor's account during the month.

_______ **6.** Checks issued and recorded that have not been paid by the bank.

_______ **7.** A form on which all cash and cash items are listed before they are placed in the bank.

_______ **8.** The process of determining why a difference exists between the firm's accounting records and the bank records and bringing them into balance.

_______ **9.** The firm or person designated on the check to receive payment.

_______ **10.** The form that contains all the information necessary for journalizing a transaction paid by check.

_______ **11.** The person or firm from whose account a check is to be paid.

_______ **12.** A check on which payment has been refused because of too few funds in the issuer's account.

Demonstration Problem

On June 2, 2010, Yorba Linda Legal Services received its May bank statement. Enclosed with the bank statement, shown below, was a debit memorandum for $140 for a NSF check issued by James White. The firm's checkbook contained the information shown below about deposits made and checks issued during May. The balance of the **Cash** account and the checkbook on May 31 was $36,885.

Instructions

1. Prepare a bank reconciliation statement for Yorba Linda Legal Services as of May 31, 2010.
2. Record general journal entries for any items on the bank reconciliation statement that must be journalized. Date the entries May 31, 2010. Number the journal as page 17.

Checkbook information:

May 1	Balance	$40,592
1	Check 177	400
1	Check 178	800
7	Deposit	2,600
8	Check 179	900
12	Check 180	6,000
17	Check 181	720
19	Deposit	680
22	Check 182	88
23	Check 183	592
26	Deposit	1,748
29	Check 184	160
31	Deposit	925
		$36,885

First California National Bank

Yorba Linda Legal Services
4312 Brea Street
Yorba Linda, CA 92885-8714

ACCOUNT NO. 77546798
PERIOD ENDING: May 31, 2010

CHECK NO.	AMOUNT	DATE	DESCRIPTION	BALANCE
			Balance last statement	40,592.00
177	400.00	6/1		40,192.00
178	800.00	6/4		39,392.00
	2,600.00	6/7	Deposit	41,992.00
179	900.00	6/8		41,092.00
180	6,000.00	6/12		35,092.00
	140.00	6/12	Debit Memorandum	34,952.00
181	720.00	6/17		34,232.00
	680.00	6/19	Deposit	34,912.00
182	88.00	6/22		34,824.00
	1,748.00	6/26	Deposit	36,572.00
	15.00	6/29	Service Charge	36,557.00

SOLUTION

Yorba Linda Legal Services

Bank Reconciliation Statement

May 31, 2010

Balance on Bank Statement		36,557.00
Additions:		
Deposit of May 31 in Transit		925.00
		37,482.00
Deductions for Outstanding Checks:		
Check 183 of May 23	592.00	
Check 184 of May 29	160.00	
Total Checks Outstanding		752.00
Adjusted Bank Balance		36,730.00
Balance in Books		36,885.00
Deductions:		
NSF Check	140.00	
Bank Service Charge	15.00	155.00
Adjusted Book Balance		36,730.00

GENERAL JOURNAL PAGE 17

	DATE		DESCRIPTION	POST. REF.	DEBIT	CREDIT	
1	2010						1
2	May	31	Accounts Receivable/James White		140.00		2
3			Cash			140.00	3
4			To record NSF check returned by bank				4
5							5
6		31	Miscellaneous Expense		15.00		6
7			Cash			15.00	7
8			To record bank service charge for May				8
9							9

WORKING PAPERS

Name ______________________________

EXERCISES 9.1, 9.2

EXERCISE 9.1

CASH RECEIPTS JOURNAL

PAGE ______

DATE	DESCRIPTION	POST. REF.	ACCOUNTS RECEIVABLE CREDIT	SALES TAX PAYABLE CREDIT	SALES CREDIT	OTHER ACCOUNTS CREDIT			CASH DEBIT
						ACCOUNT NAME	POST. REF.	AMOUNT	

EXERCISE 9.2

CASH PAYMENTS JOURNAL

PAGE ______

DATE	CK. NO.	DESCRIPTION	POST. REF.	ACCOUNTS PAYABLE DEBIT	OTHER ACCOUNTS DEBIT			PURCHASES DISCOUNT CREDIT	CASH CREDIT
					ACCOUNT NAME	POST. REF.	AMOUNT		

Name ______________________

EXERCISES 9.3, 9.4

EXERCISE 9.3

CASH PAYMENTS JOURNAL

PAGE ______

DATE		CK. NO.	DESCRIPTION	POST. REF.	ACCOUNTS PAYABLE DEBIT	OTHER ACCOUNTS DEBIT			PURCHASES DISCOUNT CREDIT	CASH CREDIT
						ACCOUNT NAME	POST. REF.	AMOUNT		

EXERCISE 9.4

CASH PAYMENTS JOURNAL

PAGE ______

DATE		CK. NO.	DESCRIPTION	POST. REF.	ACCOUNTS PAYABLE DEBIT	OTHER ACCOUNTS DEBIT			PURCHASES DISCOUNT CREDIT	CASH CREDIT
						ACCOUNT NAME	POST. REF.	AMOUNT		

Name

EXERCISE 9.5

GENERAL JOURNAL

PAGE

DATE		DESCRIPTION	POST. REF.	DEBIT	CREDIT

Name ______________________

EXERCISE 9.6

	Bank Balance	Book Balance	Accounting Entry
1.			
2.			
3.			
4.			
5.			
6.			
7.			

EXTRA FORM

GENERAL JOURNAL

PAGE ______

	DATE		DESCRIPTION	POST. REF.	DEBIT	CREDIT	
1							1
2							2
3							3
4							4
5							5
6							6
7							7
8							8
9							9
10							10
11							11
12							12
13							13
14							14

Name

EXERCISE 9.7

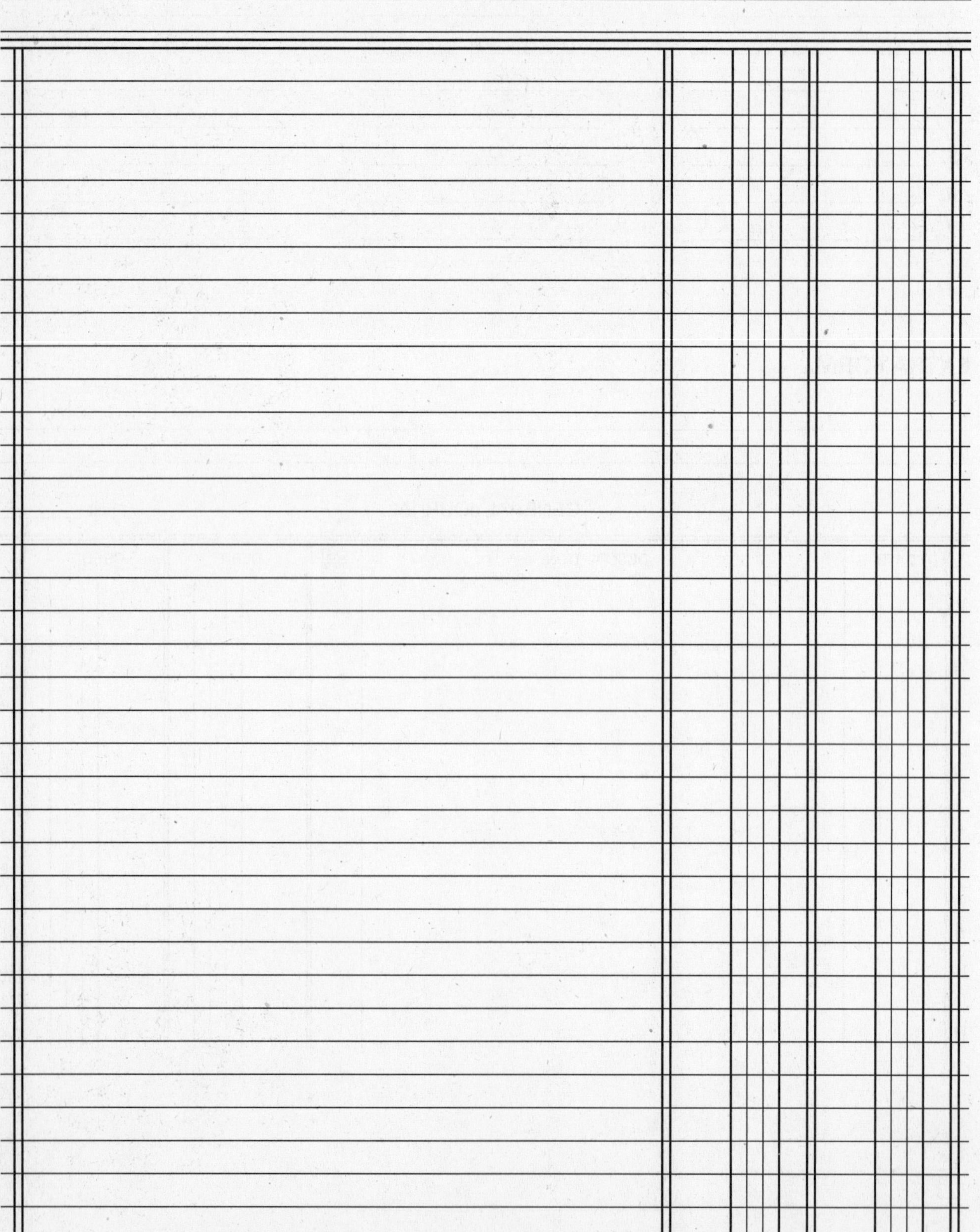

Name ______________________________

EXERCISE 9.7 (continued)

GENERAL JOURNAL PAGE ______

	DATE	DESCRIPTION	POST. REF.	DEBIT	CREDIT	
1						1
2						2
3						3
4						4
5						5
6						6
7						7
8						8
9						9
10						10
11						11
12						12

Name ____________________

PROBLEM 9.1A or 9.1B

CASH RECEIPTS JOURNAL

PAGE ____

DATE	DESCRIPTION	POST. REF.	ACCOUNTS RECEIVABLE CREDIT	SALES TAX PAYABLE CREDIT	SALES CREDIT	OTHER ACCOUNTS CREDIT			CASH DEBIT
						ACCOUNT NAME	POST. REF.	AMOUNT	

Name ______________________

PROBLEM 9.1A or 9.1B (continued)

GENERAL LEDGER

ACCOUNT ______________________ ACCOUNT NO. ________

DATE	DESCRIPTION	POST. REF.	DEBIT	CREDIT	BALANCE	
					DEBIT	CREDIT

ACCOUNT ______________________ ACCOUNT NO. ________

DATE	DESCRIPTION	POST. REF.	DEBIT	CREDIT	BALANCE	
					DEBIT	CREDIT

ACCOUNT ______________________ ACCOUNT NO. ________

DATE	DESCRIPTION	POST. REF.	DEBIT	CREDIT	BALANCE	
					DEBIT	CREDIT

ACCOUNT ______________________ ACCOUNT NO. ________

DATE	DESCRIPTION	POST. REF.	DEBIT	CREDIT	BALANCE	
					DEBIT	CREDIT

ACCOUNT ______________________ ACCOUNT NO. ________

DATE	DESCRIPTION	POST. REF.	DEBIT	CREDIT	BALANCE	
					DEBIT	CREDIT

Name ____________________

PROBLEM 9.1A or 9.1B (continued)

GENERAL LEDGER

ACCOUNT ____________________ ACCOUNT NO. __________

DATE	DESCRIPTION	POST. REF.	DEBIT	CREDIT	BALANCE	
					DEBIT	CREDIT

ACCOUNT ____________________ ACCOUNT NO. __________

DATE	DESCRIPTION	POST. REF.	DEBIT	CREDIT	BALANCE	
					DEBIT	CREDIT

ACCOUNT ____________________ ACCOUNT NO. __________

DATE	DESCRIPTION	POST. REF.	DEBIT	CREDIT	BALANCE	
					DEBIT	CREDIT

ACCOUNT ____________________ ACCOUNT NO. __________

DATE	DESCRIPTION	POST. REF.	DEBIT	CREDIT	BALANCE	
					DEBIT	CREDIT

Analyze: ____________________

Name ______________________________

PROBLEM 9.2A or 9.2B

CASH PAYMENTS JOURNAL

PAGE ______

DATE	CK. NO.	DESCRIPTION	POST. REF.	ACCOUNTS PAYABLE DEBIT	OTHER ACCOUNTS DEBIT			PURCHASES DISCOUNT CREDIT	CASH CREDIT
					ACCOUNT NAME	POST. REF.	AMOUNT		

Name ____________________

PROBLEM 9.2A or 9.2B (continued)

PETTY CASH ANALYSIS SHEET

PAGE ______

DATE	VOU. NO.	DESCRIPTION	RECEIPTS	PAYMENTS	DISTRIBUTION OF PAYMENTS				
					SUPPLIES DEBIT	DELIVERY EXPENSE DEBIT	MISC. EXPENSE DEBIT	OTHER ACCOUNTS DEBIT	
								ACCOUNT NAME	AMOUNT

Name ______________________

PROBLEM 9.2A or 9.2B (continued)

GENERAL LEDGER

ACCOUNT ______________________ ACCOUNT NO. ________

DATE	DESCRIPTION	POST. REF.	DEBIT	CREDIT	BALANCE DEBIT	BALANCE CREDIT

ACCOUNT ______________________ ACCOUNT NO. ________

DATE	DESCRIPTION	POST. REF.	DEBIT	CREDIT	BALANCE DEBIT	BALANCE CREDIT

ACCOUNT ______________________ ACCOUNT NO. ________

DATE	DESCRIPTION	POST. REF.	DEBIT	CREDIT	BALANCE DEBIT	BALANCE CREDIT

ACCOUNT ______________________ ACCOUNT NO. ________

DATE	DESCRIPTION	POST. REF.	DEBIT	CREDIT	BALANCE DEBIT	BALANCE CREDIT

ACCOUNT ______________________ ACCOUNT NO. ________

DATE	DESCRIPTION	POST. REF.	DEBIT	CREDIT	BALANCE DEBIT	BALANCE CREDIT

Name ______________________

PROBLEM 9.2A or 9.2B (continued)

GENERAL LEDGER

ACCOUNT ______________________ ACCOUNT NO. ______

DATE		DESCRIPTION	POST. REF.	DEBIT	CREDIT	BALANCE	
						DEBIT	CREDIT

ACCOUNT ______________________ ACCOUNT NO. ______

DATE		DESCRIPTION	POST. REF.	DEBIT	CREDIT	BALANCE	
						DEBIT	CREDIT

ACCOUNT ______________________ ACCOUNT NO. ______

DATE		DESCRIPTION	POST. REF.	DEBIT	CREDIT	BALANCE	
						DEBIT	CREDIT

ACCOUNT ______________________ ACCOUNT NO. ______

DATE		DESCRIPTION	POST. REF.	DEBIT	CREDIT	BALANCE	
						DEBIT	CREDIT

ACCOUNT ______________________ ACCOUNT NO. ______

DATE		DESCRIPTION	POST. REF.	DEBIT	CREDIT	BALANCE	
						DEBIT	CREDIT

Name

PROBLEM 9.2A or 9.2B (continued)

GENERAL LEDGER

ACCOUNT ______ ACCOUNT NO. ______

DATE	DESCRIPTION	POST. REF.	DEBIT	CREDIT	BALANCE DEBIT	BALANCE CREDIT

ACCOUNT ______ ACCOUNT NO. ______

DATE	DESCRIPTION	POST. REF.	DEBIT	CREDIT	BALANCE DEBIT	BALANCE CREDIT

ACCOUNT ______ ACCOUNT NO. ______

DATE	DESCRIPTION	POST. REF.	DEBIT	CREDIT	BALANCE DEBIT	BALANCE CREDIT

ACCOUNT ______ ACCOUNT NO. ______

DATE	DESCRIPTION	POST. REF.	DEBIT	CREDIT	BALANCE DEBIT	BALANCE CREDIT

ACCOUNT ______ ACCOUNT NO. ______

DATE	DESCRIPTION	POST. REF.	DEBIT	CREDIT	BALANCE DEBIT	BALANCE CREDIT

Analyze: ______

Name

PROBLEM 9.3A or 9.3B

SALES JOURNAL

PAGE

	DATE	INVOICE NO.	CUSTOMER'S NAME	POST. REF.	ACCOUNTS RECEIVABLE DR./ SALES CR.	
1						1
2						2
3						3
4						4
5						5
6						6
7						7
8						8
9						9
10						10
11						11

CASH RECEIPTS JOURNAL

PAGE

DATE	DESCRIPTION	POST. REF.	ACCOUNTS RECEIVABLE CREDIT	SALES CREDIT	OTHER ACCOUNTS CREDIT			SALES DISCOUNTS DEBIT	CASH DEBIT
					ACCOUNT NAME	POST. REF.	AMOUNT		

Name ______________________

PROBLEM 9.3A or 9.3B (continued)

GENERAL JOURNAL

PAGE ______

	DATE		DESCRIPTION	POST. REF.	DEBIT	CREDIT	
1							1
2							2
3							3
4							4
5							5
6							6
7							7
8							8
9							9
10							10
11							11
12							12

GENERAL LEDGER (PARTIAL)

ACCOUNT ______________________ ACCOUNT NO. ______

DATE		DESCRIPTION	POST. REF.	DEBIT	CREDIT	BALANCE	
						DEBIT	CREDIT

ACCOUNT ______________________ ACCOUNT NO. ______

DATE		DESCRIPTION	POST. REF.	DEBIT	CREDIT	BALANCE	
						DEBIT	CREDIT

ACCOUNT ______________________ ACCOUNT NO. ______

DATE		DESCRIPTION	POST. REF.	DEBIT	CREDIT	BALANCE	
						DEBIT	CREDIT

Name

PROBLEM 9.3A or 9.3B (continued)

GENERAL LEDGER (PARTIAL)

ACCOUNT ______ ACCOUNT NO. ______

DATE		DESCRIPTION	POST. REF.	DEBIT	CREDIT	BALANCE DEBIT	BALANCE CREDIT

ACCOUNT ______ ACCOUNT NO. ______

DATE		DESCRIPTION	POST. REF.	DEBIT	CREDIT	BALANCE DEBIT	BALANCE CREDIT

ACCOUNT ______ ACCOUNT NO. ______

DATE		DESCRIPTION	POST. REF.	DEBIT	CREDIT	BALANCE DEBIT	BALANCE CREDIT

Analyze: ______

PROBLEM 9.4A or 9.4B

PURCHASES JOURNAL

PAGE

DATE		PURCHASED FROM	INVOICE NUMBER	INVOICE DATE	TERMS	POST. REF.	PURCHASES DR./ ACCOUNTS PAYABLE CR.

GENERAL JOURNAL

PAGE

	DATE		DESCRIPTION	POST. REF.	DEBIT	CREDIT	
1							1
2							2
3							3
4							4
5							5
6							6
7							7
8							8
9							9
10							10
11							11
12							12
13							13
14							14
15							15
16							16
17							17
18							18
19							19
20							20
21							21
22							22
23							23

Name

PROBLEM 9.4A or 9.4B (continued)

CASH PAYMENTS JOURNAL

PAGE ____

DATE	CK. NO.	DESCRIPTION	POST. REF.	ACCOUNTS PAYABLE DEBIT	OTHER ACCOUNTS DEBIT			PURCHASES DISCOUNT CREDIT	CASH CREDIT
					ACCOUNT NAME	POST. REF.	AMOUNT		

Name ____________________

PROBLEM 9.4A or 9.4B (continued)

GENERAL LEDGER

ACCOUNT ____________________ ACCOUNT NO. ________

DATE		DESCRIPTION	POST. REF.	DEBIT	CREDIT	BALANCE	
						DEBIT	CREDIT

ACCOUNT ____________________ ACCOUNT NO. ________

DATE		DESCRIPTION	POST. REF.	DEBIT	CREDIT	BALANCE	
						DEBIT	CREDIT

ACCOUNT ____________________ ACCOUNT NO. ________

DATE		DESCRIPTION	POST. REF.	DEBIT	CREDIT	BALANCE	
						DEBIT	CREDIT

ACCOUNT ____________________ ACCOUNT NO. ________

DATE		DESCRIPTION	POST. REF.	DEBIT	CREDIT	BALANCE	
						DEBIT	CREDIT

Name ____________________

PROBLEM 9.4A or 9.4B (continued)

GENERAL LEDGER

ACCOUNT ____________________ ACCOUNT NO. ________

DATE		DESCRIPTION	POST. REF.	DEBIT	CREDIT	BALANCE DEBIT	BALANCE CREDIT

ACCOUNT ____________________ ACCOUNT NO. ________

DATE		DESCRIPTION	POST. REF.	DEBIT	CREDIT	BALANCE DEBIT	BALANCE CREDIT

ACCOUNT ____________________ ACCOUNT NO. ________

DATE		DESCRIPTION	POST. REF.	DEBIT	CREDIT	BALANCE DEBIT	BALANCE CREDIT

ACCOUNT ____________________ ACCOUNT NO. ________

DATE		DESCRIPTION	POST. REF.	DEBIT	CREDIT	BALANCE DEBIT	BALANCE CREDIT

ACCOUNT ____________________ ACCOUNT NO. ________

DATE		DESCRIPTION	POST. REF.	DEBIT	CREDIT	BALANCE DEBIT	BALANCE CREDIT

ACCOUNT ____________________ ACCOUNT NO. ________

DATE		DESCRIPTION	POST. REF.	DEBIT	CREDIT	BALANCE DEBIT	BALANCE CREDIT

Name

PROBLEM 9.4A or 9.4B (continued)

Analyze:

EXTRA FORM

Name

PROBLEM 9.5A or 9.5B

GENERAL JOURNAL PAGE

	DATE		DESCRIPTION	POST. REF.	DEBIT	CREDIT	
1							1
2							2
3							3
4							4
5							5
6							6
7							7
8							8
9							9
10							10
11							11
12							12
13							13

Analyze:

Name

PROBLEM 9.6A or 9.6B

Name ____________________

PROBLEM 9.6A or 9.6B (continued)

GENERAL JOURNAL

PAGE ____

	DATE	DESCRIPTION	POST. REF.	DEBIT	CREDIT	
1						1
2						2
3						3
4						4
5						5
6						6
7						7
8						8
9						9
10						10
11						11
12						12
13						13
14						14
15						15
16						16
17						17
18						18
19						19
20						20
21						21
22						22
23						23
24						24
25						25
26						26
27						27
28						28

Analyze: ____________________

Name

PROBLEM 9.7A or 9.7B

GENERAL JOURNAL PAGE

	DATE		DESCRIPTION	POST. REF.	DEBIT	CREDIT	
1							1
2							2
3							3
4							4
5							5
6							6
7							7
8							8
9							9
10							10
11							11
12							12
13							13

Analyze:

Name ____________________

CRITICAL THINKING PROBLEM 9.1

SALES JOURNAL

PAGE ______

	DATE	SALES SLIP NO.	CUSTOMER'S NAME	POST. REF.	ACCOUNTS RECEIVABLE DEBIT	SALES TAX PAYABLE CREDIT	SALES CREDIT	
1								1
2								2
3								3
4								4
5								5
6								6
7								7
8								8
9								9
10								10
11								11
12								12
13								13
14								14
15								15
16								16

PURCHASES JOURNAL

PAGE ______

DATE	PURCHASED FROM	INVOICE NUMBER	INVOICE DATE	TERMS	POST. REF.	ACCOUNTS PAYABLE CREDIT	PURCHASES DEBIT	FREIGHT IN DEBIT

Name ____________________

CRITICAL THINKING PROBLEM 9.1 (continued)

GENERAL JOURNAL

PAGE ______

	DATE	DESCRIPTION	POST. REF.	DEBIT	CREDIT	
1						1
2						2
3						3
4						4
5						5
6						6
7						7
8						8
9						9
10						10
11						11
12						12
13						13
14						14
15						15
16						16
17						17
18						18
19						19
20						20
21						21
22						22
23						23
24						24
25						25
26						26
27						27
28						28
29						29
30						30
31						31
32						32
33						33
34						34
35						35
36						36
37						37

Name ____________________

CRITICAL THINKING PROBLEM 9.1 (continued)

CASH RECEIPTS JOURNAL

PAGE ____

DATE	DESCRIPTION	POST. REF.	ACCOUNTS RECEIVABLE CREDIT	SALES TAX PAYABLE CREDIT	SALES CREDIT	OTHER ACCOUNTS CREDIT			CASH DEBIT
						ACCOUNT NAME	POST. REF.	AMOUNT	

Name ____________________

CRITICAL THINKING PROBLEM 9.1 (continued)

CASH PAYMENTS JOURNAL

PAGE ____

DATE	CK. NO.	DESCRIPTION	POST. REF.	ACCOUNTS PAYABLE DEBIT	OTHER ACCOUNTS DEBIT			PURCHASES DISCOUNTS CREDIT	CASH CREDIT
					ACCOUNT NAME	POST. REF.	AMOUNT		

Name

CRITICAL THINKING PROBLEM 9.1 (continued)

GENERAL LEDGER

ACCOUNT ______ ACCOUNT NO. ______

DATE	DESCRIPTION	POST. REF.	DEBIT	CREDIT	BALANCE DEBIT	BALANCE CREDIT

ACCOUNT ______ ACCOUNT NO. ______

DATE	DESCRIPTION	POST. REF.	DEBIT	CREDIT	BALANCE DEBIT	BALANCE CREDIT

ACCOUNT ______ ACCOUNT NO. ______

DATE	DESCRIPTION	POST. REF.	DEBIT	CREDIT	BALANCE DEBIT	BALANCE CREDIT

ACCOUNT ______ ACCOUNT NO. ______

DATE	DESCRIPTION	POST. REF.	DEBIT	CREDIT	BALANCE DEBIT	BALANCE CREDIT

ACCOUNT ______ ACCOUNT NO. ______

DATE	DESCRIPTION	POST. REF.	DEBIT	CREDIT	BALANCE DEBIT	BALANCE CREDIT

ACCOUNT ______ ACCOUNT NO. ______

DATE	DESCRIPTION	POST. REF.	DEBIT	CREDIT	BALANCE DEBIT	BALANCE CREDIT

Name ____________________

CRITICAL THINKING PROBLEM 9.1 (continued)

GENERAL LEDGER

ACCOUNT ____________________ ACCOUNT NO. __________

DATE		DESCRIPTION	POST. REF.	DEBIT	CREDIT	BALANCE DEBIT	BALANCE CREDIT

ACCOUNT ____________________ ACCOUNT NO. __________

DATE		DESCRIPTION	POST. REF.	DEBIT	CREDIT	BALANCE DEBIT	BALANCE CREDIT

ACCOUNT ____________________ ACCOUNT NO. __________

DATE		DESCRIPTION	POST. REF.	DEBIT	CREDIT	BALANCE DEBIT	BALANCE CREDIT

ACCOUNT ____________________ ACCOUNT NO. __________

DATE		DESCRIPTION	POST. REF.	DEBIT	CREDIT	BALANCE DEBIT	BALANCE CREDIT

ACCOUNT ____________________ ACCOUNT NO. __________

DATE		DESCRIPTION	POST. REF.	DEBIT	CREDIT	BALANCE DEBIT	BALANCE CREDIT

Name ____________________

CRITICAL THINKING PROBLEM 9.1 (continued)

GENERAL LEDGER

ACCOUNT ____________________ ACCOUNT NO. ________

DATE		DESCRIPTION	POST. REF.	DEBIT	CREDIT	BALANCE DEBIT	BALANCE CREDIT

ACCOUNT ____________________ ACCOUNT NO. ________

DATE		DESCRIPTION	POST. REF.	DEBIT	CREDIT	BALANCE DEBIT	BALANCE CREDIT

ACCOUNT ____________________ ACCOUNT NO. ________

DATE		DESCRIPTION	POST. REF.	DEBIT	CREDIT	BALANCE DEBIT	BALANCE CREDIT

ACCOUNT ____________________ ACCOUNT NO. ________

DATE		DESCRIPTION	POST. REF.	DEBIT	CREDIT	BALANCE DEBIT	BALANCE CREDIT

ACCOUNT ____________________ ACCOUNT NO. ________

DATE		DESCRIPTION	POST. REF.	DEBIT	CREDIT	BALANCE DEBIT	BALANCE CREDIT

Name ____________________

CRITICAL THINKING PROBLEM 9.1 (continued)

GENERAL LEDGER

ACCOUNT ____________________ ACCOUNT NO. ________

DATE		DESCRIPTION	POST. REF.	DEBIT	CREDIT	BALANCE	
						DEBIT	CREDIT

ACCOUNT ____________________ ACCOUNT NO. ________

DATE		DESCRIPTION	POST. REF.	DEBIT	CREDIT	BALANCE	
						DEBIT	CREDIT

ACCOUNT ____________________ ACCOUNT NO. ________

DATE		DESCRIPTION	POST. REF.	DEBIT	CREDIT	BALANCE	
						DEBIT	CREDIT

ACCOUNTS RECEIVABLE SUBSIDIARY LEDGER

NAME ____________________ TERMS ________

DATE		DESCRIPTION	POST. REF.	DEBIT	CREDIT	BALANCE

NAME ____________________ TERMS ________

DATE		DESCRIPTION	POST. REF.	DEBIT	CREDIT	BALANCE

Name

CRITICAL THINKING PROBLEM 9.1 (continued)

ACCOUNTS RECEIVABLE SUBSIDIARY LEDGER

NAME ______ TERMS ______

DATE		DESCRIPTION	POST. REF.	DEBIT	CREDIT	BALANCE

NAME ______ TERMS ______

DATE		DESCRIPTION	POST. REF.	DEBIT	CREDIT	BALANCE

NAME ______ TERMS ______

DATE		DESCRIPTION	POST. REF.	DEBIT	CREDIT	BALANCE

NAME ______ TERMS ______

DATE		DESCRIPTION	POST. REF.	DEBIT	CREDIT	BALANCE

NAME ______ TERMS ______

DATE		DESCRIPTION	POST. REF.	DEBIT	CREDIT	BALANCE

Name

CRITICAL THINKING PROBLEM 9.1 (continued)

ACCOUNTS PAYABLE SUBSIDIARY LEDGER

NAME TERMS

DATE		DESCRIPTION	POST. REF.	DEBIT	CREDIT	BALANCE

NAME TERMS

DATE		DESCRIPTION	POST. REF.	DEBIT	CREDIT	BALANCE

NAME TERMS

DATE		DESCRIPTION	POST. REF.	DEBIT	CREDIT	BALANCE

NAME TERMS

DATE		DESCRIPTION	POST. REF.	DEBIT	CREDIT	BALANCE

Name

CRITICAL THINKING PROBLEM 9.1 (continued)

NAME ______ TERMS ______

DATE		DESCRIPTION	POST. REF.	DEBIT	CREDIT	BALANCE

NAME ______ TERMS ______

DATE		DESCRIPTION	POST. REF.	DEBIT	CREDIT	BALANCE

ACCOUNTS PAYABLE SUBSIDIARY LEDGER

NAME ______ TERMS ______

DATE		DESCRIPTION	POST. REF.	DEBIT	CREDIT	BALANCE

Analyze: ______

Name

CRITICAL THINKING PROBLEM 9.2

Name

CRITICAL THINKING PROBLEM 9.2 (continued)

Chapter 9 Practice Test Answer Key

Part A True-False

1.	F	12.	F
2.	F	13.	T
3.	T	14.	T
4.	F	15.	T
5.	F	16.	F
6.	F	17.	T
7.	T	18.	F
8.	T	19.	T
9.	T	20.	F
10.	T	21.	T
11.	T		

Part B Matching

1. k
2. l
3. j
4. b
5. e
6. c
7. i
8. d
9. g
10. f
11. h
12. a

CHAPTER 10

Payroll Computations, Records, and Payment

STUDY GUIDE

STUDY GUIDE

Understanding the Chapter

Objectives

1. Explain the major federal laws relating to employee earnings and withholding. **2.** Compute gross earnings of employees. **3.** Determine employee deductions for social security taxes. **4.** Determine employee deductions for Medicare taxes. **5.** Determine employee deductions for income taxes. **6.** Enter gross earnings, deductions, and net pay in the payroll register. **7.** Journalize payroll transactions in the general journal. **8.** Maintain an earnings record for each employee. **9.** Define the accounting terms new to this chapter.

Reading Assignment

Read Chapter 10 in the textbook. Complete the Section Self Review as you finish reading each section of the chapter, and the Comprehensive Self Review at the end of the chapter. Refer to the Chapter 10 Glossary or to the Glossary at the end of the book to find definitions for terms that are not familiar to you.

Activities

❑ **Thinking Critically** — Answer the *Thinking Critically* questions for Clif Bar and Managerial Implications.

❑ **Discussion Questions** — Answer each assigned review question in Chapter 10.

❑ **Exercises** — Complete each assigned exercise in Chapter 10. Use the forms provided in this SGWP. The objectives covered by an exercise are given after the exercise number. If you need help with an exercise, review the portion of the chapter related to the objective(s) covered.

❑ **Problems A/B** — Complete each assigned problem in Chapter 10. Use the forms provided in this SGWP. The objectives covered by a problem are given after the problem number. If you need help with a problem, review the portion of the chapter related to the objective(s) covered.

❑ **Critical Thinking Problems** — Complete the critical thinking problems as assigned. Use the forms provided in this SGWP.

❑ **Business Connections** — Complete the Business Connections activities as assigned to gain a deeper understanding of Chapter 10 concepts.

Practice Tests

Complete the Practice Tests, which cover the main points in your reading assignment. Compare your answers with those in the Practice Test Answer Key for Chapter 10 at the end of this chapter. If you have answered any questions incorrectly, review the related section of the text.

STUDY GUIDE

Part A True-False *For each of the following statements, circle T in the answer column if the statement is true or F if the statement is false.*

T F **1.** A company hires Michael Sestini, CPA, to prepare monthly financial statements. Sestini comes to the company's office, reviews source documents, and later returns the statements. Sestini would be classified as an employee.

T F **2.** An employee worked 45 hours during the week. Her regular hourly pay is $9 per hour. Her gross pay for the week is $405.00.

T F **3.** The payroll register provides all the information required to make a general journal entry to record the payroll.

T F **4.** The workers' compensation program is a federal program.

T F **5.** The state unemployment tax rate can be reduced by the rate charged by the federal government in the federal unemployment tax program.

T F **6.** The employer is required to contribute the same amount of federal unemployment tax as the amount withheld from the employee's earnings.

T F **7.** The employee's marital status, number of exemptions, earnings for the pay period, and length of pay period are all factors in determining the amount of social security tax to be withheld.

T F **8.** The Medicare tax is in addition to the social security tax (FICA).

T F **9.** Most employers determine the amount of income tax to be withheld from the employee's pay by using withholding tables.

T F **10.** Employees can choose whether they want to be covered by the social security laws.

T F **11.** The Fair Labor Standards Act fixes a minimum wage for supervisory employees paid a monthly salary.

T F **12.** Payroll taxes apply to salaries and wages paid employees, but not to amounts paid independent contractors.

Part B Matching *For each numbered item, choose the matching term from the box and write the identifying letter in the answer column.*

Answer	Item
________	**1.** The form that employees file in order to claim the number of allowances to which they are entitled.
________	**2.** Provides for funding of retirement and disability benefits.
________	**3.** Time worked in excess of 40 hours per week
________	**4.** A columnar record that shows each employee's earnings, deductions, and net pay.
________	**5.** Wages paid in a year above the base amount subject to a tax.
________	**6.** Wages before deductions
________	**7.** A government publication containing withholding tables for employee taxes.
________	**8.** A tax levied on the employer to provide benefits to employees who lose their jobs.
________	**9.** Deductions to pay for medical benefits for retired persons.
________	**10.** A record for each employee showing the person's earnings and deductions for the period, along with cumulative data.

- **a.** Employee earnings record
- **b.** Payroll register
- **c.** Exempt wages
- **d.** Workers' compensation insurance
- **e.** Overtime
- **f.** Circular E
- **g.** Medicare premiums
- **h.** Unemployment tax
- **i.** Federal Insurance Contributions Act
- **j.** Employee's Withholding Allowance Certificate Form W4
- **k.** Gross pay

Demonstration Problem

Santa Barbara Consulting Company pays its employees monthly. Payments made by the company on November 30, 2010, follow. Cumulative amounts paid to the persons named prior to November 30 are also given.

1. John Arrow, President, gross monthly salary of $17,000; gross earnings prior to November 30, $170,000.
2. Virginia Richey, Vice President, gross monthly salary of $14,000; gross earnings paid prior to November 30, $140,000.
3. Kathryn Price, independent accountant who audits the company's accounts and performs consulting services, $17,500; gross amounts paid prior to November 30, $35,000.
4. Cheryl Wang, Treasurer, gross monthly salary of $9,000; gross earnings prior to November 30, $90,000.
5. Payment to Hankins Research Services for monthly services of Robert Hankins, a tax and financial accounting consultant, $7,000; amount paid to Hankins Research Services prior to November 30, $24,000.

Instructions

1. Use an earnings ceiling of $97,500, and a tax rate of 6.2 percent for social security taxes and a tax rate of 1.45 percent on all earnings for medicare taxes. Prepare a schedule showing:
   - **a.** Each employee's cumulative earnings prior to November 30.
   - **b.** Each employee's gross earnings for November.
   - **c.** The amounts to be withheld for each payroll tax from each employee's earnings; the employee's income tax withholdings are Arrow, $5,500; Richey, $3,250; Wang, $1,175.
   - **d.** The net amount due each employee.
   - **e.** The total gross earnings, the total of each payroll tax deduction, and the total net amount payable to employees.
2. Give the general journal entry to record the company's payroll on November 30. Use journal page 24. Omit description.
3. Give the general journal entry to record payments to employees on November 30.

SOLUTION

EARNINGS SCHEDULE

EMPLOYEE NAME	CUMULATIVE EARNINGS	MONTHLY PAY	SOCIAL SECURITY	MEDICARE	EMPLOYEE INCOME TAX WITHHOLDING	NET PAY
John Arrow	**$170,000.00**	**$17,000.00**	**—**	**$246.50**	**$5,500.00**	**$11,253.50**
Virginia Richey	**140,000.00**	**14,000.00**	**—**	**203.00**	**3,250.00**	**10,547.00**
Cheryl Wang	**90,000.00**	**9,000.00**	**465.00**	**130.50**	**1,175.00**	**7,229.50**
Totals	**$400,000.00**	**$40,000.00**	**$465.00**	**$580.00**	**$9,925.00**	**$29,030.00**

Kathryn Price and Robert Hankins are not employees of Santa Barbara Consulting Company.

GENERAL JOURNAL — PAGE **24**

	DATE		DESCRIPTION	POST. REF.	DEBIT	CREDIT	
1	**2010**						1
2	**Nov.**	**30**	**Salaries Expense**		**40 0 0 0 00**		2
3			**Social Security Tax Payable**			**4 6 5 00**	3
4			**Medicare Tax Payable**			**5 8 0 00**	4
5			**Employee Income Tax Payable**			**9 9 2 5 00**	5
6			**Salaries Payable**			**29 0 3 0 00**	6
7							7
8		**30**	**Salaries Payable**		**29 0 3 0 00**		8
9			**Cash**			**29 0 3 0 00**	9
10							10

WORKING PAPERS

Name ______________________

EXERCISE 10.1

EMPLOYEE NO.	HOURLY RATE	HOURS WORKED	GROSS EARNINGS

EXERCISE 10.2

HOURLY RATE	OVERTIME RATE	REGULAR HOURS WORKED	OVERTIME HOURS WORKED	REGULAR PAY	OVERTIME PAY	GROSS PAY

EXERCISE 10.3

EMPLOYEE NO.	DECEMBER SALARY	YEAR TO DATE EARNINGS THROUGH NOVEMBER 30	SOC. SEC. TAXABLE EARNINGS-DECEMBER	SOCIAL SECURITY TAX 6.20%

EXERCISE 10.4

EMPLOYEE NO.	DECEMBER SALARY	MEDICARE TAXABLE EARNINGS-DECEMBER	MEDICARE TAX 1.45%

EXERCISE 10.5

EMPLOYEE NO.	MARITAL STATUS	WITHHOLDING ALLOWANCES	WEEKLY SALARY	INCOME TAX WITHHOLDING

Name ______________________

EXERCISE 10.6

GENERAL JOURNAL — PAGE ______

	DATE		DESCRIPTION	POST. REF.	DEBIT	CREDIT	
1							1
2							2
3							3
4							4
5							5
6							6
7							7
8							8
9							9
10							10
11							11
12							12
13							13
14							14
15							15

EXERCISE 10.7

GENERAL JOURNAL — PAGE ______

	DATE		DESCRIPTION	POST. REF.	DEBIT	CREDIT	
1							1
2							2
3							3
4							4
5							5
6							6
7							7
8							8
9							9
10							10
11							11
12							12
13							13
14							14
15							15

Name ____________________

PROBLEM 10.1A or 10.1B

EMPLOYEE NO.	REGULAR HOURS, HOURLY RATE	HOURS WORKED	REGULAR TIME EARNINGS	OVERTIME EARNINGS	GROSS EARNINGS

Gross Pay ____________

Social Security Tax ____________

Medicare Tax ____________

Income Tax Withholding ____________

Health & Disability ____________

United Way ____________

U.S. Savings Bond ____________

Net Pay ____________

GENERAL JOURNAL

PAGE ________

	DATE		DESCRIPTION	POST. REF.	DEBIT	CREDIT	
1							1
2							2
3							3
4							4
5							5

Analyze: ____________________

Name ______________________________

PROBLEM 10.2A or 10.2B

PAYROLL REGISTER WEEK BEGINNING ________ AND ENDING ________ PAID ________

NAME	NO. OF ALLOW.	MARITAL STATUS	CUMULATIVE EARNINGS	NO. OF HRS.	RATE	EARNINGS			CUMULATIVE EARNINGS	TAXABLE WAGES			DEDUCTIONS			NET AMOUNT	CHECK NO.	DISTRIBUTION	
						REGULAR TIME EARNINGS	OVERTIME EARNINGS	GROSS AMOUNT		SOCIAL SECURITY	MEDICARE	FUTA	SOCIAL SECURITY	MEDICARE	INCOME TAX			THEATER WAGES	OFFICE WAGES

Name ____________________

PROBLEM 10.2A or 10.2B (continued)

GENERAL JOURNAL

PAGE ______

DATE		DESCRIPTION	POST. REF.	DEBIT	CREDIT

Analyze: ____________________

Name

PROBLEM 10.3A or 10.3B

PAYROLL REGISTER WEEK BEGINNING ______ AND ENDING ______ PAID ______

NAME	NO. OF ALLOW.	MARITAL STATUS	CUMULATIVE EARNINGS	NO. OF HRS.	RATE	EARNINGS			CUMULATIVE EARNINGS
						REGULAR TIME EARNINGS	OVERTIME EARNINGS	GROSS AMOUNT	

TAXABLE WAGES		FUTA	DEDUCTIONS			NET AMOUNT	CHECK NO.	DISTRIBUTION	
SOCIAL SECURITY	MEDICARE		SOCIAL SECURITY	MEDICARE	INCOME TAX			OFFICE WAGES	DELIVERY WAGES

Name ______________________

PROBLEM 10.3A or 10.3B (continued)

GENERAL JOURNAL PAGE ______

DATE	DESCRIPTION	POST. REF.	DEBIT	CREDIT

Analyze: ______________________

Name ____________________

PROBLEM 10.4A or 10.4B

EMPLOYEE NAME	CUMULATIVE EARNINGS	MONTHLY PAY	SOCIAL SECURITY	MEDICARE	EMPLOYEE INCOME TAX WITHHOLDING	NET PAY
Totals						

GENERAL JOURNAL

PAGE ______

DATE	DESCRIPTION	POST. REF.	DEBIT	CREDIT

Analyze: ____________________

Name ____________________

CRITICAL THINKING PROBLEM 10.1

EMPLOYEE NAME	CUMULATIVE EARNINGS	MONTHLY PAY	SOCIAL SECURITY	MEDICARE	EMPLOYEE INCOME TAX WITHHOLDING	NET PAY

GENERAL JOURNAL PAGE ______

	DATE		DESCRIPTION	POST. REF.	DEBIT	CREDIT	
1							1
2							2
3							3
4							4
5							5
6							6
7							7
8							8
9							9
10							10
11							11
12							12
13							13
14							14
15							15

Analyze: ____________________

Name

CRITICAL THINKING PROBLEM 10.2

Chapter 10 Practice Test Answer Key

Part A True-False

1. F
2. F
3. T
4. F
5. F
6. F
7. F
8. T
9. T
10. F
11. F
12. T

Part B Matching

1. j
2. i
3. e
4. b
5. c
6. k
7. f
8. h
9. g
10. a

CHAPTER 11

Payroll Taxes, Deposits, and Reports

STUDY GUIDE

Understanding the Chapter

Objectives

1. Explain how and when payroll taxes are paid to the government. **2.** Compute and record the employer's social security and Medicare taxes. **3.** Record deposit of social security, Medicare, and employee income taxes. **4.** Prepare an Employer's Quarterly Federal Tax Return, Form 941. **5.** Prepare Wage and Tax Statement (Form W-2) and Annual Transmittal of Wage and Tax Statements (Form W-3). **6.** Compute and record liability for federal and state unemployment taxes and record payment of the taxes. **7.** Prepare an Employer's Federal Unemployment Tax Return, Form 940 or 940-EZ. **8.** Compute and record workers' compensation insurance premiums. **9.** Define the accounting terms new to this chapter.

Reading Assignment

Read Chapter 11 in the textbook. Complete the textbook Section Self Review as you finish reading each section of the chapter, and Comprehensive Self Review at the end of the chapter. Refer to the Chapter 11 Glossary or to the Glossary at the end of the book to find definitions for terms that are not familiar to you.

Activities

- ❑ **Thinking Critically** — Answer the *Thinking Critically* questions for Ikea and Managerial Implications.
- ❑ **Discussion Questions** — Answer each assigned discussion question in Chapter 11.
- ❑ **Exercises** — Complete each assigned exercise in Chapter 11. Use the forms provided in this SGWP. The objectives covered by an exercise are given after the exercise number. If you need help with an exercise, review the portion of the chapter related to the objective(s) covered.
- ❑ **Problems A/B** — Complete each assigned problem in Chapter 11. Use the forms provided in this SGWP. The objectives covered by a problem are given after the problem number. If you need help with a problem, review the portion of the chapter related to the objective(s) covered.
- ❑ **Critical Thinking Problems** — Complete the critical thinking problems as assigned. Use the forms provided in this SGWP.
- ❑ **Business Connections** — Complete the Business Connections activities as assigned to gain a deeper understanding of Chapter 11 concepts.

Practice Tests

Complete the Practice Tests, which cover the main points in your reading assignment. Compare your answers with those in the Practice Test Answer Key for Chapter 11 at the end of this chapter. If you have answered any questions incorrectly, review the related section of the text.

STUDY GUIDE

Part A True-False *For each of the following statements, circle T in the answer column if the statement is true or F if the statement is false.*

T F **1.** Social security taxes are paid equally by the employer and employee.

T F **2.** Each employer subject to the Federal Unemployment Compensation Tax Act must file an annual return on Form 940 by January 15 of the following year.

T F **3.** The employee must attach a Form W-3 to his or her federal income tax return.

T F **4.** Payments of social security tax, Medicare tax, and employee income tax withheld for a year may be deposited without penalty in an authorized depository at any time up to January 31 of the following year.

T F **5.** Only the amount of each employee's earnings up to $7,000 each year is subject to Medicare tax.

T F **6.** Employees' individual earnings records provide much of the information needed to prepare the Employer's Quarterly Federal Tax Return, Form 941.

T F **7.** On each date of payment of an employee's wages, the employer must provide the employee with a statement, on Form W-2, of earnings and taxes withheld.

T F **8.** During the month immediately following the close of each calendar quarter, an employer is required to file a quarterly tax report and pay in or deposit any balance owed for social security and Medicare taxes and employees' income tax withheld.

T F **9.** A business firm pays income tax withholding at the same rate and on the same taxable wages as employees.

T F **10.** The employer's payroll taxes are usually recorded at the end of each payroll period, even though the cash will not be paid out until later.

T F **11.** Most states allow a credit against the FUTA for amounts paid to the federal government as SUTA.

T F **12.** The federal government grants a lower federal unemployment rate under an experience rating system to those employers who provide stable employment.

T F **13.** Under a typical state plan, the federal government actually receives 0.6 percent of the taxable wages because the employer is allowed credits for payments made to the state.

T F **14.** The federal unemployment tax for the year is based on an audit of the payroll for the year.

T F **15.** Premiums on workers' compensation insurance vary with the type of work performed by employees.

T F **16.** The premium on workers' compensation insurance is based on the federal unemployment tax.

T F **17.** The credit against the federal unemployment tax is the amount actually paid to the state under its unemployment compensation insurance program.

T F **18.** Employers with a small number of employees are frequently required to deposit the entire amount of estimated workers' compensation insurance premiums early in the year.

Part B Matching *For each number item, choose the matching term from the box and write the identifying letter in the answer column.*

Answer		Item
______	1.	A tax borne equally by the employer and employee.
______	2.	An IRS publication containing tax rates and other information about payroll taxes.
______	3.	A tax paid solely by the employer.
______	4.	A plan under which the SUTA is adjusted to reflect the unemployment experience of the employer.
______	5.	Plan providing benefits to employees who are injured or become ill on the job.
______	6.	A statement of earnings and deductions for each employee.
______	7.	A yearly form sent to the U.S. government summarizing earnings and payroll taxes withheld for the year.
______	8.	A quarterly report to the federal government summarizing taxable wages and payroll taxes due for the quarter.
______	9.	An annual report to the federal government summarizing the employer's unemployment compensation tax for the year.
______	10.	A deposit "coupon" accompanying the employer's deposit of taxes in a commercial bank.

a. Workers' compensation
b. Form 8109
c. Form 941
d. Form 940
e. Form W-3
f. Form W-2
g. Experience rating system
h. Publication 15, Circular E
i. Federal unemployment tax
j. Medicare tax

STUDY GUIDE

Demonstration Problem

The payroll register of the Quick Copy Center showed employee earnings of $14,460 for the month ended January 31, 2010. Employee income tax withholding was $3,700. Tax rates are: social security, 6.2 percent, and Medicare, 1.45 percent.

Instructions

1. Compute the employees' social security and Medicare taxes.
2. Record the payroll for January in the general journal, page 3.
3. Compute the employer's payroll taxes for the period.
4. Prepare a general journal entry to record the employer's payroll taxes for the period.
5. Prepare a general journal entry to record the February 4 deposit of the social security, Medicare, and employee income taxes for the month.

SOLUTION

CALCULATION OF EMPLOYEE TAXES

Social security: 0.062 × $14,460	**$896.52**
Medicare: 0.0145 × $14,460	**209.67**
	$1,106.19

CALCULATION OF EMPLOYER TAXES

Social security: 0.062 × $14,460	**$896.52**
Medicare: 0.0145 × $14,460	**209.67**
	$1,106.19

SOLUTION (continued)

GENERAL JOURNAL

PAGE 3

DATE		DESCRIPTION	POST. REF.	DEBIT	CREDIT
2010					
Jan.	31	Salaries Expense		14,460.00	
		Social Security Tax Payable			896.52
		Medicare Tax Payable			209.67
		Employee Income Tax Payable			3,700.00
		Salaries Payable			9,653.81
		Payroll for January			
	31	Payroll Tax Expense		1,106.19	
		Social Security Tax Payable			896.52
		Medicare Tax Payable			209.67
		Payroll for January			
Feb.	4	Social Security Tax Payable		1,793.04	
		Medicare Tax Payable		419.34	
		Employee Income Tax Payable		3,700.00	
		Cash			5,912.38
		Deposit of payroll taxes withholding			

WORKING PAPERS

Name ________________________________

EXERCISE 11.1

____

____

____

____

____

EXERCISE 11.2

GENERAL JOURNAL

PAGE ________

	DATE		DESCRIPTION	POST. REF.	DEBIT	CREDIT	
1							1
2							2
3							3
4							4
5							5
6							6
7							7

EXERCISE 11.3

TAX	BASE	RATE	AMOUNT

EXERCISE 11.4

GENERAL JOURNAL

PAGE ________

	DATE		DESCRIPTION	POST. REF.	DEBIT	CREDIT	
1							1
2							2
3							3
4							4
5							5
6							6
7							7

Name ____________________

EXERCISE 11.5

____

____

____

EXERCISE 11.6

GENERAL JOURNAL PAGE ______

	DATE	DESCRIPTION	POST. REF.	DEBIT	CREDIT	
1						1
2						2
3						3
4						4
5						5
6						6
7						7

EXERCISE 11.7

____

____

____

____

EXERCISE 11.8

WORK CLASSIFICATION	ESTIMATED EARNINGS	RATE	ESTIMATED PREMIUM

Name ____________________

PROBLEM 11.1A or 11.1B

TAX	BASE	RATE	AMOUNT

GENERAL JOURNAL PAGE 28

	DATE		DESCRIPTION	POST. REF.	DEBIT	CREDIT	
1							1
2							2
3							3
4							4
5							5
6							6
7							7
8							8
9							9
10							10
11							11
12							12

Analyze: ____________________

Name

PROBLEM 11.2A or 11.2B

GENERAL JOURNAL

PAGE

DATE		DESCRIPTION	POST. REF.	DEBIT	CREDIT

Analyze:

Name ____________________

PROBLEM 11.3A or 11.3B

GENERAL JOURNAL PAGE ______

	DATE		DESCRIPTION	POST. REF.	DEBIT	CREDIT	
1							1
2							2
3							3
4							4
5							5
6							6
7							7
8							8
9							9
10							10
11							11
12							12
13							13
14							14
15							15
16							16
17							17
18							18
19							19
20							20
21							21
22							22
23							23
24							24
25							25
26							26
27							27
28							28
29							29
30							30
31							31
32							32
33							33

Analyze: ____________________

Name ______________________

PROBLEM 11.3A or 11.3B (continued)

Form **941 for 2010: Employer's Quarterly Federal Tax Return** 9901

(Rev. January 2005) Department of the Treasury — Internal Revenue Service OMB No. 1545-0029

Employer identification number ☐☐ – ☐☐☐☐☐☐☐

Name *(not your trade name)* ______

Trade name *(if any)* ______

Address ______
Number Street Suite or room number
______
City State ZIP code

Report for this Quarter ...
(Check one.)

- ☐ **1:** January, February, March
- ☒ **2:** April, May, June
- ☐ **3:** July, August, September
- ☐ **4:** October, November, December

Read the separate instructions before you fill out this form. Please type or print within the boxes.

Part 1: Answer these questions for this quarter.

1 **Number of employees who received wages, tips, or other compensation for the pay period including:** ***Mar. 12*** **(Quarter 1),** ***June 12*** **(Quarter 2),** ***Sept. 12*** **(Quarter 3),** ***Dec. 12*** **(Quarter 4)** 1 ______

2 **Wages, tips, and other compensation** . . . . 2 ______ .

3 **Total income tax withheld from wages, tips, and other compensation** . . . . . . 3 ______ .

4 **If no wages, tips, and other compensation are subject to social security or Medicare tax** . ☐ Check and go to line 6.

5 **Taxable social security and Medicare wages and tips:**

	Column 1		Column 2
5a **Taxable social security wages**	.	× .124 =	.
5b **Taxable social security tips**	.	× .124 =	.
5c **Taxable Medicare wages & tips**	.	× .029 =	.

5d **Total social security and Medicare taxes** (*Column 2,* lines 5a + 5b + 5c = line 5d) . 5d ______ .

6 **Total taxes before adjustments** (lines 3 + 5d = line 6) . . . . 6 ______ .

7 **Tax adjustments** (If your answer is a negative number, write it in brackets.):

7a **Current quarter's fractions of cents** . . . . ______ .

7b **Current quarter's sick pay** . . . . ______ .

7c **Current quarter's adjustments for tips and group-term life insurance** ______ .

7d **Current year's income tax withholding** (Attach Form 941c) . . ______ .

7e **Prior quarters' social security and Medicare taxes** (Attach Form 941c) ______ .

7f **Special additions to federal income tax** (reserved use) . . . . ______ .

7g **Special additions to social security and Medicare** (reserved use) ______ .

7h **Total adjustments** (Combine all amounts: lines 7a through 7g.) . . . . 7h ______ .

8 **Total taxes after adjustments** (Combine lines 6 and 7h.) . . . . 8 ______ .

9 **Advance earned income credit (EIC) payments made to employees** . . . . 9 ______ .

10 **Total taxes after adjustment for advance EIC** (lines 8 – 9 = line 10) . . . . 10 ______ .

11 **Total deposits for this quarter, including overpayment applied from a prior quarter** . . 11 ______ .

12 **Balance due** (lines 10 – 11 = line 12) Make checks payable to the *United States Treasury* . 12 ______ .

13 **Overpayment** (If line 11 is more than line 10, write the difference here.) ______ . Check one ☐ Apply to next return. ☐ Send a refund.

Next ➔

For Privacy Act and Paperwork Reduction Act Notice, see the back of the Payment Voucher. Cat. No. 17001Z Form **941**

Name

PROBLEM 11.3A or 11.3B (continued)

990212

Name *(not your trade name)* | Employer identification number

Part 2: Tell us about your deposit schedule for this quarter.

If you are unsure about whether you are a monthly schedule depositor or a semiweekly schedule depositor, see *Pub. 15 (Circular E),* section 11.

14 ☐☐ **Write the state abbreviation for the state where you made your deposits** OR **write "MU" if you made your deposits in *multiple* states.**

15 **Check one:** ☐ **Line 10 is less than $2,500.** Go to Part 3.

☐ **You were a monthly schedule depositor for the entire quarter. Fill out your tax liability for each month.** Then go to Part 3.

Tax liability: **Month 1** .

Month 2 .

Month 3 .

Total . **Total must equal line 10.**

☐ **You were a semiweekly schedule depositor for any part of this quarter.** Fill out *Schedule B (Form 941): Report of Tax Liability for Semiweekly Schedule Depositors,* and attach it to this form.

Part 3: Tell us about your business. If a question does NOT apply to your business, leave it blank.

16 **If your business has closed and you do not have to file returns in the future** . . . . ☐ Check here, and

enter the final date you paid wages / / .

17 **If you are a seasonal employer and you do not have to file a return for every quarter of the year** . ☐ Check here.

Part 4: May we contact your third-party designee?

Do you want to allow an employee, a paid tax preparer, or another person to discuss this return with the IRS? See the instructions for details.

☐ Yes. Designee's name

Phone ( ) – Personal Identification Number (PIN) ☐☐☐☐☐

☐ No.

Part 5: Sign here

Under penalties of perjury, I declare that I have examined this return, including accompanying schedules and statements, and to the best of my knowledge and belief, it is true, correct, and complete.

X Sign your name here

Print name and title

Date / / Phone ( ) –

Part 6: For paid preparers only *(optional)*

Preparer's signature

Firm's name

Address EIN

ZIP code

Date / / Phone ( ) – SSN/PTIN

☐ Check if you are self-employed.

Name ______________________

PROBLEM 11.4A or 11.4B

GENERAL JOURNAL PAGE ______

	DATE	DESCRIPTION	POST. REF.	DEBIT	CREDIT	
1						1
2						2
3						3
4						4
5						5
6						6
7						7
8						8
9						9
10						10
11						11
12						12
13						13
14						14
15						15
16						16
17						17
18						18
19						19
20						20
21						21
22						22
23						23
24						24
25						25
26						26
27						27
28						28
29						29

Analyze: ______________________

Name ______________________

PROBLEM 11.5A or 11.5B

GENERAL JOURNAL

PAGE ______

DATE	DESCRIPTION	POST. REF.	DEBIT	CREDIT

Analyze: ______________________

Name

PROBLEM 11.5A or 11.5B (continued)

Form **940-EZ**

Department of the Treasury
Internal Revenue Service

Employer's Annual Federal Unemployment (FUTA) Tax Return

▶ See the separate Instructions for Form 940-EZ for information on completing this form.

OMB No. 1545-1110

2010

T	
FF	
FD	
FP	
I	
T	

You must complete this section. ▶

Name (as distinguished from trade name) | Calendar year

Trade name, if any | Employer identification number (EIN)

Address (number and street) | City, state, and ZIP code

*Answer the questions under **Who May Use Form 940-EZ** on page 2. If you cannot use Form 940-EZ, you must use Form 940.*

A Enter the amount of contributions paid to your state unemployment fund (see the separate instructions) . . ▶ $

B (1) Enter the name of the state where you have to pay contributions . . . . ▶

(2) Enter your state reporting number as shown on your state unemployment tax return ▶

If you will not have to file returns in the future, check here (see **Who Must File** in separate instructions) **and complete and sign the return.** ▶ ☐

If this is an Amended Return, check here (see **Amended Returns** in the separate instructions) . . . . ▶ ☐

Part I **Taxable Wages and FUTA Tax**

1	Total payments (including payments shown on lines 2 and 3) during the calendar year for services of employees		1	
2	Exempt payments. (Explain all exempt payments, attaching additional sheets if necessary.) ▶	2		
3	Payments of more than $7,000 for services. Enter only amounts over the first $7,000 paid to each employee **(see the separate instructions)**	3		
4	Add lines 2 and 3		4	
5	**Total taxable wages** (subtract line 4 from line 1) . . . . ▶		5	
6	**FUTA tax.** Multiply the wages on line 5 by .008 and enter here. **(If the result is over $100, also complete Part II.)**		6	
7	Total FUTA tax deposited for the year, including any overpayment applied from a prior year		7	
8	**Balance due** (subtract line 7 from line 6). Pay to the "United States Treasury." . . . . ▶ If you owe more than $100, see **Depositing FUTA tax** in the separate instructions.		8	
9	**Overpayment** (subtract line 6 from line 7). Check if it is to be: ☐ **Applied to next return** or ☐ **Refunded** ▶		9	

Part II **Record of Quarterly Federal Unemployment Tax Liability** (Do not include state liability.) **Complete only if line 6 is over $100.**

Quarter	First (Jan. 1 – Mar. 31)	Second (Apr. 1 – June 30)	Third (July 1 – Sept. 30)	Fourth (Oct. 1 – Dec. 31)	Total for year
Liability for quarter					

Third-Party Designee

Do you want to allow another person to discuss this return with the IRS (see the separate instructions)? ☐ **Yes.** Complete the following. ☐ **No**

Designee's name ▶ | Phone no. ▶ ( ) | Personal identification number (PIN) ▶

Under penalties of perjury, I declare that I have examined this return, including accompanying schedules and statements, and, to the best of my knowledge and belief, it is true, correct, and complete, and that no part of any payment made to a state unemployment fund claimed as a credit was, or is to be, deducted from the payments to employees.

Signature ▶ **Title (Owner, etc.)** ▶ **Date** ▶

For Privacy Act and Paperwork Reduction Act Notice, see the separate instructions. ▼ **DETACH HERE** ▼ Cat. No. 10983G Form **940-EZ**

Form **940-V(EZ)**

Department of the Treasury
Internal Revenue Service

Payment Voucher

Use this voucher only when making a payment with your return.

OMB No. 1545-1110

2010

Complete boxes 1, 2, and 3. Do not send cash, and do not staple your payment to this voucher. Make your check or money order payable to the "United States Treasury." Be sure to enter your employer identification number (EIN), "Form 940-EZ," and "2004" on your payment.

1 Enter your employer identification number (EIN).	2 **Enter the amount of your payment.** ▶	Dollars	Cents

3 Enter your business name (individual name for sole proprietors).

Enter your address.

Enter your city, state, and ZIP code.

Name ______________________

PROBLEM 11.6A or 11.6B

WORK CLASSIFICATION	ESTIMATED EARNINGS	INSURANCE RATE	ESTIMATED PREMIUMS

WORK CLASSIFICATION	ACTUAL EARNINGS	INSURANCE RATE	ACTUAL PREMIUMS

Name

PROBLEM 11.6A or 11.6B (continued)

GENERAL JOURNAL PAGE

	DATE		DESCRIPTION	POST. REF.	DEBIT	CREDIT	
1							1
2							2
3							3
4							4
5							5
6							6
7							7
8							8
9							9
10							10
11							11
12							12
13							13
14							14
15							15
16							16
17							17
18							18
19							19

Analyze:

Name

CRITICAL THINKING PROBLEM 11.1

1.

2.

3.

4.

5.

Analyze:

CRITICAL THINKING PROBLEM 11.2

1.

2. YEARLY COST—CURRENT SYSTEM

Name

CRITICAL THINKING PROBLEM 11.2 (continued)

YEARLY COST—PROPOSED SYSTEM

3.

Chapter 11 Practice Test Answer Key

Part A True-False

1.	**T**	**10.**	**T**
2.	**F**	**11.**	**F**
3.	**F**	**12.**	**F**
4.	**F**	**13.**	**F**
5.	**F**	**14.**	**F**
6.	**T**	**15.**	**T**
7.	**F**	**16.**	**F**
8.	**T**	**17.**	**F**
9.	**F**	**18.**	**T**

Part B Matching

1. j
2. h
3. i
4. g
5. a
6. f
7. e
8. c
9. d
10. b

CHAPTER 12

Accruals, Deferrals, and the Worksheet

STUDY GUIDE

STUDY GUIDE

Understanding the Chapter

Objectives

1. Determine the adjustment for merchandise inventory and enter the adjustment on the worksheet. **2.** Compute adjustments for accrued and prepaid expense items and enter the adjustments on the worksheet. **3.** Compute adjustments for accrued and deferred income items and enter the adjustments on the worksheet. **4.** Complete a ten-column worksheet. **5.** Define the accounting terms new to this chapter.

Reading Assignment

Read Chapter 12 in the textbook. Complete the textbook Section Self Review as you finish reading each section of the chapter, and the Comprehensive Self Review at the end of the chapter. Refer to the Chapter 12 Glossary or to the Glossary at the end of the book to find definitions for terms that are not familiar to you.

Activities

- ❑ **Thinking Critically** — Answer the *Thinking Critically* questions for American Eagle Outfitters and Managerial Implications.
- ❑ **Discussion Questions** — Answer each assigned discussion question in Chapter 12.
- ❑ **Exercises** — Complete each assigned exercise in Chapter 12. Use the forms provided in this SGWP. The objectives covered by an exercise are given after the exercise number. If you need help with an exercise, review the portion of the chapter related to the objective(s) covered.
- ❑ **Problems A/B** — Complete each assigned problem in Chapter 12. Use the forms provided in this SGWP. The objectives covered by a problem are given after the problem number. If you need help with a problem, review the portion of the chapter related to the objective(s) covered.
- ❑ **Critical Thinking Problems** — Complete the critical thinking problems as assigned. Use the forms provided in this SGWP.
- ❑ **Business Connections** — Complete the Business Connections activities as assigned to gain a deeper understanding of Chapter 12 concepts.

Practice Tests

Complete the Practice Tests, which cover the main points in your reading assignment. Compare your answers with those in the Practice Test Answer Key for Chapter 12 at the end of this chapter. If you have answered any questions incorrectly, review the related section of the text.

Part A True-False *For each of the following statements, circle T in the answer column if the statement is true or F if the statement is false.*

T F **1.** The accounts should be adjusted when preparing monthly or quarterly statements.

T F **2.** A prepaid expense incorrectly charged to expense in an accounting period results in an understatement of net income in that period and an overstatement of net income in the following period.

T F **3.** In preparing financial statements, it is unnecessary to make adjustments for relatively small items because they are immaterial and will not affect the statements.

T F **4.** The financial statements are prepared directly from the worksheet.

T F **5.** The statement of owner's equity should be prepared before the income statement is prepared.

T F **6.** The **Drawing** account balance is extended to the Debit column in the Income Statement section.

T F **7.** The beginning merchandise inventory does not appear in the Adjusted Trial Balance.

T F **8.** Adjusting entries are recorded in the general journal after the worksheet and the financial statements are completed.

T F **9.** Deferred income has been earned but not recorded, while accrued income has been recorded but not earned.

T F **10.** The entry to record accrued interest on notes payable is a debit to **Interest Expense** and a credit to **Interest Payable.**

T F **11.** **Interest Receivable** is usually classified as a revenue account.

T F **12.** In most cases, **Prepaid Interest Expense** will be classified as a current asset on the balance sheet.

T F **13.** The **Interest Expense** account must be adjusted if an interest-bearing note payable is outstanding at the end of the fiscal period and interest has not been paid on that date.

T F **14.** Under the accrual basis of accounting, purchases are recorded when the title to the goods passes to the buyer.

T F **15.** In the "adjustments" column of the worksheet, the **Merchandise Inventory** is debited for the amount of ending inventory and credited for the amount of beginning inventory.

T F **16.** The **Unearned Subscriptions Income** account will appear in the Assets section of the balance sheet.

T F **17.** The unadjusted trial balance figures for accumulated depreciation accounts contain the depreciation for the current period.

T F **18.** At the end of an accounting period, an adjustment is needed to record as an expense any part of the balance in an asset account that has been used up or has expired.

T F **19.** On the trial balance, the **Store Supplies** account shows a debit balance of $300. A physical count showed supplies on hand of $80. The adjusting entry includes a debit of $80 to the **Store Supplies Expense** account.

T F **20.** An adjustment for depreciation results in an entry debiting the **Depreciation Expense** account and crediting the **Equipment** account.

T F **21.** Office or store supplies that have been paid for in cash do not need any adjusting entries.

T F **22.** The net income for the business is entered as a debit entry in the Balance Sheet section and as a credit entry in the Income Statement section of the worksheet.

T F **23.** The accountant completes the worksheet and prepares the financial statements as soon as all adjustments have been entered on the worksheet.

T F **24.** The Adjusted Trial Balance column of the worksheet tests only the arithmetic accuracy of the worksheet to that point in the worksheet and statement preparation process.

T F **25.** After the amounts shown in the Adjusted Trial Balance section have been extended, the difference between the total debits and total credits in the balance sheet section represents the net income or loss for the period.

Part B Exercise *In each of the following independent cases give the general journal entry to adjust the accounts for the year on December 31, 2010. Omit the descriptions.*

1. Store supplies costing $1,450 were purchased during the year and were charged to the **Store Supplies** account. At the end of the year, supplies costing $300 were on hand.

GENERAL JOURNAL PAGE ______

	DATE		DESCRIPTION	POST. REF.	DEBIT	CREDIT	
1							1
2							2

2. On December 1, 2010 the company gave a $5,000 note payable to a supplier. The note bears interest at 9 percent.

GENERAL JOURNAL PAGE ______

	DATE		DESCRIPTION	POST. REF.	DEBIT	CREDIT	
1							1
2							2

3. On October 1, 2010, the company received a four-month, 12 percent note for $2,500 from settlement of an overdue account. No interest has been recorded on the note.

GENERAL JOURNAL PAGE ______

	DATE		DESCRIPTION	POST. REF.	DEBIT	CREDIT	
1							1
2							2

4. On November 1, 2010, the company purchased a one-year insurance policy for $1,800. The amount was charged to **Prepaid Insurance.**

GENERAL JOURNAL PAGE ______

	DATE		DESCRIPTION	POST. REF.	DEBIT	CREDIT	
1							1
2							2

Demonstration Problem

The trial balance for Pietro's Imports on December 31, 2010, the end of its accounting period, is shown on the worksheet.

Instructions

1. Complete the worksheet for the year, using the following information:
   - **a-b.** Ending merchandise inventory, $108,570.
   - **c.** Uncollectible accounts expense, $900.
   - **d.** Supplies on hand December 31, 2010, $680.
   - **e.** Depreciation on store equipment, $8,100.
   - **f.** Depreciation on office equipment, $3,050.
   - **g.** Accrued sales salaries, $4,000; accrued office salaries, $750.
   - **h.** Tax on accrued salaries: social security, $294.50; Medicare, $68.88.
2. Journalize the adjusting entries on page 16 of the general journal.

SOLUTION

Pietro's Imports

Worksheet

December 31, 2010

	ACCOUNT NAME	TRIAL BALANCE DEBIT	TRIAL BALANCE CREDIT	ADJUSTMENTS DEBIT	ADJUSTMENTS CREDIT
1	Cash	9,810.00			
2	Accounts Receivable	32,340.00			
3	Allowance for Doubtful Accounts		5,060.00		(c) 900.00
4	Merchandise Inventory	116,780.00		(b) 108,570.00	(a) 116,780.00
5	Supplies	10,600.00			(d) 9,920.00
6	Store Equipment	84,000.00			
7	Accumulated Depreciation—Store Equip.		16,590.00		(e) 8,100.00
8	Office Equipment	25,700.00			
9	Accumulated Depreciation—Office Equip.		7,033.00		(f) 3,050.00
10	Accounts Payable		22,560.00		
11	Salaries Payable				(g) 4,750.00
12	Social Security Tax Payable				(h) 294.50
13	Medicare Tax Payable				(h) 68.88
14	Pietro Canzone, Capital		230,764.00		
15	Pietro Canzone, Drawing	26,000.00			
16	Income Summary			(a) 116,780.00	(b) 108,570.00
17	Sales		394,642.00		
18	Sales Returns and Allowances	8,155.00			
19	Purchases	197,534.00			
20	Purchase Returns and Allowances		1,200.00		
21	Purchase Discounts		600.00		
22	Freight In	12,260.00			
23	Sales Salaries Expense	94,580.00		(g) 4,000.00	
24	Rent Expense	31,000.00			
25	Advertising Expense	12,045.00			
26	Supplies Expense			(d) 9,920.00	
27	Depreciation Expense—Store Equipment			(e) 8,100.00	
28	Office Salaries Expense	17,645.00		(g) 750.00	
29	Payroll Taxes Expense			(h) 363.38	
30	Depreciation Expense—Office Equipment			(f) 3,050.00	
31	Uncollectible Accounts Expense			(c) 900.00	
32		678,449.00	678,449.00	252,433.38	252,433.38
33	Net Loss				
34					
35					

SOLUTION (continued)

Adjusted Trial Balance Debit	Adjusted Trial Balance Credit	Income Statement Debit	Income Statement Credit	Balance Sheet Debit	Balance Sheet Credit	
9,810.00				9,810.00		1
32,340.00				32,340.00		2
	5,960.00				5,960.00	3
108,570.00				108,570.00		4
680.00				680.00		5
84,000.00				84,000.00		6
	24,690.00				24,690.00	7
25,700.00				25,700.00		8
	10,083.00				10,083.00	9
	22,560.00				22,560.00	10
	4,750.00				4,750.00	11
	294.50				294.50	12
	68.88				68.88	13
	230,764.00				230,764.00	14
26,000.00				26,000.00		15
116,780.00	108,570.00	116,780.00	108,570.00			16
	394,642.00		394,642.00			17
8,155.00		8,155.00				18
197,534.00		197,534.00				19
	1,200.00		1,200.00			20
	600.00		600.00			21
12,260.00		12,260.00				22
98,580.00		98,580.00				23
31,000.00		31,000.00				24
12,045.00		12,045.00				25
9,920.00		9,920.00				26
8,100.00		8,100.00				27
18,395.00		18,395.00				28
363.38		363.38				29
3,050.00		3,050.00				30
900.00		900.00				31
804,182.38	804,182.38	517,082.38	505,012.00	287,100.00	299,170.38	32
			12,070.38	12,070.38		33
		517,082.38	517,082.38	299,170.38	299,170.38	34
						35

SOLUTION (continued)

GENERAL JOURNAL PAGE 16

DATE		DESCRIPTION	POST. REF.	DEBIT	CREDIT
2010					
		(a)			
Dec.	31	Income Summary		116780.00	
		Merchandise Inventory			116780.00
		Close beginning merchandise inventory			
		(b)			
	31	Merchandise Inventory		108570.00	
		Income Summary			108570.00
		Record ending merchandise inventory			
		(c)			
	31	Uncollectible Accounts Expense		900.00	
		Allowance for Doubtful Accounts			900.00
		Record estimated uncollectible accounts expense			
		(d)			
	31	Supplies Expense		9920.00	
		Supplies			9920.00
		Record supplies used during year			
		(e)			
	31	Depreciation Expense—Store Equipment		8100.00	
		Accumulated Depreciation—Store Equipment			8100.00
		Record depreciation on store equipment for year			
		(f)			
	31	Depreciation Expense—Office Equipment		3050.00	
		Accumulated Depreciation—Office Equipment			3050.00
		Record depreciation on office equipment for year			
		(g)			
	31	Sales Salaries Expense		4000.00	
		Office Salaries Expense		750.00	
		Salaries Payable			4750.00
		Record accrued salaries			
		(h)			
	31	Payroll Taxes Expense		363.38	
		Social Security Tax Payable			294.50
		Medicare Tax Payable			68.88
		Record accrued payroll taxes			

WORKING PAPERS

Name ______________________

EXERCISE 12.1

GENERAL JOURNAL PAGE ______

	DATE		DESCRIPTION	POST. REF.	DEBIT	CREDIT	
1							1
2							2
3							3
4							4
5							5
6							6
7							7

EXERCISE 12.2

EXERCISE 12.3

GENERAL JOURNAL PAGE ______

	DATE		DESCRIPTION	POST. REF.	DEBIT	CREDIT	
1							1
2							2
3							3
4							4
5							5
6							6
7							7
8							8
9							9
10							10
11							11
12							12
13							13
14							14
15							15
16							16
17							17
18							18

Name ______________________

EXERCISE 12.4

GENERAL JOURNAL PAGE ______

	DATE	DESCRIPTION	POST. REF.	DEBIT	CREDIT	
1						1
2						2
3						3
4						4
5						5
6						6
7						7
8						8
9						9
10						10
11						11
12						12
13						13

EXERCISE 12.5

GENERAL JOURNAL PAGE ______

	DATE	DESCRIPTION	POST. REF.	DEBIT	CREDIT	
1						1
2						2
3						3
4						4
5						5
6						6
7						7
8						8

EXERCISE 12.6

GENERAL JOURNAL PAGE ______

	DATE	DESCRIPTION	POST. REF.	DEBIT	CREDIT	
1						1
2						2
3						3
4						4

Name ____________________

EXERCISE 12.7

GENERAL JOURNAL

PAGE ______

	DATE	DESCRIPTION	POST. REF.	DEBIT	CREDIT	
1						1
2						2
3						3
4						4
5						5
6						6
7						7
8						8
9						9
10						10
11						11
12						12
13						13

Name ______________________________

PROBLEM 12.1A or 12.1B

GENERAL JOURNAL

PAGE 1

DATE		DESCRIPTION	POST. REF.	DEBIT	CREDIT

Name ____________________

PROBLEM 12.1A or 12.1B (continued)

GENERAL JOURNAL

PAGE 2

	DATE		DESCRIPTION	POST. REF.	DEBIT	CREDIT	
1							1
2							2
3							3
4							4
5							5
6							6
7							7
8							8
9							9
10							10
11							11
12							12
13							13
14							14
15							15
16							16
17							17
18							18
19							19
20							20
21							21
22							22
23							23
24							24
25							25
26							26
27							27
28							28
29							29
30							30
31							31
32							32
33							33
34							34

Analyze: ____________________

Name ______________________

PROBLEM 12.2A or 12.2B

	ACCOUNT NAME	TRIAL BALANCE		ADJUSTMENTS	
		DEBIT	CREDIT	DEBIT	CREDIT
1					
2					
3					
4					
5					
6					
7					
8					
9					
10					
11					
12					
13					
14					
15					
16					
17					
18					
19					
20					
21					
22					
23					
24					
25					
26					
27					
28					
29					
30					
31					
32					

Name

PROBLEM 12.2A or 12.2B (continued)

ADJUSTED TRIAL BALANCE		INCOME STATEMENT		BALANCE SHEET		
DEBIT	CREDIT	DEBIT	CREDIT	DEBIT	CREDIT	
						1
						2
						3
						4
						5
						6
						7
						8
						9
						10
						11
						12
						13
						14
						15
						16
						17
						18
						19
						20
						21
						22
						23
						24
						25
						26
						27
						28
						29
						30
						31
						32

Analyze:

Name

PROBLEM 12.3A or 12.3B

	ACCOUNT NAME	TRIAL BALANCE		ADJUSTMENTS	
		DEBIT	CREDIT	DEBIT	CREDIT
1					
2					
3					
4					
5					
6					
7					
8					
9					
10					
11					
12					
13					
14					
15					
16					
17					
18					
19					
20					
21					
22					
23					
24					
25					
26					
27					
28					
29					
30					
31					
32					
33					
34					

Name ______________________

PROBLEM 12.3A or 12.3B (continued)

ADJUSTED TRIAL BALANCE		INCOME STATEMENT		BALANCE SHEET	
DEBIT	CREDIT	DEBIT	CREDIT	DEBIT	CREDIT

Name

PROBLEM 12.3A or 12.3B (continued)

	ACCOUNT NAME	TRIAL BALANCE		ADJUSTMENTS	
		DEBIT	CREDIT	DEBIT	CREDIT
1					
2					
3					
4					
5					
6					
7					
8					
9					
10					
11					
12					
13					
14					
15					
16					
17					
18					
19					
20					
21					
22					
23					
24					
25					
26					
27					
28					
29					
30					
31					
32					

PROBLEM 12.3A or 12.3B (continued)

ADJUSTED TRIAL BALANCE		INCOME STATEMENT		BALANCE SHEET		
DEBIT	CREDIT	DEBIT	CREDIT	DEBIT	CREDIT	
						1
						2
						3
						4
						5
						6
						7
						8
						9
						10
						11
						12
						13
						14
						15
						16
						17
						18
						19
						20
						21
						22
						23
						24
						25
						26
						27
						28
						29
						30
						31
						32

Analyze:

Name

PROBLEM 12.4A or 12.4B

	ACCOUNT NAME	TRIAL BALANCE DEBIT	TRIAL BALANCE CREDIT	ADJUSTMENTS DEBIT	ADJUSTMENTS CREDIT
1					
2					
3					
4					
5					
6					
7					
8					
9					
10					
11					
12					
13					
14					
15					
16					
17					
18					
19					
20					
21					
22					
23					
24					
25					
26					
27					
28					
29					
30					
31					
32					
33					
34					

Name

PROBLEM 12.4A or 12.4B (continued)

ADJUSTED TRIAL BALANCE		INCOME STATEMENT		BALANCE SHEET	
DEBIT	CREDIT	DEBIT	CREDIT	DEBIT	CREDIT

Name

PROBLEM 12.4A or 12.4B (continued)

	ACCOUNT NAME	TRIAL BALANCE DEBIT	TRIAL BALANCE CREDIT	ADJUSTMENTS DEBIT	ADJUSTMENTS CREDIT
1					
2					
3					
4					
5					
6					
7					
8					
9					
10					
11					
12					
13					
14					
15					
16					
17					
18					
19					
20					
21					
22					
23					
24					
25					
26					
27					
28					
29					
30					
31					
32					

Name

PROBLEM 12.4A or 12.4B (continued)

ADJUSTED TRIAL BALANCE		INCOME STATEMENT		BALANCE SHEET		
DEBIT	CREDIT	DEBIT	CREDIT	DEBIT	CREDIT	
						1
						2
						3
						4
						5
						6
						7
						8
						9
						10
						11
						12
						13
						14
						15
						16
						17
						18
						19
						20
						21
						22
						23
						24
						25
						26
						27
						28
						29
						30
						31
						32

Analyze:

Name ____________________

CRITICAL THINKING PROBLEM 12.1

	ACCOUNT NAME	TRIAL BALANCE		ADJUSTMENTS	
		DEBIT	CREDIT	DEBIT	CREDIT
1					
2					
3					
4					
5					
6					
7					
8					
9					
10					
11					
12					
13					
14					
15					
16					
17					
18					
19					
20					
21					
22					
23					
24					
25					
26					
27					
28					
29					
30					
31					
32					
33					

Name

CRITICAL THINKING PROBLEM 12.1 (continued)

ADJUSTED TRIAL BALANCE		INCOME STATEMENT		BALANCE SHEET		
DEBIT	CREDIT	DEBIT	CREDIT	DEBIT	CREDIT	
						1
						2
						3
						4
						5
						6
						7
						8
						9
						10
						11
						12
						13
						14
						15
						16
						17
						18
						19
						20
						21
						22
						23
						24
						25
						26
						27
						28
						29
						30
						31
						32
						33

Name

CRITICAL THINKING PROBLEM 12.1 (continued)

	ACCOUNT NAME	TRIAL BALANCE		ADJUSTMENTS	
		DEBIT	CREDIT	DEBIT	CREDIT
1					
2					
3					
4					
5					
6					
7					
8					
9					
10					
11					
12					
13					
14					
15					
16					
17					
18					
19					
20					
21					
22					
23					
24					
25					
26					
27					
28					
29					
30					
31					
32					

Name

CRITICAL THINKING PROBLEM 12.1 (continued)

ADJUSTED TRIAL BALANCE		INCOME STATEMENT		BALANCE SHEET		
DEBIT	CREDIT	DEBIT	CREDIT	DEBIT	CREDIT	
						1
						2
						3
						4
						5
						6
						7
						8
						9
						10
						11
						12
						13
						14
						15
						16
						17
						18
						19
						20
						21
						22
						23
						24
						25
						26
						27
						28
						29
						30
						31
						32

Name ____________________

CRITICAL THINKING PROBLEM 12.1 (continued)

GENERAL JOURNAL PAGE 30

DATE		DESCRIPTION	POST. REF.	DEBIT	CREDIT

Name

CRITICAL THINKING PROBLEM 12.1 (continued)

GENERAL JOURNAL PAGE 32

DATE	DESCRIPTION	POST. REF.	DEBIT	CREDIT

Name

CRITICAL THINKING PROBLEM 12.1 (continued)

a. Net Sales

b. Net Delivered Cost of Purchases

c. Cost of Goods Sold

d. Net Income (from worksheet)

e. Capital, December 31

Analyze:

Name

CRITICAL THINKING PROBLEM 12.2

1.

2.

Name ____________________

Chapter 12 Practice Test Answer Key

Part A True-False

1. T
2. T
3. F
4. T
5. F
6. F
7. T
8. T
9. F
10. T
11. F
12. T
13. T
14. T
15. T
16. F
17. F
18. T
19. F
20. F
21. F
22. F
23. T
24. T
25. T

Part B Exercises

GENERAL JOURNAL PAGE______

	DATE		DESCRIPTION	POST. REF.	DEBIT	CREDIT	
1			**Adjusting Entries**				1
2	2010		(Adjustment 1)				2
3	Dec.	31	Supplies Expense		1,150.00		3
4			Store Supplies			1,150.00	4
5			(Adjustment 2)				5
6		31	Interest Expense		37.50		6
7			Interest Payable			37.50	7
8			(Adjustment 3)				8
9		31	Interest Receivable		75.00		9
10			Interest Income			75.00	10
11			(Adjustment 4)				11
12		31	Insurance Expense		300.00		12
13			Prepaid Insurance			300.00	13
14							14
15							

CHAPTER 13 Financial Statements and Closing Procedures

STUDY GUIDE

Understanding the Chapter

Objectives

1. Prepare a classified income statement from the worksheet. **2.** Prepare a statement of owner's equity from the worksheet. **3.** Prepare a classified balance sheet from the worksheet. **4.** Journalize and post the adjusting entries. **5.** Journalize and post the closing entries. **6.** Prepare a postclosing trial balance. **7.** Journalize and post reversing entries. **8.** Define the accounting terms new to this chapter.

Reading Assignment

Read Chapter 13 in the textbook. Complete the textbook Section Self Review as you finish reading each section of the chapter, and the Comprehensive Self Review at the end of the chapter. Refer to the Chapter 13 Glossary or to the Glossary at the end of the book to find definitions for terms that are not familiar to you.

Activities

❑ **Thinking Critically** — Answer the *Thinking Critically* questions for Whole Foods Market and Managerial Implications.

❑ **Discussion Questions** — Answer each assigned discussion question in Chapter 13.

❑ **Exercises** — Complete each assigned exercise in Chapter 13. Use the forms provided in this SGWP. The objectives covered by an exercise are given after the exercise number. If you need help with an exercise, review the portion of the chapter related to the objective(s) covered.

❑ **Problems A/B** — Complete each assigned problem in Chapter 13. Use the forms provided in this SGWP. The objectives covered by a problem are given after the problem number. If you need help with a problem review the portion of the chapter related to the objective(s) covered.

❑ **Critical Thinking Problems** — Complete the critical thinking problems as assigned. Use the forms provided in this SGWP.

❑ **Business Connections** — Complete the Business Connections activities as assigned to gain a deeper understanding of Chapter 13 concepts.

Practice Tests

Complete the Practice Tests, which cover the main points in your reading assignment. Compare your answers with those in the Practice Test Answer Key for Chapter 13 at the end of this chapter. If you have answered any questions incorrectly, review the related section of text.

STUDY GUIDE

Part A True-False *True-False For each of the following statements, circle T in the answer column if the statement is true or F if the statement is false.*

T F **1.** The drawing account is closed into the **Income Summary** account as one of the last closing entries.

T F **2.** After completing the worksheet and the financial statements, adjustments are entered in the general journal.

T F **3.** After all adjustments have been journalized and posted, the ledger account balances should be the same as the post-closing trial balance amounts.

T F **4.** The revenue and expense accounts are the only accounts carried forward from one year to the next.

T F **5.** The information needed to close the revenue and expense accounts is taken directly from the ledger accounts to ensure accuracy.

T F **6.** Asset and liability accounts are the only accounts carried forward from one year to the next.

T F **7.** The **Income Summary** account is closed at the end of the period.

T F **8.** It is desirable to prepare a postclosing trial balance after the adjusting and closing entries have been journalized and posted.

T F **9.** The postclosing trial balance shows essentially the same account balances that appear in the balance sheet.

T F **10.** Short-term notes receivable, cash, accounts receivable, merchandise inventory and prepaid expense items appear in the Current Assets section of the classified balance sheet.

T F **11.** The gross profit on sales shown on the classified income statement is the difference between the net sales and the operating expenses.

T F **12.** Current liabilities are debts that are due for payment after one year from the balance sheet date.

T F **13.** The Cost of Goods Sold section of the classified income statement includes information about the beginning and ending merchandise inventory and the purchases and net sales made during the year.

T F **14.** The net income or loss from operations shown on the classified income statement is the difference between gross profit on sales and total operating expenses.

T F **15.** The depreciation expense for the store equipment appears in the Plant and Equipment section of the classified balance sheet.

T F **16.** Adjustments are posted from the worksheet to the general ledger accounts.

T F **17.** The ending merchandise inventory is recorded in the accounting records by an adjusting entry.

T F **18.** **Income Summary** is credited for the total of the expenses and the beginning inventory.

T F **19.** Closing journal entries for December 31, 2010 should be reversed on January 1, 2011.

T F **20.** In closing the **Income Summary** account, the net income or loss is closed into the owner's capital account.

T F **21.** Reversing entries are not required, but are highly recommended in order to improve efficiency and reduce errors.

T F **22.** Cash, accounts receivable, merchandise inventory and equipment are classified as current assets.

T F **23.** **Interest Payable** and **Depreciation Expense** are typical of accounts that do not require reversing entries.

T F **24.** Some accounts adjusted in the Adjustment columns of the worksheet do not require a reversing entry.

T F **25.** A company reported net sales of $1,000,000 and cost of goods sold of $600,000. The gross profit percentage is 60%.

Demonstration Problem

A partial worksheet showing the end-of-year operating results for Sports Warehouse for 2010 follows.

Instructions

1. Prepare a classified income statement. Sports Warehouse does not classify its operating expenses as selling and administrative expenses.
2. Prepare a statement of owner's equity. No additional investments were made during the period.
3. Prepare a classified balance sheet as of December 31, 2010. All notes payable are due within one year.
4. Journalize the closing entries on page 45 of the general journal.
5. Compute the gross profit percentage for the year ended December 31, 2010. Round your answer to one decimal.
6. Compute the current ratio at December 31, 2010.

DEMONSTRATION PROBLEM (continued)

Sports Warehouse
Worksheet (Partial)
Year Ended December 31, 2010

	ACCOUNT NAME	INCOME STATEMENT		BALANCE SHEET	
		DEBIT	CREDIT	DEBIT	CREDIT
1	Cash			24,285.00	
2	Accounts Receivable			56,258.00	
3	Allowance for Doubtful Accounts				5,840.00
4	Merchandise Inventory			197,214.00	
5	Supplies			3,612.00	
6	Prepaid Insurance			37,000.00	
7	Equipment			83,290.00	
8	Accumulated Depreciation—Equipment				24,330.00
9	Notes Payable				47,500.00
10	Accounts Payable				41,860.00
11	Social Security Tax Payable				2,683.00
12	Medicare Tax Payable				845.00
13	Salaries Payable				6,530.00
14	Interest Payable				3,660.00
15	Raul Flores, Capital				260,730.00
16	Raul Flores, Drawing			50,000.00	
17	Income Summary	201,345.00	197,214.00		
18	Sales		620,690.00		
19	Sales Returns and Allowances	11,950.00			
20	Purchases	277,174.00			
21	Purchases Returns and Allowances		10,440.00		
22	Freight In	11,410.00			
23	Purchases Discounts		11,921.00		
24	Telephone Expense	4,171.00			
25	Salaries Expense	240,380.00			
26	Payroll Tax Expense	13,104.00			
27	Supplies Expense	5,960.00			
28	Insurance Expense	5,000.00			
29	Depreciation Expense—Equipment	7,420.00			
30	Uncollectible Accounts Expense	2,510.00			
31	Interest Expense	2,160.00			
32	Totals	782,584.00	840,265.00	451,659.00	393,978.00
33	Net Income	57,681.00			57,681.00
34		840,265.00	840,265.00	451,659.00	451,659.00
35					

SOLUTION

(1.)

Sports Warehouse
Income Statement
Year Ended December 31, 2010

Operating Revenue				
Sales				620 690 00
Less Sales Returns and Allowances				11 950 00
Net Sales				608 740 00
Cost of Goods Sold				
Merchandise Inventory, Jan. 1, 2010			201 345 00	
Purchases		277 174 00		
Freight In		11 410 00		
Delivered Cost of Purchases		288 584 00		
Less Purchase Returns and Allow.	10 440 00			
Purchase Discounts	11 921 00	22 361 00		
Net Delivered Cost of Purchases			266 223 00	
Total Merchandise Available for Sale			467 568 00	
Less Merchandise Inv., Dec. 31, 2010			197 214 00	
Cost of Goods Sold				270 354 00
Gross Profit on Sales				338 386 00
Operating Expenses				
Telephone Expense			4 171 00	
Salaries Expense			240 380 00	
Payroll Tax Expense			13 104 00	
Supplies Expense			5 960 00	
Insurance Expense			5 000 00	
Depreciation Expense—Equipment			7 420 00	
Uncollectible Accounts Expense			2 510 00	
Total Operating Expenses				278 545 00
Income from Operations				59 841 00
Other Expenses				
Interest Expense				2 160 00
Net Income for Year				57 681 00

SOLUTION (continued)

(2.)

Sports Warehouse
Statement of Owner's Equity
Year Ended December 31, 2010

Raul Flores, Capital, Jan. 1, 2010			260 730 00
Net Income for Year		57 681 00	
Less Withdrawals for the Year		50 000 00	
Increase in Capital			7 681 00
Raul Flores, Capital, Dec. 31, 2010			268 411 00

(3.)

Sports Warehouse
Balance Sheet
December 31, 2010

Assets			
Current Assets			
Cash			24 285 00
Accounts Receivable		56 258 00	
Less Allowance for Doubtful Accounts		5 840 00	50 418 00
Merchandise Inventory			197 214 00
Prepaid Expenses			
Supplies		3 612 00	
Prepaid Insurance		37 000 00	40 612 00
Total Current Assets			312 529 00
Plant and Equipment			
Equipment	83 290 00		
Less Accumulated Depreciation	24 330 00	58 960 00	
Total Plant and Equipment			58 960 00
Total Assets			371 489 00
Liabilities and Owner's Equity			
Current Liabilities			
Notes Payable		47 500 00	
Accounts Payable		41 860 00	
Interest Payable		3 660 00	
Social Security Tax Payable		2 683 00	
Medicare Tax Payable		845 00	
Salaries Payable		6 530 00	
Total Current Liabilities			103 078 00
Owner's Equity			
Raul Flores, Capital			268 411 00
Total Liabilities and Owner's Equity			371 489 00

SOLUTION (continued)

(4.)

GENERAL JOURNAL PAGE 45

DATE		DESCRIPTION	POST. REF.	DEBIT	CREDIT
		Closing Entries			
2010					
Dec.	31	Sales		620,690.00	
		Purchase Returns and Allowances		10,440.00	
		Purchases Discounts		11,921.00	
		Income Summary			643,051.00
	31	Income Summary		581,239.00	
		Sales Returns and Allowances			11,950.00
		Purchases			277,174.00
		Freight In			11,410.00
		Telephone Expense			4,171.00
		Salaries Expense			240,380.00
		Payroll Taxes Expense			13,104.00
		Supplies Expense			5,960.00
		Insurance Expense			5,000.00
		Depreciation Expense—Equipment			7,420.00
		Uncollectible Accounts Expense			2,510.00
		Interest Expense			2,160.00
	31	Income Summary		57,681.00	
		Raul Flores, Capital			57,681.00
	31	Raul Flores, Capital		50,000.00	
		Raul Flores, Drawing			50,000.00

(5.) The gross profit percentage for the year ended December 31, 2010 is 55.6% ($338,386/$608,740).

(6.) The current ratio at December 31, 2010 is 3.03:1 ($312,529/$103,078).

WORKING PAPERS

Name ______________________

EXERCISE 13.1

1. Rent Expense ____________
2. Depreciation Expense—Store Equipment ____________
3. Sales ____________
4. Interest Expense ____________
5. Merchandise Inventory ____________
6. Interest Income ____________
7. Purchases ____________
8. Sales Returns and Allowances ____________
9. Utilities Expense ____________
10. Purchase Returns and Allowances ____________

EXERCISE 13.2

1. Rent Payable ____________
2. Cash ____________
3. Raja Julia, Capital ____________
4. Merchandise Inventory ____________
5. Accounts Payable ____________
6. Store Supplies ____________
7. Sales Tax Payable ____________
8. Prepaid Insurance ____________
9. Delivery Van ____________
10. Accounts Receivable ____________

EXERCISE 13.3

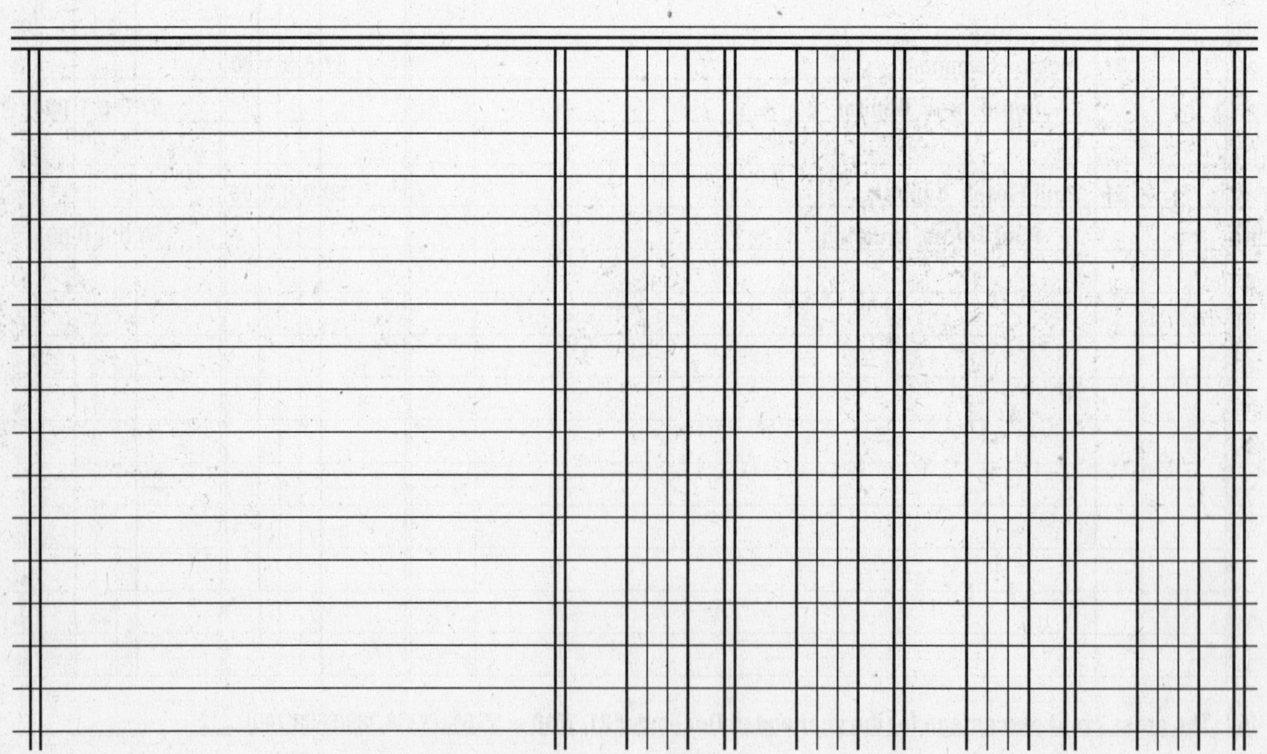

(continued)

Name

EXERCISE 13.3 (continued)

EXERCISE 13.4

Name

EXERCISE 13.5

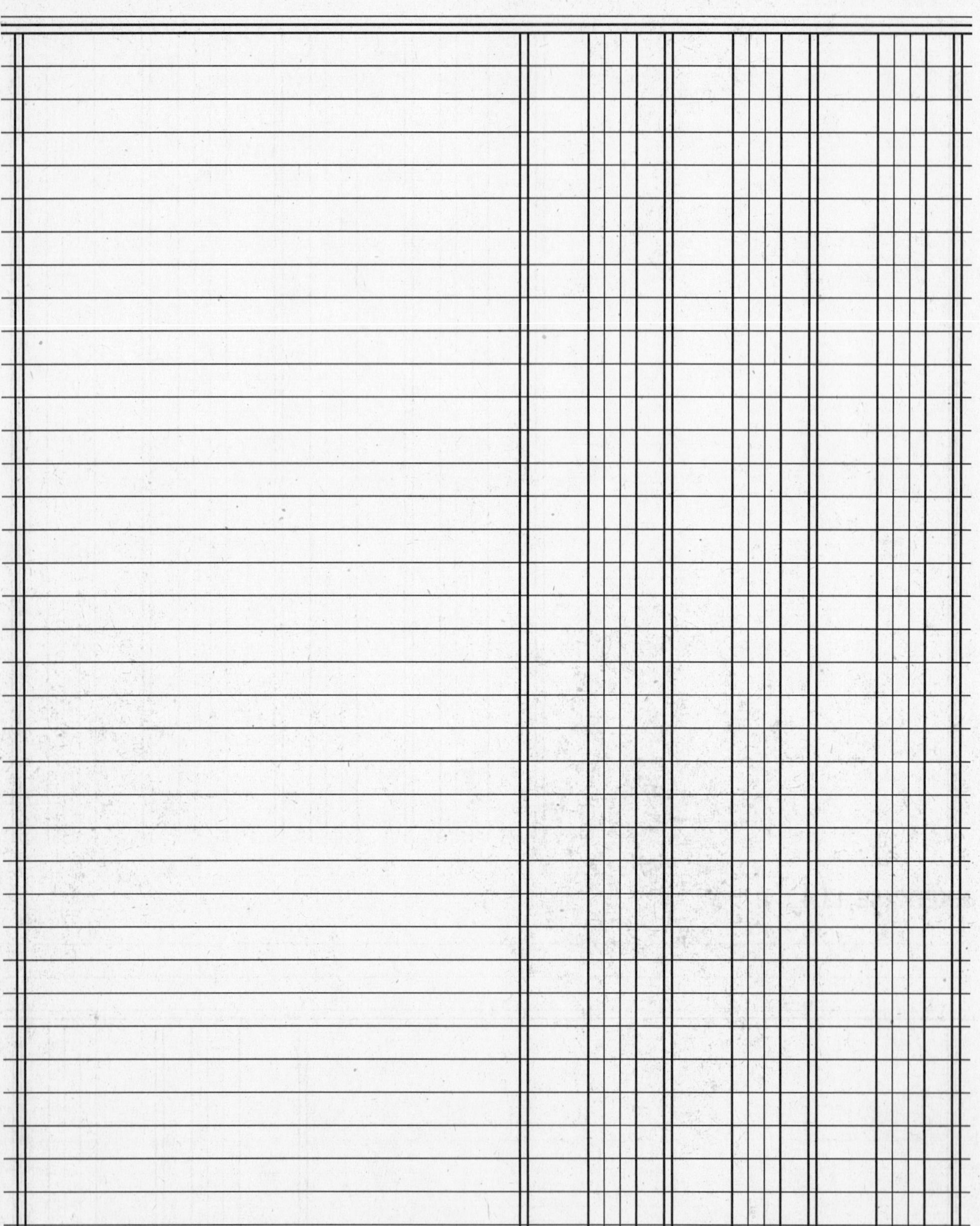

Name ____________________

EXERCISE 13.6

GENERAL JOURNAL

PAGE ________

	DATE		DESCRIPTION	POST. REF.	DEBIT	CREDIT	
1							1
2							2
3							3
4							4
5							5
6							6
7							7
8							8
9							9
10							10
11							11
12							12
13							13
14							14
15							15
16							16
17							17
18							18
19							19
20							20
21							21
22							22
23							23
24							24
25							25
26							26
27							27
28							28
29							29
30							30
31							31
32							32
33							33
34							34
35							35
36							36
37							37

Name ____________________

EXERCISE 13.7

GENERAL JOURNAL

PAGE ______

DATE		DESCRIPTION	POST. REF.	DEBIT	CREDIT

Name

EXERCISE 13.8

ACCOUNT NAME	DEBIT	CREDIT

Name

EXERCISE 13.9

a. Net Sales is

Gross profit is

The gross profit percentages is

b. Current assets are

Current liabilities are

Working capital is

Name

EXERCISE 13.9 (continued)

c. The current ratio is

d. The inventory turnover is

Name

PROBLEM 13.1A or 13.1B

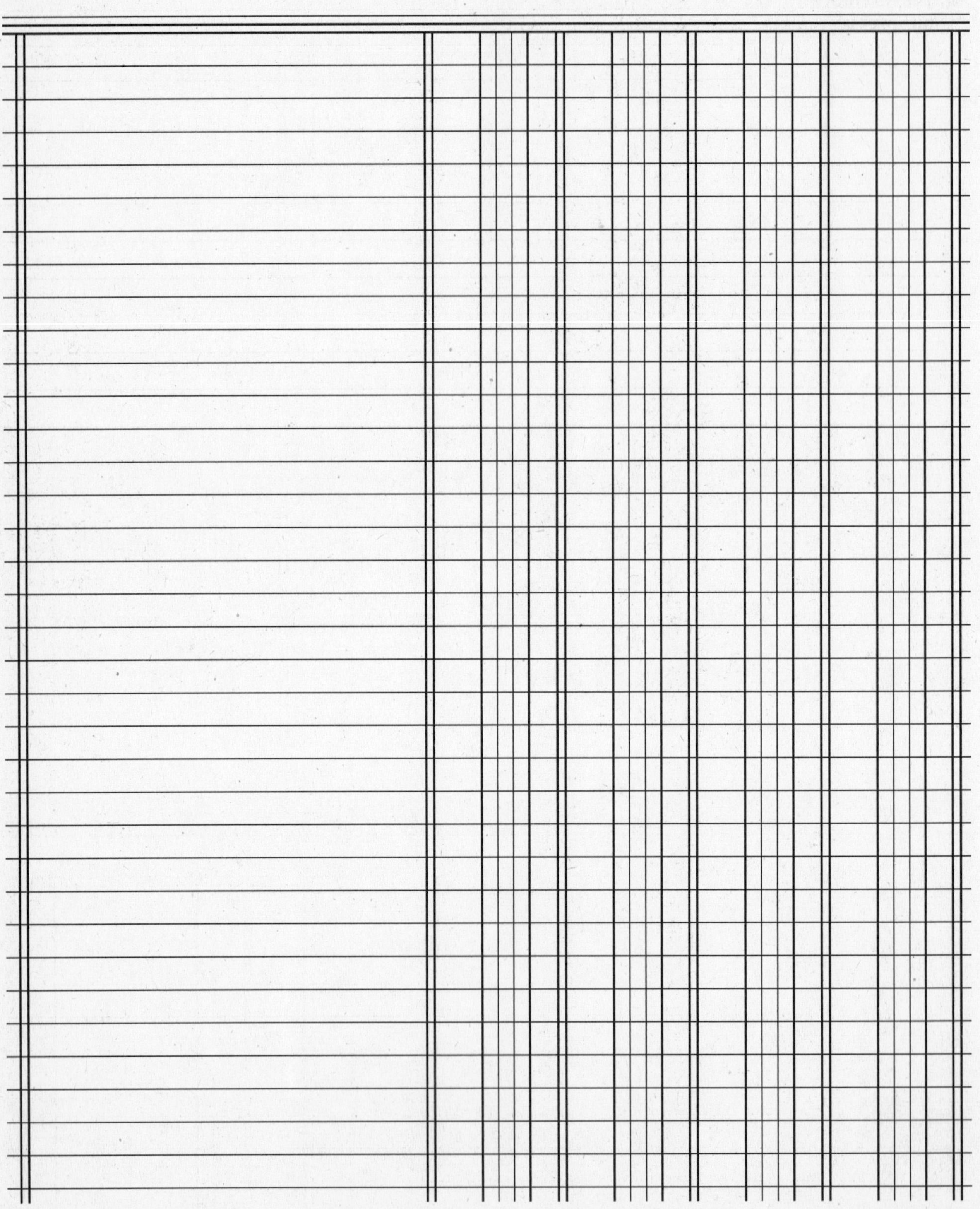

(continued)

Name

PROBLEM 13.1A or 13.1B (continued)

Name

PROBLEM 13.1A or 13.1B (continued)

(continued)

Name

PROBLEM 13.1A or 13.1B (continued)

Analyze:

Name

PROBLEM 13.2A or 13.2B

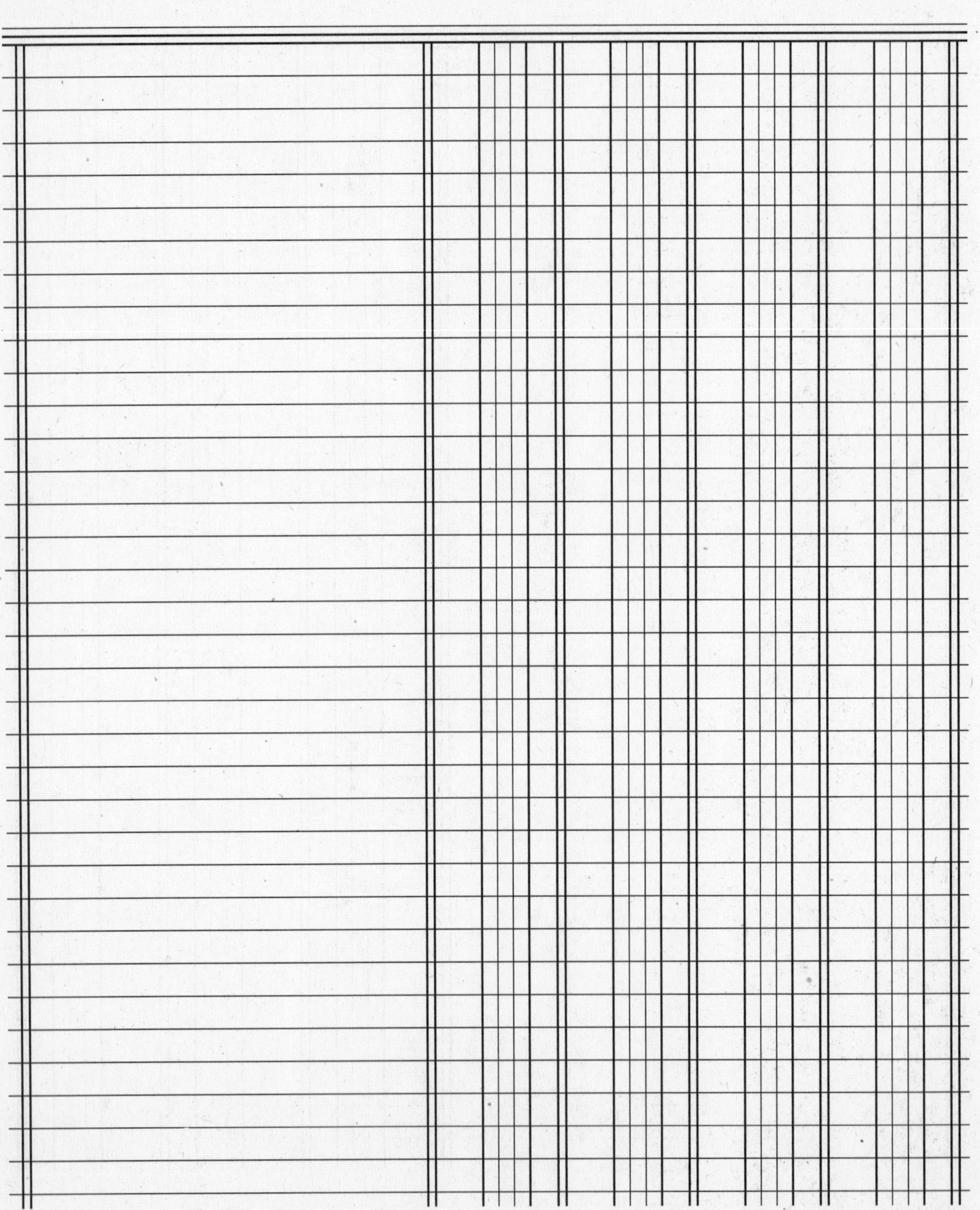

(continued)

Name

PROBLEM 13.2A or 13.2B (continued)

Name

PROBLEM 13.2A or 13.2B (continued)

(continued)

Name

PROBLEM 13.2A or 13.2B (continued)

Analyze:

Name ____________________

PROBLEM 13.3A or 13.3B

GENERAL JOURNAL

PAGE ______

DATE	DESCRIPTION	POST. REF.	DEBIT	CREDIT

Name ______________________

PROBLEM 13.3A or 13.3B (continued)

GENERAL JOURNAL

PAGE ______

DATE		DESCRIPTION	POST. REF.	DEBIT	CREDIT

Name

PROBLEM 13.3A or 13.3B (continued)

GENERAL JOURNAL

PAGE

DATE		DESCRIPTION	POST. REF.	DEBIT	CREDIT

Name

PROBLEM 13.3A or 13.3B (continued)

GENERAL JOURNAL

PAGE

DATE		DESCRIPTION	POST. REF.	DEBIT	CREDIT

Analyze:

PAGE

DATE		DESCRIPTION	POST. REF.	DEBIT	CREDIT

Name ____________________

PROBLEM 13.4A or 13.4B

GENERAL JOURNAL

PAGE ______

	DATE	DESCRIPTION	POST. REF.	DEBIT	CREDIT	
1						1
2						2
3						3
4						4
5						5
6						6
7						7
8						8
9						9
10						10
11						11
12						12
13						13
14						14
15						15
16						16
17						17
18						18
19						19
20						20
21						21
22						22
23						23
24						24
25						25
26						26
27						27
28						28
29						29
30						30
31						31
32						32
33						33
34						34
35						35
36						36

Name ______________________

PROBLEM 13.4A or 13.4B (continued)

GENERAL JOURNAL PAGE ______

	DATE	DESCRIPTION	POST. REF.	DEBIT	CREDIT	
1						1
2						2
3						3
4						4
5						5
6						6
7						7
8						8
9						9
10						10
11						11
12						12
13						13
14						14
15						15
16						16

Analyze: ______________________

EXTRA FORM

GENERAL JOURNAL PAGE ______

	DATE	DESCRIPTION	POST. REF.	DEBIT	CREDIT	
1						1
2						2
3						3
4						4
5						5
6						6
7						7
8						8
9						9
10						10
11						11
12						12
13						13

Name

CRITICAL THINKING PROBLEM 13.1

	ACCOUNT NAME	TRIAL BALANCE DEBIT	TRIAL BALANCE CREDIT	ADJUSTMENTS DEBIT	ADJUSTMENTS CREDIT
1					
2					
3					
4					
5					
6					
7					
8					
9					
10					
11					
12					
13					
14					
15					
16					
17					
18					
19					
20					
21					
22					
23					
24					
25					
26					
27					
28					
29					
30					
31					
32					
33					
34					
35					
36					

Name ______________________

CRITICAL THINKING PROBLEM 13.1 (continued)

ADJUSTED TRIAL BALANCE		INCOME STATEMENT		BALANCE SHEET		
DEBIT	CREDIT	DEBIT	CREDIT	DEBIT	CREDIT	
						1
						2
						3
						4
						5
						6
						7
						8
						9
						10
						11
						12
						13
						14
						15
						16
						17
						18
						19
						20
						21
						22
						23
						24
						25
						26
						27
						28
						29
						30
						31
						32
						33
						34
						35
						36

Name

CRITICAL THINKING PROBLEM 13.1 (continued)

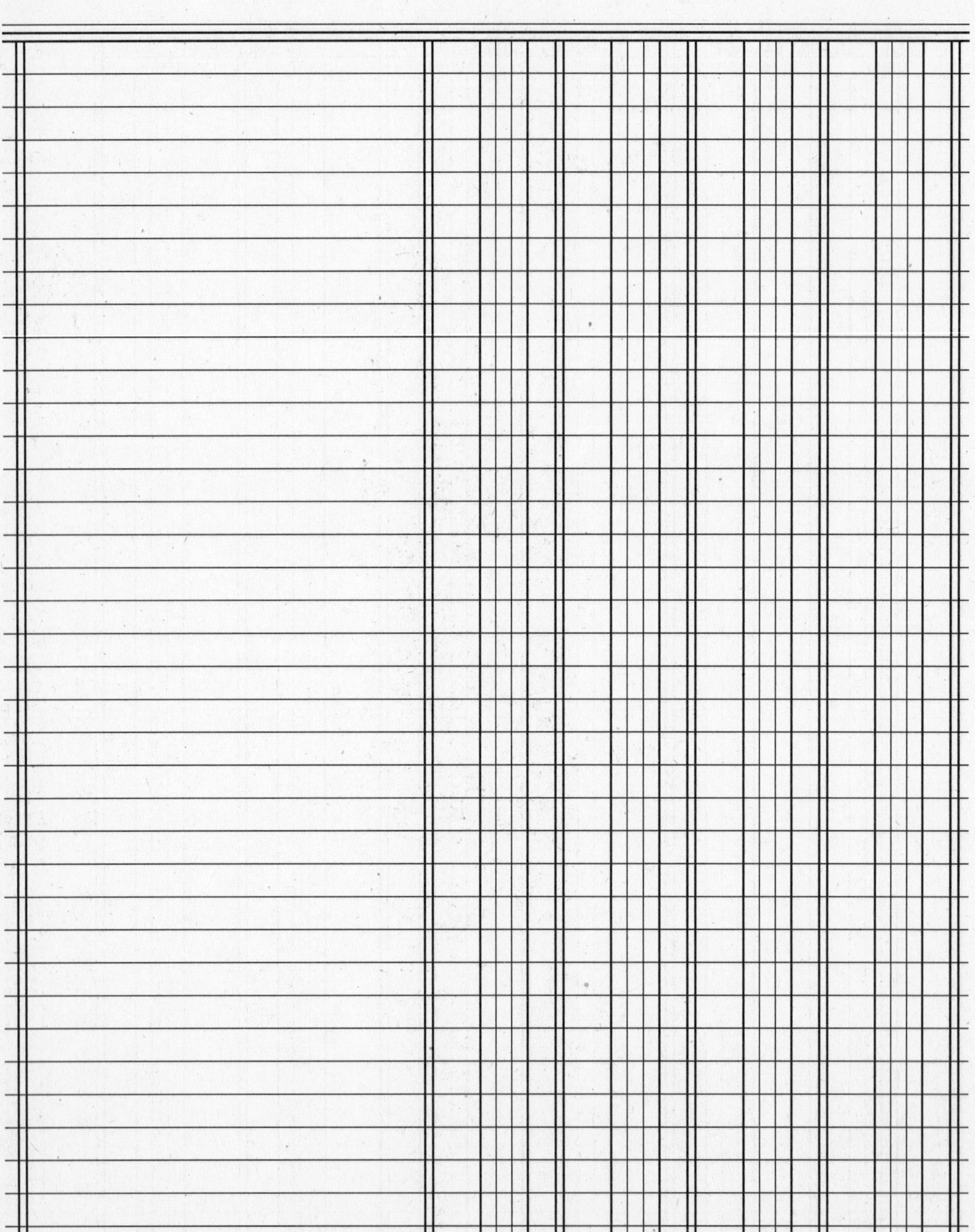

Name

CRITICAL THINKING PROBLEM 13.1 (continued)

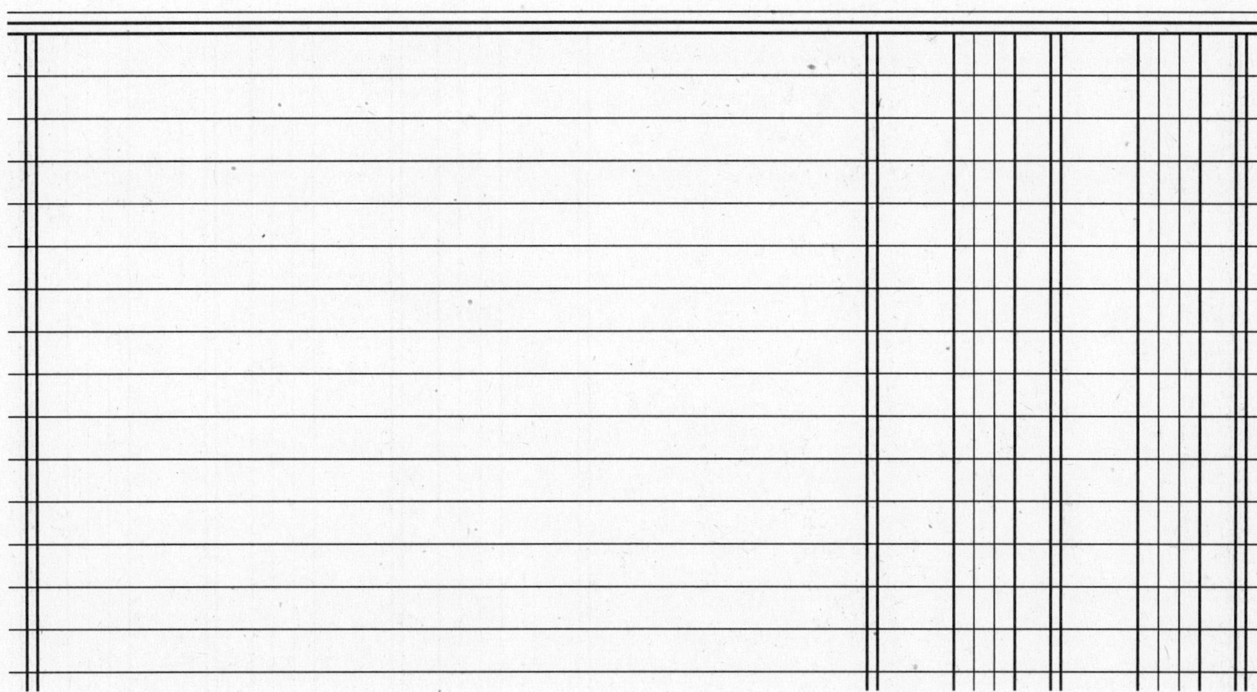

EXTRA FORM

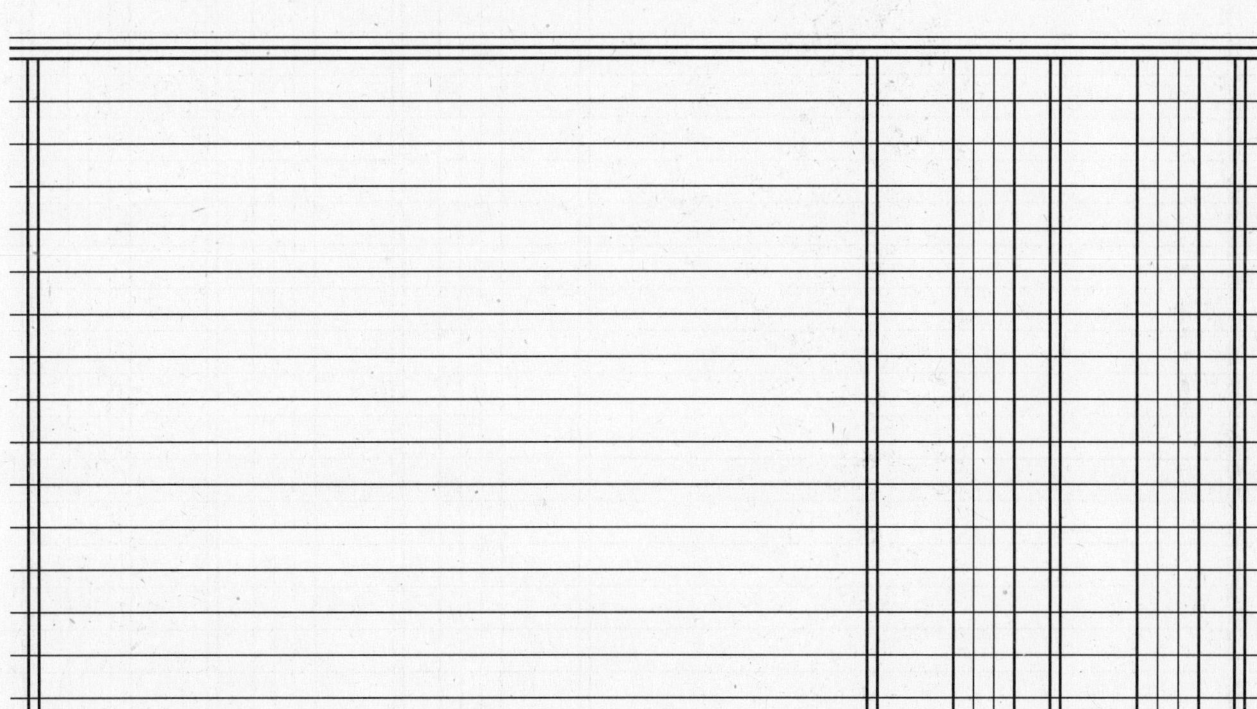

Name

CRITICAL THINKING PROBLEM 13.1 (continued)

Name ______________________

CRITICAL THINKING PROBLEM 13.1 (continued)

GENERAL JOURNAL PAGE ______

DATE	DESCRIPTION	POST. REF.	DEBIT	CREDIT

Name

CRITICAL THINKING PROBLEM 13.1 (continued)

GENERAL JOURNAL

PAGE ________

DATE	DESCRIPTION	POST. REF.	DEBIT	CREDIT

Name ____________________

CRITICAL THINKING PROBLEM 13.1 (continued)

GENERAL JOURNAL — PAGE ______

DATE	DESCRIPTION	POST. REF.	DEBIT	CREDIT

Name

CRITICAL THINKING PROBLEM 13.1 (continued)

GENERAL JOURNAL PAGE

	DATE	DESCRIPTION	POST. REF.	DEBIT	CREDIT	
1						1
2						2
3						3
4						4
5						5
6						6
7						7
8						8
9						9
10						10
11						11
12						12
13						13
14						14
15						15
16						16
17						17
18						18
19						19
20						20
21						21
22						22
23						23
24						24
25						25
26						26
27						27
28						28
29						29
30						30
31						31
32						32
33						33
34						34

Analyze:

Name

CRITICAL THINKING PROBLEM 13.2

1.

2.

Name

CHAPTER 13 CRITICAL THINKING PROBLEM (continued)

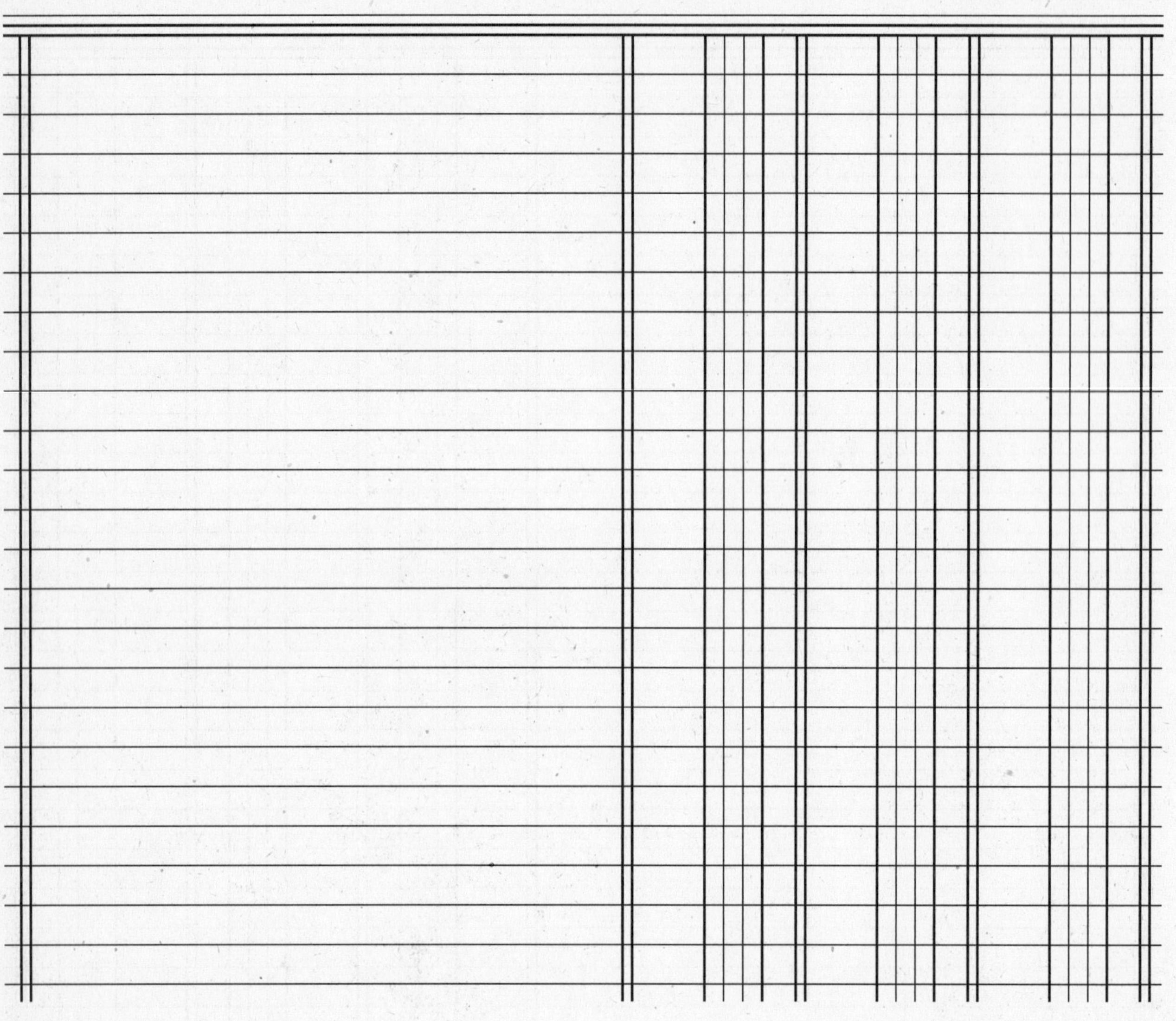

3.

Chapter 13 Practice Test Answer Key

Part A True-False

1. F	6. F	11. F	16. F	21. T
2. T	7. T	12. F	17. T	22. F
3. T	8. T	13. F	18. F	23. F
4. F	9. T	14. T	19. F	24. T
5. F	10. T	15. F	20. T	25. F

Name ____________________

MINI-PRACTICE SET 2

Merchandising Business Accounting Cycle

SALES JOURNAL

PAGE ________

	DATE	SALES SLIP NO.	CUSTOMER'S NAME	POST. REF.	ACCOUNTS RECEIVABLE DEBIT	SALES TAX PAYABLE CREDIT	SALES CREDIT	
1								1
2								2
3								3
4								4
5								5
6								6
7								7
8								8
9								9
10								10
11								11
12								12
13								13
14								14

PURCHASES JOURNAL

PAGE ________

DATE	PURCHASED FROM	INVOICE NUMBER	INVOICE DATE	TERMS	POST. REF.	PURCHASES DR./ ACCOUNTS PAYABLE CREDIT

 Name ____________________

CASH RECEIPTS JOURNAL

PAGE ______

DATE	DESCRIPTION	POST. REF.	ACCOUNTS RECEIVABLE CREDIT	SALES TAX PAYABLE CREDIT	SALES CREDIT	OTHER ACCOUNTS CREDIT			CASH DEBIT
						ACCOUNT NAME	POST. REF.	AMOUNT	

Name ______________________________

CASH PAYMENTS JOURNAL

PAGE ______

DATE	CK. NO.	DESCRIPTION	POST. REF.	ACCOUNTS PAYABLE DEBIT	OTHER ACCOUNTS DEBIT			PURCHASES DISCOUNTS CREDIT	CASH CREDIT
					ACCOUNT NAME	POST. REF.	AMOUNT		

 Name ______________________

GENERAL JOURNAL

PAGE ______

DATE	DESCRIPTION	POST. REF.	DEBIT	CREDIT

 Name ____________________

GENERAL JOURNAL

PAGE ______

DATE		DESCRIPTION	POST. REF.	DEBIT	CREDIT

 Name

GENERAL JOURNAL

PAGE

DATE		DESCRIPTION	POST. REF.	DEBIT	CREDIT

 Name

GENERAL LEDGER

ACCOUNT ______ ACCOUNT NO. ______

DATE		DESCRIPTION	POST. REF.	DEBIT	CREDIT	BALANCE	
						DEBIT	CREDIT

ACCOUNT ______ ACCOUNT NO. ______

DATE		DESCRIPTION	POST. REF.	DEBIT	CREDIT	BALANCE	
						DEBIT	CREDIT

ACCOUNT ______ ACCOUNT NO. ______

DATE		DESCRIPTION	POST. REF.	DEBIT	CREDIT	BALANCE	
						DEBIT	CREDIT

ACCOUNT ______ ACCOUNT NO. ______

DATE		DESCRIPTION	POST. REF.	DEBIT	CREDIT	BALANCE	
						DEBIT	CREDIT

 Name

GENERAL LEDGER

ACCOUNT ______ ACCOUNT NO. ______

DATE		DESCRIPTION	POST. REF.	DEBIT	CREDIT	BALANCE DEBIT	BALANCE CREDIT

ACCOUNT ______ ACCOUNT NO. ______

DATE		DESCRIPTION	POST. REF.	DEBIT	CREDIT	BALANCE DEBIT	BALANCE CREDIT

ACCOUNT ______ ACCOUNT NO. ______

DATE		DESCRIPTION	POST. REF.	DEBIT	CREDIT	BALANCE DEBIT	BALANCE CREDIT

ACCOUNT ______ ACCOUNT NO. ______

DATE		DESCRIPTION	POST. REF.	DEBIT	CREDIT	BALANCE DEBIT	BALANCE CREDIT

ACCOUNT ______ ACCOUNT NO. ______

DATE		DESCRIPTION	POST. REF.	DEBIT	CREDIT	BALANCE DEBIT	BALANCE CREDIT

Name

GENERAL LEDGER

ACCOUNT ACCOUNT NO.

DATE		DESCRIPTION	POST. REF.	DEBIT	CREDIT	BALANCE DEBIT	BALANCE CREDIT

ACCOUNT ACCOUNT NO.

DATE		DESCRIPTION	POST. REF.	DEBIT	CREDIT	BALANCE DEBIT	BALANCE CREDIT

ACCOUNT ACCOUNT NO.

DATE		DESCRIPTION	POST. REF.	DEBIT	CREDIT	BALANCE DEBIT	BALANCE CREDIT

ACCOUNT ACCOUNT NO.

DATE		DESCRIPTION	POST. REF.	DEBIT	CREDIT	BALANCE DEBIT	BALANCE CREDIT

 Name ______________________

GENERAL LEDGER

ACCOUNT ______________________ ACCOUNT NO. ________

DATE		DESCRIPTION	POST. REF.	DEBIT	CREDIT	BALANCE DEBIT	BALANCE CREDIT

ACCOUNT ______________________ ACCOUNT NO. ________

DATE		DESCRIPTION	POST. REF.	DEBIT	CREDIT	BALANCE DEBIT	BALANCE CREDIT

ACCOUNT ______________________ ACCOUNT NO. ________

DATE		DESCRIPTION	POST. REF.	DEBIT	CREDIT	BALANCE DEBIT	BALANCE CREDIT

ACCOUNT ______________________ ACCOUNT NO. ________

DATE		DESCRIPTION	POST. REF.	DEBIT	CREDIT	BALANCE DEBIT	BALANCE CREDIT

ACCOUNT ______________________ ACCOUNT NO. ________

DATE		DESCRIPTION	POST. REF.	DEBIT	CREDIT	BALANCE DEBIT	BALANCE CREDIT

 Name

GENERAL LEDGER

ACCOUNT ______________ ACCOUNT NO. ______

DATE		DESCRIPTION	POST. REF.	DEBIT	CREDIT	BALANCE	
						DEBIT	CREDIT

ACCOUNT ______________ ACCOUNT NO. ______

DATE		DESCRIPTION	POST. REF.	DEBIT	CREDIT	BALANCE	
						DEBIT	CREDIT

ACCOUNT ______________ ACCOUNT NO. ______

DATE		DESCRIPTION	POST. REF.	DEBIT	CREDIT	BALANCE	
						DEBIT	CREDIT

ACCOUNT ______________ ACCOUNT NO. ______

DATE		DESCRIPTION	POST. REF.	DEBIT	CREDIT	BALANCE	
						DEBIT	CREDIT

 Name ______________________

GENERAL LEDGER

ACCOUNT ______________________ ACCOUNT NO. ________

DATE		DESCRIPTION	POST. REF.	DEBIT	CREDIT	BALANCE DEBIT	BALANCE CREDIT

ACCOUNT ______________________ ACCOUNT NO. ________

DATE		DESCRIPTION	POST. REF.	DEBIT	CREDIT	BALANCE DEBIT	BALANCE CREDIT

ACCOUNT ______________________ ACCOUNT NO. ________

DATE		DESCRIPTION	POST. REF.	DEBIT	CREDIT	BALANCE DEBIT	BALANCE CREDIT

ACCOUNT ______________________ ACCOUNT NO. ________

DATE		DESCRIPTION	POST. REF.	DEBIT	CREDIT	BALANCE DEBIT	BALANCE CREDIT

ACCOUNT ______________________ ACCOUNT NO. ________

DATE		DESCRIPTION	POST. REF.	DEBIT	CREDIT	BALANCE DEBIT	BALANCE CREDIT

 Name

GENERAL LEDGER

ACCOUNT ______ ACCOUNT NO. ______

DATE		DESCRIPTION	POST. REF.	DEBIT	CREDIT	BALANCE	
						DEBIT	CREDIT

ACCOUNT ______ ACCOUNT NO. ______

DATE		DESCRIPTION	POST. REF.	DEBIT	CREDIT	BALANCE	
						DEBIT	CREDIT

ACCOUNT ______ ACCOUNT NO. ______

DATE		DESCRIPTION	POST. REF.	DEBIT	CREDIT	BALANCE	
						DEBIT	CREDIT

ACCOUNT ______ ACCOUNT NO. ______

DATE		DESCRIPTION	POST. REF.	DEBIT	CREDIT	BALANCE	
						DEBIT	CREDIT

ACCOUNT ______ ACCOUNT NO. ______

DATE		DESCRIPTION	POST. REF.	DEBIT	CREDIT	BALANCE	
						DEBIT	CREDIT

 Name ______________________

GENERAL LEDGER

ACCOUNT ______________________ ACCOUNT NO. ________

DATE		DESCRIPTION	POST. REF.	DEBIT	CREDIT	BALANCE	
						DEBIT	CREDIT

ACCOUNT ______________________ ACCOUNT NO. ________

DATE		DESCRIPTION	POST. REF.	DEBIT	CREDIT	BALANCE	
						DEBIT	CREDIT

ACCOUNT ______________________ ACCOUNT NO. ________

DATE		DESCRIPTION	POST. REF.	DEBIT	CREDIT	BALANCE	
						DEBIT	CREDIT

ACCOUNT ______________________ ACCOUNT NO. ________

DATE		DESCRIPTION	POST. REF.	DEBIT	CREDIT	BALANCE	
						DEBIT	CREDIT

ACCOUNT ______________________ ACCOUNT NO. ________

DATE		DESCRIPTION	POST. REF.	DEBIT	CREDIT	BALANCE	
						DEBIT	CREDIT

 Name

ACCOUNTS RECEIVABLE SUBSIDIARY LEDGER

NAME ______ TERMS ______

DATE		DESCRIPTION	POST. REF.	DEBIT	CREDIT	BALANCE

NAME ______ TERMS ______

DATE		DESCRIPTION	POST. REF.	DEBIT	CREDIT	BALANCE

NAME ______ TERMS ______

DATE		DESCRIPTION	POST. REF.	DEBIT	CREDIT	BALANCE

NAME ______ TERMS ______

DATE		DESCRIPTION	POST. REF.	DEBIT	CREDIT	BALANCE

NAME ______ TERMS ______

DATE		DESCRIPTION	POST. REF.	DEBIT	CREDIT	BALANCE

Name

ACCOUNTS RECEIVABLE SUBSIDIARY LEDGER

NAME   TERMS

DATE	DESCRIPTION	POST. REF.	DEBIT	CREDIT	BALANCE

NAME   TERMS

DATE	DESCRIPTION	POST. REF.	DEBIT	CREDIT	BALANCE

ACCOUNTS PAYABLE SUBSIDIARY LEDGER

NAME   TERMS

DATE	DESCRIPTION	POST. REF.	DEBIT	CREDIT	BALANCE

NAME   TERMS

DATE	DESCRIPTION	POST. REF.	DEBIT	CREDIT	BALANCE

 Name

ACCOUNTS PAYABLE SUBSIDIARY LEDGER

NAME TERMS

DATE		DESCRIPTION	POST. REF.	DEBIT	CREDIT	BALANCE

 Name

	ACCOUNT NAME	TRIAL BALANCE		ADJUSTMENTS	
		DEBIT	CREDIT	DEBIT	CREDIT
1					
2					
3					
4					
5					
6					
7					
8					
9					
10					
11					
12					
13					
14					
15					
16					
17					
18					
19					
20					
21					
22					
23					
24					
25					
26					
27					
28					
29					
30					
31					
32					
33					
34					
35					
36					

 Name

ADJUSTED TRIAL BALANCE		INCOME STATEMENT		BALANCE SHEET	
DEBIT	CREDIT	DEBIT	CREDIT	DEBIT	CREDIT

 Name

	ACCOUNT NAME	TRIAL BALANCE DEBIT	TRIAL BALANCE CREDIT	ADJUSTMENTS DEBIT	ADJUSTMENTS CREDIT
1					
2					
3					
4					
5					
6					
7					
8					
9					
10					
11					
12					
13					
14					
15					
16					
17					
18					
19					
20					
21					
22					
23					
24					
25					
26					
27					
28					
29					
30					
31					
32					
33					
34					
35					
36					

 Name ______________________

ADJUSTED TRIAL BALANCE		INCOME STATEMENT		BALANCE SHEET		
DEBIT	CREDIT	DEBIT	CREDIT	DEBIT	CREDIT	
						1
						2
						3
						4
						5
						6
						7
						8
						9
						10
						11
						12
						13
						14
						15
						16
						17
						18
						19
						20
						21
						22
						23
						24
						25
						26
						27
						28
						29
						30
						31
						32
						33
						34
						35
						36

Name

Name

Name

 Name

ACCOUNT NAME	DEBIT	CREDIT

 Name

EXTRA FORMS

	ACCOUNT NAME	TRIAL BALANCE		ADJUSTMENTS	
		DEBIT	CREDIT	DEBIT	CREDIT
1					
2					
3					
4					
5					
6					
7					
8					
9					
10					
11					
12					
13					
14					
15					
16					
17					
18					
19					
20					
21					
22					
23					
24					
25					
26					
27					
28					
29					
30					
31					
32					
33					
34					

 Name ____________________

ADJUSTED TRIAL BALANCE		INCOME STATEMENT		BALANCE SHEET		
DEBIT	CREDIT	DEBIT	CREDIT	DEBIT	CREDIT	
						1
						2
						3
						4
						5
						6
						7
						8
						9
						10
						11
						12
						13
						14
						15
						16
						17
						18
						19
						20
						21
						22
						23
						24
						25
						26
						27
						28
						29
						30
						31
						32
						33
						34

MINI-PRACTICE SET 2 (continued)

Name ______________________

EXTRA FORM

GENERAL JOURNAL

PAGE ________

DATE		DESCRIPTION	POST. REF.	DEBIT	CREDIT

CHAPTER 14

Accounting Principles and Reporting Standards

STUDY GUIDE

STUDY GUIDE

Understanding the Chapter

Objectives

1. Understand the process used to develop generally accepted accounting principles. **2.** Identify the major accounting standards-setting bodies and their roles in the standards-setting process. **3.** Describe the users and uses of financial reports. **4.** Identify and explain the qualitative characteristics of accounting information. **5.** Describe and explain the basic assumptions about accounting reports. **6.** Explain and apply the basic principles of accounting. **7.** Describe and apply the modifying constraints on accounting principles. **8.** Define the accounting terms new to this chapter.

Reading Assignment

Read Chapter 14 in the textbook. Complete the textbook Section Self Review as you finish reading each section of the chapter, and the Comprehensive Self Review at the end of the chapter. Refer to the Chapter 14 Glossary or to the Glossary at the end of the book to find definitions for terms that are not familiar to you.

Activities

- ❑ **Thinking Critically** — Answer the *Thinking Critically* questions for Goodyear and Managerial Implications.
- ❑ **Discussion Questions** — Answer each assigned discussion question in Chapter 14.
- ❑ **Exercises** — Complete each assigned exercise in Chapter 14. Use the forms provided in this SGWP. The objectives covered by an exercise are given after the exercise number. If you need help with an exercise, review the portion of the chapter related to the objective(s) covered.
- ❑ **Problems A/B** — Complete each assigned problem in Chapter 14. Use the forms provided in this SGWP. The objectives covered by a problem are given after the problem number. If you need help with a problem, review the portion of the chapter related to the objective(s) covered.
- ❑ **Critical Thinking Problems** — Complete the critical thinking problems as assigned. Use the forms provided in this SGWP.
- ❑ **Business Connections** — Complete the Business Connections activities as assigned to gain a deeper understanding of Chapter 14 concepts.

Practice Tests

Complete the Practice Tests, which cover the main points in your reading assignment. Compare your answers with those in the Practice Test Answer Key for Chapter 14 at the end of this chapter. If you have answered any questions incorrectly, review the related section of the text.

STUDY GUIDE

Part A True-False *For each of the following statements, circle T in the answer column if the statement is true or F if the statement is false.*

T F **1.** The "stable monetary unit" assumption simplifies accounting records.

T F **2.** The Securities and Exchange Commission has little power to dictate accounting methods used by companies whose stocks are traded on the stock exchanges.

T F **3.** The SEC discourages disclosures outside the financial statements.

T F **4.** Statement users have the right to assume that the figures in audited statements are objective and are based on verifiable evidence.

T F **5.** Revenue should not be recognized until cash is received.

T F **6.** The "constraints" serve to modify basic principles of accounting.

T F **7.** An overstatement of an expense account in one accounting period results in an understatement of profit in the succeeding period or periods.

T F **8.** There is a conflict between the "going concern" concept and the historical cost principle.

T F **9.** In order for information to be reliable, it must be verifiable.

T F **10.** Adjusting entries are necessary because of the matching principle.

T F **11.** The matching principle requires that all known costs be charged to the current period of operations.

T F **12.** There is only one accepted method of accounting for each transaction.

T F **13.** For convenience, accountants assume that the value of money is stable or that changes in its value are insignificant.

T F **14.** The traits of objectivity and verifiability reduce subjective decisions.

T F **15.** The Conceptual Framework assumes that readers of financial reports know little about accounting and financial reporting.

T F **16.** Long-term assets are usually carried in the accounts at market value, less depreciation, until used up or disposed of.

T F **17.** The Sarbanes-Oxley Act reaffirms the SEC's option to depend on a private sector organization in developing accounting principles and standards and the SEC has chosen the FASB as that organization.

T F **18.** The statements of the Financial Accounting Standards Board are binding on the members of the American Institute of Certified Public Accountants.

T F **19.** The Financial Accounting Standards Board is a governmental organization.

T F **20.** Because of the separate entity assumption, the personal activities of the owner of a sole proprietorship should be combined with his or her business activities in the accounting records.

STUDY GUIDE

Part B Completion *In the answer column, supply the missing word or words needed to complete each of the following statements.*

______________ **1.** Matching revenues and expenses of specific fiscal periods is called the ______ basis of accounting.

______________ **2.** If the accounting records are kept on the accrual basis, income is recognized in the period in which it has been ______ and ______.

______________ **3.** The notes to the financial statements illustrate application of the principle of ______.

______________ **4.** Under the modifying convention of ______, assets are sometimes stated at a lower amount than they might be stated if other principles could be logically applied under GAAP.

______________ **5.** The ______ constraint may make it possible for a transaction with small value to be exempt from GAAP.

______________ **6.** The idea that the same accounting principles should be followed each year is called the ______ characteristic.

______________ **7.** The ______ assumption permits carrying forward the un-depreciated cost of assets to be charged against future operations.

______________ **8.** The ______ quality of financial statements permits the reports of different entities to be compared meaningfully with one another.

______________ **9.** The ______ assumption implies that an enterprise's economic activities can be divided into time periods.

______________ **10.** The assumption that permits the cost of assets acquired to be included in the same account is the ____________ assumption.

______________ **11.** The agency with statutory authority to establish accounting standards for publicly-held corporations is the ______.

______________ **12.** The international body that was established to develop accounting rules that might be followed on a world-wide basis is the ______ ______.

______________ **13.** The business enterprise is normally thought of by the accountant as a ______ entity.

______________ **14.** ______ refers to the significance of an item in relation to other items in the financial statements.

______________ **15.** Before the FASB was established, the ____________ was recognized as the private sector source of GAAP.

______________ **16.** The organization that has the authority to monitor CPA firms that audit publicly held companies is the ____________.

STUDY GUIDE

Part C Exercise *Answer each of the following in the space provided. Make your answers complete but as brief as possible.*

1. Does the separate entity assumption conform to the legal obligations of a sole proprietor? Explain.

2. In its accounting, Frank Company has been following a FASB Standard issued three years ago. It discovers in November 2010 that the International Accounting Standards Board has issued a "Standard" with greatly different reporting requirements from those of the FASB. What must Frank Company do?

3. Explain the tests that must be met for revenue to be recognized.

4. Explain why the accountant assumes continuity in the operation of the business?

5. Explain the role of the FASB's conceptual framework of accounting.

Demonstration Problem

You are an independent CPA performing audits of financial statements. In your work you encounter the independent situations described in items 1–6. For each situation, indicate which accounting assumption, principle or constraint is most relevant. If the treatment described conforms to GAAP, explain why. If the treatment does not conform, explain which concept is violated and how the situation should be reported.

1. Viola Company has been sued in court by customers for defective merchandise. The company's attorney expects a liability of $2 million is reasonably possible. In the statements, the lawsuits are not mentioned.
2. Bigtown Company's income statement shows only sales, cost of sales, total expenses and net profit.
3. During 2010 Morris received and reported as income $1 million in deposits accompanying orders for products to be manufactured and delivered in 2011.
4. Orange Company occupies a building purchased 5 years ago. Because the value of the building has increased each year, no depreciation has been taken.
5. Happy Days Holidays spends a large sum on sales promotions during this year. Management thinks the advertising will generate revenues for three years, so has charged to expense only one-third of the amount spent this year. The remainder will be charged off in equal amounts in the next two years.
6. Modern BioLabs has constructed special-purpose equipment designed for research use. The equipment may be used for several different research projects in the future. Because of its special use, this equipment has virtually no resale value to any other company. Therefore, Modern BioLabs charged the entire cost to build the equipment, $4,500,000, to expense in the year it was put into service.

STUDY GUIDE

SOLUTION

1. Full disclosure. Assuming that this is a material amount, disclosure of the lawsuits should be given in the footnotes to the financial statements. It probably is not reasonable to expect the company to reveal the attorney's attitude toward the case. However, disclosure of the amount of the suit, with some indication of the impact of a decision in favor of the plaintiffs should be made.

2. Full disclosure. The disclosure of such few items does not provide the user with information needed. The components of the net income are important to users who are trying to evaluate the business, and in this instance the disclosures should take the form of inclusion in the income statement. Even though it is appropriate to make a summary of income and costs in the income statement, without all the details, the procedure being followed is not satisfactory.

3. Revenue recognition and matching. Revenue should be reported only if it has been realized (which it has) and earned (which it has not). The revenue should be deferred and matched against costs to be incurred in the next year.

4. Matching. Historical cost principle. The cost of the building should be depreciated over its useful life. This is also part of the historical cost framework of accounting.

5. Objectivity and verifiability. To defer a cost such as advertising, there must be verification that a future benefit has been created and it must be possible to objectively measure the benefit. Neither of these factors appears to be present, so the costs should be charged to expense in the year incurred.

6. Going concern, matching and historical cost concepts. The accounting concept framework assumes a going concern. Therefore historical cost of an asset is entered in the accounts and depreciated over the useful life of the asset. There is no intent to sell the asset, but to use it in the business. There is no indication that the asset has lost its usefulness or even that its usefulness has decreased.

EXTRA FORM

WORKING PAPERS

Name ______________________

EXERCISE 14.1

1. ______________________

2. ______________________

3. ______________________

EXERCISE 14.2

1. ______________________

2. ______________________

3. ______________________

Name ____________________

EXERCISE 14.3

1. ____________________

2. ____________________

3. ____________________

EXERCISE 14.4

1. ____________________

2. ____________________

3. ____________________

Name

EXERCISE 14.5

EXERCISE 14.6

EXTRA FORM

Name

PROBLEM 14.1A or 14.1B

1.
2.
3.
4.
5.
6.
7.
8.
9.
10.

EXTRA FORM

Name

PROBLEM 14.2A or 14.2B

Handled Properly?	Basic Concept	Proper Presentation
1.		
2.		
3.		
4.		
5.		
6.		

Analyze:

Name

PROBLEM 14.3A or 14.3B

Name

PROBLEM 14.3A or 14.3B (continued)

COMPUTATIONS

Analyze:

Name

PROBLEM 14.4A or 14.4B

Name

PROBLEM 14.4A or 14.4B (continued)

NOTES

Analyze:

Name

PROBLEM 14.5A or 14.5B

Analyze:

Name

CRITICAL THINKING PROBLEM 14.1

Analyze:

Name

CRITICAL THINKING PROBLEM 14.2

Name ______________________________

Chapter 14 Practice Test Answer Key

Part A True-False

1. T	8. F	15. F
2. F	9. T	16. F
3. F	10. T	17. T
4. T	11. F	18. T
5. F	12. F	19. F
6. T	13. T	20. F
7. F	14. T	

Part B Completion

1. accrual
2. earned and realized
3. full disclosure
4. conservatism
5. cost-benefit
6. consistency
7. going concern
8. comparability
9. periodicity of income
10. stable monetary unit
11. Securities and Exchange Commission
12. International Accounting Standards Board
13. separate
14. materiality
15. American Institute of CPAs (Accounting Principles Board)
16. Public Company Accounting Oversight Board (PCAOB)

Part C Exercise

1. No. The owner of a sole proprietorship is generally legally liable for the debts and other obligations of the business as well as for personal debts.
2. Assuming Frank is an American company, it must use the rules of the FASB.
3. For revenue to be recognized, it must have been (1) realized (cash or other assets must have been received or debts liquidated) and (2) earned, which means that goods or services have been delivered and the costs related to the revenue have been incurred.
4. If continuity were not assumed, the accounting records would have to be kept on the assumption that the business is about to liquidate—presumably reflecting estimated value.
5. The conceptual framework is designed to provide a sound basis for developing accounting standards and rules. It permits development of a coherent set of standards based on the same assumptions, basic principles and constraints.

CHAPTER 15

Accounts Receivable and Uncollectible Accounts

STUDY GUIDE

Understanding the Chapter

Objectives **1.** Record the estimated expense from uncollectible accounts receivable using the allowance method. **2.** Charge off uncollectible accounts using the allowance method. **3.** Record the collection of accounts previously written off using the allowance method. **4.** Record losses from uncollectible accounts using the direct charge-off method. **5.** Record the collection of accounts previously written off using the direct charge-off method. **6.** Recognize common internal controls for accounts receivable. **7.** Define the accounting terms new to this chapter.

Reading Assignment Read Chapter 15 in the textbook. Complete the textbook Section Self Review as you finish reading each section of the chapter, and the Comprehensive Self Review at the end of the chapter. Refer to the Chapter 15 Glossary or to the Glossary at the end of the book to find definitions for terms that are not familiar to you.

Activities

- ❑ **Thinking Critically** Answer the *Thinking Critically* questions for FedEx Corporation and Managerial Implications.
- ❑ **Discussion Questions** Answer each assigned discussion question in Chapter 15.
- ❑ **Exercises** Complete each assigned exercise in Chapter 15. Use the forms provided in this SGWP. The objectives covered by an exercise are given after the exercise number. If you need help with an exercise, review the portion of the chapter related to the objective(s) covered.
- ❑ **Problems A/B** Complete each assigned problem in Chapter 15. Use the forms provided in this SGWP. The objectives covered by a problem are given after the problem number. If you need help with a problem, review the portion of the chapter related to the objective(s) covered.
- ❑ **Critical Thinking Problems** Complete the critical thinking problems as assigned. Use the forms provided in this SGWP.
- ❑ **Business Connections** Complete the Business Connections activities as assigned to gain a deeper understanding of Chapter 15 concepts.

Practice Tests

Complete the Practice Tests, which cover the main points in your reading assignment. Compare your answers with those in the Practice Test Answer Key for Chapter 15 at the end of this chapter. If you have answered any questions incorrectly, review the related section of the text.

Part A True-False *For each of the following statements, circle T in the answer column if the answer is true or F if the statement is false.*

T F **1.** Under the allowance method, the entry to record estimated expenses from uncollectible accounts is a debit to **Uncollectible Accounts Expense** and a credit to **Accounts Receivable.**

T F **2.** The collection of an account previously written off is recorded in the general journal and the cash receipts journal.

T F **3.** The direct charge-off method of recording losses from uncollectible accounts is required by generally accepted accounting principles.

T F **4.** Aging the accounts receivable will provide useful information for determining the loss from uncollectible accounts.

T F **5.** The experience of other firms in the same line of business may be used in estimating losses from uncollectible accounts for a new firm.

T F **6.** Providing for losses from uncollectible accounts before they occur permits the seller to match the estimated amount of uncollectible accounts against the sales revenue earned during the same accounting period.

T F **7.** **The Allowance for Doubtful Accounts** decreases during the year as individual accounts receivable are deemed to be uncollectible and written off.

T F **8.** Allowance for Doubtful Accounts is called a valuation account.

T F **9.** Basing the estimated uncollectible accounts on net credit sales is the method for estimating uncollectible accounts that emphasizes the valuation of assets.

T F **10.** Losses resulting from uncollectible accounts should be considered when evaluating the operating efficiency of a firm's credit department.

T F **11.** Generally, as accounts receivable get older a lower percent of the receivables will be uncollectible.

T F **12.** Allowance for Doubtful Accounts is an expense account.

T F **13.** In the balance sheet, the balance of Allowance for Doubtful Accounts is added to the Accounts Receivable account balance to arrive at the net value of the firm's receivables.

T F **14.** When losses from uncollectible accounts are recorded using the direct charge-off method, **Uncollectible Accounts Expense** is debited and **Allowance for Doubtful Accounts** and the customers' accounts are credited.

T F **15.** Uncollectible Accounts Expense should be deducted from the Sales account in the Revenue section of the income statement.

T F **16.** Given that the direct charge-off method is being used, if an account is charged off in 2010, but is recovered in 2011, the credit entry to reinstate the customer's account should be to **Uncollectible Accounts Expense.**

T F **17.** When a part of an account previously written off is collected, an entry should be made reversing the original write-off of the entire amount written off if the allowance method is being used.

T F **18.** If the provision for estimated losses from uncollectible accounts is based on a percent of net sales, the balance of the allowance account is adjusted so that it equals the product of the percentage of net sales.

T F **19.** When there is a partial collection of a balance previously written off, only the amount expected to be recoverable should be reversed in the creditor's accounting records.

Part B Exercise I *Determining the amount of uncollectible accounts expense using the allowance method.*

In each of the following cases, compute the amount of the adjusting entry to be debited to **Uncollectible Accounts Expense** and enter the amount in the space provided. Round all calculations to the nearest dollar.

The balance of the Accounts Receivable account on December 31 is $125,000. Total sales for the year were $1.5 million. Total sales returns and allowances were $35,000. Gross credit sales were $980,000, and returns of credit sales were $22,700.

_______ **1. Allowance for Doubtful Accounts** has a credit balance of $100. Losses from uncollectible accounts are estimated as eight-tenths of one percent of net credit sales.

_______ **2. Allowance for Doubtful Accounts** has a debit balance of $100. Losses from uncollectible accounts are estimated to be eight-tenths of 1 percent of net credit sales.

_______ **3. Allowance for Doubtful Accounts** has a credit balance of $100. It is estimated that 5 percent of **Accounts Receivable** are uncollectible.

_______ **4.** Allowance for Doubtful Accounts has a debit balance of $100. It is estimated that 5 percent of Accounts Receivable are uncollectible.

Part C Exercise II *Prepare a schedule of accounts receivable by age, based on the information that follows. Use the form provided.*

At the end of its first year of operations, on December 31, 2010, Network Distributors had accounts receivable totaling $35,800. The accounts and amounts outstanding are shown below. Sales terms are 2/10, net 30 days.

John Ameche

Invoice of 10/3	$3,500
Invoice of 12/04	2,500
Total	$6,000

Kim Duong

Invoice of 9/15	$4,500
Invoice of 10/25	2,500
Total	$7,000

Ken Graham

Invoice of 12/08	$7,000

Harold McCartney

Invoice of 11/12	$4,800
Invoice of 11/19	2,000
Total	$6,800

Andrew Torelli

Invoice of 12/15	$9,000

Instructions: Prepare an aging schedule for the accounts receivable, using the form provided below.

ACCOUNT	BALANCE	CURRENT	PAST DUE—DAYS 1–30	31–60	OVER 60
Ameche, John					
Duong, Kim					
Graham, Ken					
McCartney, Harold					
Torelli, Andrew					

Demonstration Problem

Executive clubs is a retailer of golf clubs and other golf accessories. In 2010, its net credit sales were $28,760,000. The company's trial balance for December 31, contained the following account balances.

Accounts Receivable	$3,136,000
Allowance for Doubtful Accounts (credit)	4,600

In preparing the trial balance, the following additional accounts were identified as being uncollectible and should be charged off.

Don Baker	$1,849
Doug Chan	2,408

Instructions

(Omit explanations in journal entries. Round your entries to the nearest dollar.)

1. Record the general journal entry to charge off the two accounts identified as being uncollectible. Number the journal as page 6.
2. Assume that the company uses the percentage of sales method to estimate uncollectible accounts expense. Historical data shows that approximately 0.50 percent of net credit sales prove uncollectible. Enter the necessary adjusting journal entry to record estimated uncollectible accounts expense.
3. Assume that the company bases its estimated uncollectible accounts on accounts receivable. The company estimates that approximately three percent of accounts receivable will be uncollectible. Prepare the general journal entry to adjust the accounts on that basis.
4. Assume that the company uses the aging of accounts receivable method to estimate uncollectible accounts. Using the following information, calculate the estimated uncollectible amount on December 31, 2010, and prepare the general journal entry to adjust the accounts.

Receivable Category	Estimated Loss Rate	Amount in Receivables
Current	0.5%	$2,315,000
1–30 days past due	3.5%	543,400
31–60 days past due	16.0%	194,370
Over 60 days past due	40.0%	78,973
		$3,131,743

5. Assume that on February 8, 2011, Don Baker, whose account was charged off on December 31, 2010 (Instruction 1), sent a check for the entire amount of his account. Give the entries, in general journal form to account for this event.

SOLUTION

GENERAL JOURNAL

PAGE 6

DATE		DESCRIPTION	POST. REF.	DEBIT	CREDIT
2010		(1)			
Dec.	31	Allowance for Doubtful Accounts		4,257.00	
		Accounts Receivable/Don Baker			1,849.00
		Accounts Receivable/Doug Chan			2,408.00
		(2)			
	31	Uncollectible Accounts Expense		143,800.00	
		Allowance for Doubtful Accounts			143,800.00
		(3)			
	31	Uncollectible Accounts Expense		93,609.00	
		Allowance for Doubtful Accounts			93,609.00
		(4)			
	31	Uncollectible Accounts Expense		92,939.00	
		Allowance for Doubtful Accounts			92,939.00
2011		(5)			
Feb.	8	Accounts Receivable/Don Baker		1,849.00	
		Allowance for Doubtful Accounts			1,849.00
	8	Cash		1,849.00	
		Accounts Receivable/Don Baker			1,849.00

WORKING PAPERS

Name

EXERCISE 15.1

GENERAL JOURNAL

PAGE

	DATE		DESCRIPTION	POST. REF.	DEBIT	CREDIT	
1							1
2							2
3							3
4							4
5							5
6							6
7							7
8							8
9							9

EXERCISE 15.2

GENERAL JOURNAL

PAGE

	DATE		DESCRIPTION	POST. REF.	DEBIT	CREDIT	
1							1
2							2
3							3
4							4
5							5
6							6
7							7
8							8
9							9
10							10
11							11
12							12

Name ____________________

EXERCISE 15.3

GENERAL JOURNAL — PAGE ______

	DATE		DESCRIPTION	POST. REF.	DEBIT	CREDIT	
1							1
2							2
3							3
4							4
5							5
6							6
7							7
8							8

EXERCISE 15.4

GENERAL JOURNAL — PAGE ______

	DATE		DESCRIPTION	POST. REF.	DEBIT	CREDIT	
1							1
2							2
3							3
4							4
5							5
6							6
7							7
8							8

Name ______________________________

EXERCISE 15.5

GENERAL JOURNAL PAGE ________

	DATE		DESCRIPTION	POST. REF.	DEBIT	CREDIT	
1							1
2							2
3							3
4							4
5							5
6							6
7							7
8							8
9							9
10							10
11							11

EXERCISE 15.6

GENERAL JOURNAL PAGE ________

	DATE		DESCRIPTION	POST. REF.	DEBIT	CREDIT	
1							1
2							2
3							3
4							4
5							5
6							6
7							7
8							8
9							9
10							10

Name ______________________________

EXERCISE 15.7

GENERAL JOURNAL PAGE ______

	DATE		DESCRIPTION	POST. REF.	DEBIT	CREDIT	
1							1
2							2
3							3
4							4
5							5
6							6
7							7
8							8
9							9
10							10
11							11
12							12
13							13
14							14
15							15

EXERCISE 15.8

GENERAL JOURNAL PAGE ______

	DATE		DESCRIPTION	POST. REF.	DEBIT	CREDIT	
1							1
2							2
3							3
4							4
5							5
6							6
7							7
8							8
9							9
10							10
11							11
12							12
13							13
14							14
15							15

Name

EXERCISE 15.9

GENERAL JOURNAL

PAGE

	DATE		DESCRIPTION	POST. REF.	DEBIT	CREDIT	
1							1
2							2
3							3
4							4
5							5
6							6
7							7
8							8
9							9
10							10
11							11
12							12
13							13
14							14
15							15

Name ____________________

PROBLEM 15.1A or 15.1B

GENERAL JOURNAL PAGE ______

	DATE		DESCRIPTION	POST. REF.	DEBIT	CREDIT	
1			(2)				1
2							2
3							3
4							4
5							5
6							6
7			(4)				7
8							8
9							9
10							10
11							11
12			(5)				12
13							13
14							14
15							15
16							16
17							17
18							18

Analyze:

Name ______________________________

PROBLEM 15.2A or 15.2B

ESTIMATE OF UNCOLLECTIBLE ACCOUNTS

ADJUSTMENT FOR ESTIMATED UNCOLLECTIBLE ACCOUNTS

GENERAL JOURNAL

PAGE ______

DATE		DESCRIPTION	POST. REF.	DEBIT	CREDIT
		(3)			
		(4)			
		(5)			

Analyze: ______________________________

Name

PROBLEM 15.3A or 15.3B

1. a.

b.

2. a.

b.

Analyze:

Name ______________________

PROBLEM 15.4A or 15.4B

GENERAL JOURNAL

PAGE ______

DATE		DESCRIPTION	POST. REF.	DEBIT	CREDIT

Analyze: ______________________

Name ______________________

CRITICAL THINKING PROBLEM 15.1

GENERAL JOURNAL

PAGE ______

	DATE		DESCRIPTION	POST. REF.	DEBIT	CREDIT	
1							1
2							2
3							3
4							4
5							5
6							6
7							7
8							8
9							9
10							10
11							11
12							12
13							13
14							14
15							15
16							16
17							17
18							18
19							19
20							20
21							21

ESTIMATE OF UNCOLLECTIBLE ACCOUNTS

Allowance for Doubtful Accounts

Accounts Receivable

Name

CRITICAL THINKING PROBLEM 15.1 (continued)

Analyze:

Name ______________________

CRITICAL THINKING PROBLEM 15.2

GENERAL JOURNAL

PAGE ______

DATE		DESCRIPTION	POST. REF.	DEBIT	CREDIT

ESTIMATED UNCOLLECTIBLE ACCOUNTS

Name ______________________

CRITICAL THINKING PROBLEM 15.2 (continued)

GENERAL JOURNAL PAGE ______

	DATE		DESCRIPTION	POST. REF.	DEBIT	CREDIT	
1							1
2							2
3							3
4							4
5							5
6							6
7							7
8							8
9							9
10							10
11							11

Allowance for Doubtful Accounts

ANALYSIS BY TERRITORY

Name ______________________

EXTRA FORM

GENERAL JOURNAL

PAGE ______

	DATE	DESCRIPTION	POST. REF.	DEBIT	CREDIT	
1						1
2						2
3						3
4						4
5						5
6						6
7						7
8						8
9						9
10						10
11						11
12						12
13						13
14						14
15						15
16						16
17						17
18						18
19						19
20						20

GENERAL JOURNAL

PAGE ______

	DATE	DESCRIPTION	POST. REF.	DEBIT	CREDIT	
1						1
2						2
3						3
4						4
5						5
6						6
7						7
8						8
9						9
10						10
11						11
12						12

Name

Chapter 15 Practice Test Answer Key

Part A True-False

1. F
2. T
3. F
4. T
5. T
6. T
7. T
8. T
9. F
10. T
11. F
12. F
13. F
14. F
15. F
16. F
17. F
18. F
19. T

Part B Exercise I

1. $7,658
2. $7,658
3. $6,150
4. $6,350

Part C Exercise II

NETWORK DISTRIBUTORS
Schedule of Accounts Receivable by Age
December 31, 2010

			PAST DUE—DAYS		
ACCOUNT	BALANCE	CURRENT	1–30	31–60	OVER 60
Ameche, John	$ 6,000	$ 2,500		$3,500	
Duong, Kim	7,000			2,500	$4,500
Graham, Ken	7,000	7,000			
McCartney, Harold	6,800		$6,800		
Torelli, Andrew	9,000	9,000			
Totals	$35,800	$18,500	$6,800	$6,000	$4,500

CHAPTER 16

Notes Payable and Notes Receivable

STUDY GUIDE

STUDY GUIDE

Understanding the Chapter

Objectives

1. Determine whether an instrument meets all the requirements of negotiability. **2.** Calculate the interest on a note. **3.** Determine the maturity date of a note. **4.** Record routine notes payable transactions. **5.** Record discounted notes payable transactions. **6.** Record routine notes receivable transactions. **7.** Compute the proceeds from a discounted note receivable and record transactions related to discounting of notes receivable. **8.** Understand how to use bank drafts and trade acceptances and how to record transactions related to those instruments. **9.** Define the accounting terms new to this chapter.

Reading Assignment

Read Chapter 16 in the textbook. Complete the textbook Section Self Review as you finish reading each section of the chapter, and the Comprehensive Self Review at the end of the chapter. Refer to the Chapter 16 Glossary or to the Glossary at the end of the book to find definitions for terms that are not familiar to you.

Activities

❑ **Thinking Critically** — Answer the *Thinking Critically* questions for Bank of America and Managerial Implications.

❑ **Discussion Questions** — Answer each assigned discussion question in Chapter 16.

❑ **Exercises** — Complete each assigned exercise in Chapter 16. Use the forms provided in this SGWP. The objectives covered by an exercise are given after the exercise number. If you need help with an exercise, review the portion of the chapter related to the objective(s) covered.

❑ **Problems A/B** — Complete each assigned problem in Chapter 16. Use the forms provided in this SGWP. The objectives covered by a problem are given after the problem number. If you need help with a problem, review the portion of the chapter related to the objective(s) covered.

❑ **Critical Thinking Problems** — Complete the critical thinking problems as assigned. Use the forms provided in this SGWP.

❑ **Business Connections** — Complete the Business Connections activities as assigned to gain a deeper understanding of Chapter 16 concepts.

Practice Tests

Complete the Practice Tests, which cover the main points in your reading assignment. Compare your answers with those in the Practice Test Answer Key for Chapter 16 at the end of this chapter. If you have answered any questions incorrectly, review the related section of the text.

STUDY GUIDE

Part A True-False *For each of the following statements, circle T in the answer column if the statement is true, F if the statement is false.*

1. To be negotiable, an instrument must:

T F **a.** Be payable only to a named person

T F **b.** Be signed by the maker or drawer

T F **c.** Be payable on demand or at a future time that is fixed or that can be determined

T F **d.** Contain an unconditional promise to pay a definite sum

T F **e.** Be written on a standard note form

T F **f.** Name or identify any drawee mentioned in the instrument

T F **2.** A bank draft is a draft written by a bank on its own funds.

T F **3.** **The Notes Receivable—Discounted** account is a liability account.

T F **4.** Short-term notes receivable are listed in the Current Assets section on the balance sheet.

T F **5.** The discounting of a note receivable involves a credit to Cash.

T F **6.** The methods used in computing maturity dates and interest on a note receivable are the same as those used for a note payable.

T F **7.** The payment of a promissory note results in a debit to Notes Receivable and a credit to Notes Payable.

T F **8.** Notes Payable may appear in the Current Assets section or in the Long-Term Assets section of the balance sheet.

T F **9.** Banks deduct interest in advance when discounting a note payable.

T F **10.** The maturity value of a note is the amount of principal less any interest that is payable on the due date of the note.

T F **11.** In computing interest, a "bankers' year" of 365 days is normally used.

T F **12.** Interest = Principal × Rate × Time

13. The Elmore Company receives a $2,000 note from a customer. The note is dated July 31, matures four months later, and bears interest at 6 percent.

T F **a.** The maturity date of the note is December 1.

T F **b.** The maturity value of the note is $2,120.

T F **c.** If the note is discounted on November 1 at a discount rate of 10 percent, the proceeds will be $2,013.08.

T F **d.** If the customer dishonors the note at maturity and the bank charges a protest fee of $25, the total amount to be charged to Elmore's account by the bank will be $2,025.

Part B Exercises *Complete each of the following in the spaces provided.*

1. Fill in the blanks in each case below.

	Date of Note	Face Amount	Length of Note	Maturity Date	Interest Rate	Total Interest	Maturity Value
a.	3/8/10	$6,000	3 months	________	9%	$________	$________
b.	6/10/10	$2,400	60 days	________	________	$ 24.00	________

2. The maturity value of a note receivable is $1,800. The holder of the note discounts it at the bank with 30 days left until its maturity date. The bank charges a discount rate of 10 percent. Compute the proceeds of the note.

____

____

____

3. Give the general journal entries to record the following transactions. Omit the description.

Ron Jamison borrowed $12,000 from Northern Bank on April 10, 2010, signing a 60-day, 8 percent, interest-bearing note for that amount. On the maturity date, Jamison paid the note.

GENERAL JOURNAL PAGE ______

	DATE		DESCRIPTION	POST. REF.	DEBIT	CREDIT	
1							1
2							2
3							3
4							4
5							5
6							6

Demonstration Problem

Compute each of the amounts called for in the situations described below. Show all your computations.

1. Compute the maturity value of a $4,200 note payable. The note carries interest of 6 percent and is payable 60 days from February 27, 2010, the date of the note.

2. What is the amount of a bank's discount on a 120-day note for $9,000, discounted at 7 percent?

3. What is the maturity value of a $4,000, 6-month note receivable, bearing interest at 9 percent?

4. On July 31, 2010, Ruth discounted a $5,000 note payable at the bank. The discount rate was 10 percent. The term is three months. Give the journal entry to record the transaction.

5. Julia Chen is late paying her account of $4,000 at your business. Chen signs a note for that amount with interest at 7 percent. The note is due 60 days from July 31, the date of signing.

a. Give the general journal entry to record this transaction. Omit descriptions. Number the journal as page 12.

b. Give the general journal entry to record payment in full on the note's maturity date.

c. Suppose, instead, that the note holder discounted Chen's note at the bank with 45 days remaining on the note. The bank charged a discount rate of 9 percent. Give the general journal to record discounting of this note receivable.

SOLUTION

1. Maturity Value = Principal + Interest
   = $4,200 + ($4,200 × .06 × 60/360)
   = $4,200 + $42.00
   = $4,242.00

2. Discount = $9,000 × 0.07 × 120/360
   = $210.00

3. Maturity Value = Principal + Interest
   = $4,000 + ($4,000 × .09 × 6/12)
   = $4,000 + $180
   = $4,180

4. Discount = ($5,000 × .10 × 3/12)
   = $125
   Proceeds = $5,000 − $125
   = $4,875

GENERAL JOURNAL PAGE

	DATE		DESCRIPTION	POST. REF.	DEBIT	CREDIT	
1	2010						1
2	July	31	Cash		4 875 00		2
3			Interest Expense		125 00		3
4			Notes Payable			5 000 00	4
5							5

5. a. Notes Receivable = Amount of account balance = $4,000
   b. Maturity Value = $4,000 + ($4,000 × 0.07 × 60/360)
   = $4,000 + $46.67
   = $4,046.67
   c. Proceeds = Maturity Value − Discount
   = $4,046.67 − ($4,046.67 × 0.09 × 45/360)
   = $4,046.67 − $45.53
   = $4,001.14

GENERAL JOURNAL PAGE 12

	DATE		DESCRIPTION	POST. REF.	DEBIT	CREDIT	
1	2010						1
2	a. July	31	Notes Receivable		4 000 00		2
3			Accounts Receivable/Julia Chen			4 000 00	3
4							4
5	b. Sept.	29	Cash		4 046 67		5
6			Interest Income			46 67	6
7			Notes Receivable			4 000 00	7
8							8
9	c. Aug.	15	Cash		4 001 14		9
10			Notes Receivable Discounted			4 000 00	10
11			Interest Income			1 14	11

WORKING PAPERS

Name ______________________

EXERCISE 16.1

1. ______________________
2. ______________________
3. ______________________

EXERCISE 16.2

1. ______________________

____

____

2. ______________________

____

____

EXERCISE 16.3

1. ______________________

____

____

2. ______________________

____

____

EXERCISE 16.4

GENERAL JOURNAL

PAGE ______

	DATE		DESCRIPTION	POST. REF.	DEBIT	CREDIT	
1							1
2							2
3							3
4							4
5							5
6							6
7							7
8							8
9							9
10							10
11							11
12							12
13							13
14							14
15							15

(continued)

Name ______________________

EXERCISE 16.4 (continued)

GENERAL JOURNAL PAGE ______

	DATE		DESCRIPTION	POST. REF.	DEBIT	CREDIT	
1							1
2							2
3							3
4							4
5							5
6							6

EXERCISE 16.5

GENERAL JOURNAL PAGE ______

	DATE		DESCRIPTION	POST. REF.	DEBIT	CREDIT	
1							1
2							2
3							3
4							4
5							5
6							6

EXERCISE 16.6

GENERAL JOURNAL PAGE ______

	DATE		DESCRIPTION	POST. REF.	DEBIT	CREDIT	
1							1
2							2
3							3
4							4
5							5
6							6
7							7
8							8
9							9
10							10
11							11
12							12
13							13
14							14

Name ____________________

EXERCISE 16.7

GENERAL JOURNAL PAGE ______

DATE	DESCRIPTION	POST. REF.	DEBIT	CREDIT

EXERCISE 16.8

GENERAL JOURNAL PAGE ______

DATE	DESCRIPTION	POST. REF.	DEBIT	CREDIT

EXTRA FORM

GENERAL JOURNAL PAGE ______

DATE	DESCRIPTION	POST. REF.	DEBIT	CREDIT

Name

PROBLEM 16.1A or 16.1B

1.

2.

3.

Analyze:

PROBLEM 16.2A or 16.2B

GENERAL JOURNAL

PAGE

	DATE		DESCRIPTION	POST. REF.	DEBIT	CREDIT	
1							1
2							2
3							3
4							4
5							5
6							6
7							7
8							8
9							9
10							10
11							11
12							12
13							13
14							14
15							15
16							16
17							17
18							18
19							19
20							20
21							21

Analyze:

Name

PROBLEM 16.3A or 16.3B

Analyze:

PROBLEM 16.4A or 16.4B

Analyze:

Name

PROBLEM 16.5A or 16.5B

GENERAL JOURNAL

PAGE

	DATE		DESCRIPTION	POST. REF.	DEBIT	CREDIT	
1							1
2							2
3							3
4							4
5							5
6							6
7							7
8							8
9							9
10							10
11							11
12							12
13							13
14							14
15							15
16							16
17							17
18							18
19							19
20							20

Analyze:

Name ____________________

CRITICAL THINKING PROBLEM 16.1

Omit descriptions

GENERAL JOURNAL

PAGE ________

DATE		DESCRIPTION	POST. REF.	DEBIT	CREDIT

Name

CRITICAL THINKING PROBLEM 16.1 (continued)

Omit descriptions

GENERAL JOURNAL

PAGE

	DATE		DESCRIPTION	POST. REF.	DEBIT	CREDIT	
1							1
2							2
3							3
4							4
5							5
6							6
7							7
8							8
9							9
10							10

Analyze:

CRITICAL THINKING PROBLEM 16.2

Chapter 16 Practice Test Answer Key

Part A True-False

1. a. F	**3. F**	**10. F**	
b. T	**4. T**	**11. F**	
c. T	**5. F**	**12. T**	
d. T	**6. T**	**13. a. T**	
e. F	**7. F**	**b. F**	
f. T	**8. F**	**c. F**	
2. F	**9. T**	**d. F**	

Part B Exercises

1. a. Maturity date, 6/8/10
Total interest, $ 135
Maturity value, $6,135
b. Maturity date, 8/9/10
Interest rate 6%
Maturity value $2,424

2. Discount = $1,800 × .10 × 30/360 = $15
Proceeds = $1,800 − $15 = $1,785

3. 2010

Apr. 10	Cash	12,000.00	
	Notes Payable—Bank		12,000.00
June 9	Notes Payable—Bank	12,000.00	
	Interest Expense	160.00	
	Cash		12,160.00

CHAPTER 17

Merchandise Inventory

STUDY GUIDE

STUDY GUIDE

Understanding the Chapter

Objectives

1. Compute inventory cost by applying four commonly used costing methods. **2.** Compare the different methods of inventory costing. **3.** Compute inventory value under the lower of cost or market rule. **4.** Estimate inventory cost using the gross profit method. **5.** Estimate inventory cost using the retail method. **6.** Define the accounting terms new to this chapter.

Reading Assignment

Read Chapter 17 in the textbook. Complete the textbook Section Self Review as you finish reading each section of the chapter, and the Comprehensive Self Review at the end of the chapter. Refer to the Chapter 17 Glossary or to the Glossary at the end of the book to find definitions for terms that are not familiar to you.

Activities

- ❑ **Thinking Critically** — Answer the *Thinking Critically* questions for Circuit City Stores, Inc. and Managerial Implications.
- ❑ **Discussion Questions** — Answer each assigned discussion question in Chapter 17.
- ❑ **Exercises** — Complete each assigned exercise in Chapter 17. Use the forms provided in this SGWP. The objectives covered by an exercise are given after the exercise number. If you need help with an exercise, review the portion of the chapter related to the objective(s) covered.
- ❑ **Problems A/B** — Complete each assigned problem in Chapter 17. Use the forms provided in this SGWP. The objectives covered by a problem are given after the problem number. If you need help with a problem, review the portion of the chapter related to the objective(s) covered.
- ❑ **Critical Thinking Problems** — Complete the critical thinking problems as assigned. Use the forms provided in this SGWP.
- ❑ **Business Connections** — Complete the Business Connections activities as assigned to gain a deeper understanding of Chapter 17 concepts.

Practice Tests

Complete the Practice Tests, which cover the main points in your reading assignment. Compare your answers with those in the Practice Test Answer Key for Chapter 17 at the end of this chapter. If you have answered any questions incorrectly, review the related section of the text.

STUDY GUIDE

Part A True-False *For each of the following statements, circle T in the answer column if the statement is true or F if the statement is false.*

T F 1. During a period of rising prices, the FIFO method will yield a lower ending inventory cost than the LIFO method.

T F 2. The most conservative method of applying the lower of cost or market rule is to apply it to inventory items on a group by group basis.

T F 3. It is necessary to count the goods on hand to estimate the inventory cost under the retail method.

T F 4. Ending Merchandise Inventory appears on both the balance sheet and the income statement.

T F 5. Under the perpetual inventory system, the cost of goods on hand at any given time can be determined.

T F 6. A decline in the market value of inventory to less than its cost should be reflected in the financial statements of the period in which the decline occurs.

T F 7. The average cost method of inventory valuation will usually result in the lowest reported net income of the valuation methods that may be used.

T F 8. Applying the lower of cost or market rule on the basis of total cost and total market will generally result in a higher value than its application on the basis of individual items or groups of items.

T F 9. The gross profit method of estimating inventory and the retail method utilize the same basic concept—the relation between sales price of inventory and its cost.

T F 10. During a period of falling prices, the FIFO method of inventory valuation will result in a higher reported net income than the LIFO method.

T F 11. As used in inventory valuation, market price is the price at which an item can be bought at the inventory date through the usual channels and in the usual quantities.

T F 12. The valuation of the ending inventory has a direct effect on the net income for a period.

T F 13. LIFO inventory costing parallels the actual flow of goods in most businesses.

STUDY GUIDE

Part B Matching *For each of the numbered items, choose the matching term from the box and write the identifying letter in the answer column.*

a. Average cost
b. First in, first out
c. Last in, first out
d. Markdown
e. Markup
f. Retail method
g. Specific identification

_______ **1.** The cost of all like items available for sale during a period are averaged to determine a unit cost in valuing the ending inventory.

_______ **2.** Determining the sales value of the goods on hand and computing the approximate cost by applying the ratio of cost to the selling price during the accounting period.

_______ **3.** The inventory valuation method in which the actual cost of each individual item is determined.

_______ **4.** An inventory valuation method that assumes the oldest items of inventory are sold first.

_______ **5.** The difference between the cost and the initial retail selling price of merchandise.

_______ **6.** The inventory valuation method that attempts to match the current cost of goods purchased with current sales.

_______ **7.** Reduction of an originally established selling price.

Demonstration Problem

The Head to Head Security Company has three types of electronic security systems in its electronics department. Group S, Group U and Group V. The following data relates to January 2010 inventory transactions for the three groups.

Inventory, January 1, 2010:

Group S	8 @ $100.00
Group U	16 @ $105.00
Group V	8 @ $200.00

Purchases

Date	Group	Units	Unit Cost	Total
Jan. 7	S	31	$109.00	$3,379.00
	U	22	115.00	2,530.00
	V	33	202.00	6,666.00
Jan. 18	S	25	114.00	2,850.00
	U	26	124.00	3,224.00
	V	23	205.00	4,715.00
Jan. 29	S	19	118.00	2,242.00
	U	19	125.00	2,375.00
	V	12	218.00	2,616.00

The company uses the LIFO method of determining cost of inventory.
Sales for the month were as follows:

Group S	76 units
Group U	45 units
Group V	41 units

1. What is the cost of goods sold during the month?
2. What is the cost of the ending inventory?

STUDY GUIDE

SOLUTION

1. **Cost of Goods Sold:**

Group S	19 units @ $118.00	=	$ 2,242.00
	25 units @ $114.00	=	2,850.00
	31 units @ $109.00	=	3,379.00
	1 unit @ $100.00	=	100.00
	Total, Group S		$ 8,571.00
Group U	19 units @ $125.00	=	$ 2,375.00
	26 units @ $124.00	=	3,224.00
	Total, Group U		$ 5,599.00
Group V	12 units @ $218.00	=	$ 2,616.00
	23 units @ $205.00	=	4,715.00
	6 units @ $202.00	=	1,212.00
	Total, Group V		$ 8,543.00
Total Cost of Goods Sold			$ 22,713.00

2. **Cost of Ending Inventory**

Group S	7 units @ $100.00	=	$ 700.00
	Total, Group S	=	$ 700.00
Group U	22 units @ $115.00	=	$ 2,530.00
	16 units @ $105.00	=	1,680.00
	Total, Group U		$ 4,210.00
Group V	27 units @ $202.00	=	$ 5,454.00
	8 units @ $200.00	=	1,600.00
	Total, Group V		$ 7,054.00
Total Ending Inventory			$ 11,964.00

WORKING PAPERS

Name ______________________

EXERCISE 17.1

Description	Number of Units	Unit Cost	Total Cost

1. Average Cost Method

2. FIFO Method

3. LIFO Method

EXERCISE 17.2

Description	Quantity	Unit Cost	Market Value	Total Cost	Total Market
1. Item by Item					

Name

2. Total Cost or Total Market Value of Ending Inventory

3. By Groups

EXERCISE 17.3

EXERCISE 17.4

Name ______________________________

EXERCISE 17.5

ESTIMATED INVENTORY COST

	Cost	Retail

Name ______________________________

PROBLEM 17.1A or 17.1B

Description	Number of Units	Unit Cost	Total Cost

a. Average Cost Method

b. FIFO Method

c. LIFO Method

Analyze: ______________________________

____

Name ____________________

PROBLEM 17.2A or 17.2B

1.

Description	Number of Units	Unit Cost	Total Cost

Description	Number of Units	Unit Cost	Inventory Valuation	Cost of Goods Sold
a. FIFO Method				
b. LIFO Method				
c. Average Cost Method				

2.

Method	Number of Units	Valuation Based On: Cost	Valuation Based On: Market	Valuation Basis	Lower of Cost or Market
a. FIFO					
b. LIFO					
c. Average Cost					

Analyze: ____________________

Name ______________________

PROBLEM 17.3A or 17.3B

Description	Quantity	Unit Cost	Market Value	Total Cost	Total Market	Lower of Cost or Market

Inventory Valuations	Lower of Cost or Market

Analyze: ______________________

PROBLEM 17.4A or 17.4B

Analyze: ______________________

Name ____________________

PROBLEM 17.5A or 17.5B

Estimated Inventory	Cost	Retail

Analyze: ____________________

PROBLEM 17.6A or 17.6B

Item	Cost

Analyze: ____________________

Name

CRITICAL THINKING PROBLEM 17.1

Estimated Inventory	Cost	Retail

Analyze:

CRITICAL THINKING PROBLEM 17.2

Chapter 17 Practice Test Answer Key

Part A True-False

1. F	6. T	11. T
2. F	7. F	12. T
3. F	8. T	13. F
4. T	9. T	
5. T	10. F	

Part B Matching

1. **a** (average cost)
2. **f** (retail method)
3. **g** (specific identification)
4. **b** (First in, first out)
5. **e** (markup)
6. **c** (last in, first out)
7. **d** (markdown)

CHAPTER 18

Property, Plant, and Equipment

STUDY GUIDE

Understanding the Chapter

Objectives

1. Determine the amount to record as an asset's cost. **2.** Compute and record depreciation of property, plant, and equipment by commonly used methods. **3.** Apply the Modified Accelerated Cost Recovery System (MACRS) for federal income tax purposes. **4.** Record sales of plant and equipment. **5.** Record asset trade-ins using the financial accounting rules and income tax requirements. **6.** Compute and record depletion of natural resources. **7.** Recognize asset impairment and understand the general concepts of accounting for impairment. **8.** Compute and record amortization and impairment of intangible assets. **9.** Define the accounting terms new to this chapter.

Reading Assignment

Read Chapter 18 in the textbook. Complete the textbook Section Self Review as you finish reading each section of the chapter, and the Comprehensive Self Review at the end of the chapter. Refer to the Chapter 18 Glossary or to the Glossary at the end of the book to find definitions for terms that are not familiar to you.

Activities

- ❑ **Thinking Critically** — Answer the *Thinking Critically* questions for The Coca-Cola Company and Managerial Implications.
- ❑ **Discussion Questions** — Answer each assigned discussion question in Chapter 18.
- ❑ **Exercises** — Complete each assigned exercise in Chapter 18. Use the forms provided in this SGWP. The objectives covered by an exercise are given after the exercise number. If you need help with an exercise, review the portion of the chapter related to the objective(s) covered.
- ❑ **Problems A/B** — Complete each assigned problem in Chapter 18. Use the forms provided in this SGWP. The objectives covered by a problem are given after the problem number. If you need help with a problem, review the portion of the chapter related to the objective(s) covered.
- ❑ **Critical Thinking Problems** — Complete the critical thinking problems as assigned. Use the forms provided in this SGWP.
- ❑ **Business Connections** — Complete the Business Connections activities as assigned to gain a deeper understanding of Chapter 18 concepts.

Practice Tests

Complete the Practice Tests, which cover the main points in your reading assignment. Compare your answers with those in the Practice Test Answer Key for Chapter 18 at the end of this chapter. If you have answered any questions incorrectly, review the related section of the text.

STUDY GUIDE

Part A True-False *For each of the following statements, circle T in the answer column if the statement is true or F if the statement is false.*

T F **1.** The decline in market value of an asset each period is generally a satisfactory measure of depreciation of the asset for that period.

T F **2.** A business must use the same depreciation method for all its assets.

T F **3.** Salvage is ignored if the sum-of-years'-digits method of depreciation is used.

T F **4.** The sum-of-the-years'-digits method is an accelerated method of depreciation.

T F **5.** If the declining-balance depreciation method is used, salvage is ignored until that time at which the accumulated depreciation equals estimated salvage. From that point forward, no further depreciation is recorded.

T F **6.** The cost of installing or modifying a new asset should be charged to expense.

T F **7.** A building under construction is an example of an intangible asset.

T F **8.** **Prepaid Insurance** is included in plant and equipment.

T F **9.** At the end of an accounting period, current depreciation or depletion is debited to an expense account and credited to a contra-asset account.

T F **10.** The cost of paving a parking lot for a business is debited to the land account on which the lot is located.

T F **11.** Purchased intangibles with unlimited lives, such as goodwill, are not amortized, but are subject to an impairment test each year.

T F **12.** Costs of intangible assets having limited lives, such as patents and copyrights, should be amortized over the legal life of the intangible or its useful life, whichever is shorter.

T F **13.** Amortization of the costs of amortizable intangibles is charged to an expense account and credited directly to the asset account.

T F **14.** Under GAAP most R & D costs must be charged to expense when incurred.

T F **15.** The declining-balance method should be used in computing depletion on the cost of mineral deposits.

T F **16.** Under GAAP, a loss on the trade-in of an old asset of like kind must be recognized.

T F **17.** Neither gain nor loss is recognized for income tax purposes on the exchange or trade-in of like assets.

T F **18.** If the trade-in allowance for an old asset is greater than its book value, for financial accounting purposes a gain should be recognized on the trade-in.

T F **19.** Salvage value is ignored under the units-of-output method.

T F **20.** Depreciation should be debited to expense and credited to the asset account.

Part B Matching *For each numbered item, choose the matching term from the box and write the identifying letter in the answer column.*

a. Amortization
b. Book value
c. Declining balance method
d. Depletion
e. Depreciation
f. Goodwill
g. Impairment
h. Intangibles
i. Straight-line method
j. Unit-of-production methods

_______ **1.** The difference between the capitalized costs of an asset and the accumulated depreciation for the asset.

_______ **2.** The term used to describe the periodic transfer of capitalized costs of plant and equipment to expense.

_______ **3.** Assets such as patents, goodwill, trademarks and copyrights.

_______ **4.** A method of computing annual depreciation by dividing the depreciable cost of the asset by the expected units of production and multiplying that rate by the units produced during the year.

_______ **5.** A means of computing annual depreciation by applying a constant percentage to the book value of an asset at the beginning of the year.

_______ **6.** The value of a business in excess of its net identifiable assets.

_______ **7.** The transfer of cost of an intangible asset with a fixed life to expense.

_______ **8.** The term used to describe the situation when an asset is determined to have a market value or value-in-use less than its book value.

_______ **9.** The term used to describe the periodic transfer of acquisition costs to expense when natural resources such as ores or oil are physically removed by production.

_______ **10.** A method of computing depreciation in which the same amount is recorded for each accounting period over the useful life of an asset.

Part C Exercise

On January 1, 2010, a business acquired at a cost of $22,000 new office equipment with an estimated useful life of 8 years. Estimated salvage value at the end of that time is $2,000. Compute depreciation for 2010 and 2011 using the following methods. (Round all computations to nearest whole dollar.)

a. straight-line method.

b. the sum-of-years'-digits method.

c. double-declining-balance method.

Demonstration Problem

Discovery Company was formed in January 2010 to operate a research laboratory.

1. In January it acquired a tract of land at a cost of $96,000. In connection with the purchase, Discovery paid closing costs of $4,000. The company immediately began preparations for constructing the new laboratory. This included costs of $1,500 to demolish a shed located on the land, $1,000 to have the debris removed, $5,000 for leveling the building site, $2,000 for "clean-up of the property" required as condition of purchase, and $1,750 for drainage of low areas of land. The owners paid $23,000 for design and engineering of the building, $2,000 for legal fees associated with the building permit, and $1,500 for the city permit fee. Erecting a fence along the rear of the property cost $25,800. A parking lot was paid at a cost of $90,000 and a new building constructed at a cost of $900,000. The building was completed in December, 2010. Determine the total cost of each asset involved. Show the details of cost of each.

STUDY GUIDE

SOLUTION

Land:	
Purchase price	$96,000
Closing costs	4,000
Shed demolition	1,500
Debris removal	1,000
Property clean-up	2,000
Leveling site	5,000
Drainage	1,750
Land total	$111,250

Land Improvements:	
Paving parking lot	$ 90,000
Erect fence	25,800
Improvements total	$115,800

Building:	
Design and engineering	$ 23,000
Legal fees—permit	2,000
City permit fee	1,500
Construction contract	900,000
Building total	$926,500

2. Discovery completed the building at the end of 2010 and placed it in use on January 2, 2011. Its useful life is estimated as 30 years, with estimated net salvage value of $26,500. Three chemical research "vats," the items of equipment to be used, were installed and were put into operation on January 2, 2011. The three units are quite different in use and in physical characteristics.

a. Vat one cost $240,000 and has an estimated life of five years, and estimated net salvage value of $24,000. Because of high operating cost as the unit is used, Discovery decided to use the double-declining-balance method of depreciation on the asset.

b. Vat two cost $150,000 and has an estimated useful life of 10 years, with expected net salvage of $15,000. Because its operating costs and the hours of use are expected to be fairly constant, straight-line depreciation is used.

c. Vat three cost $350,000 and is expected to have a salvage value of $30,000, with an expected useful life of 8 years. It is decided to apply the sum-of-years'-digits method to this asset.

Compute depreciation on the building and each of these three vats for 2011 and 2012. (Round all amounts to nearest whole dollar.)

SOLUTION

Building:

2011 depreciation ($926,500 − $26,500) ÷ 30 years = $30,000

2012 depreciation ($926,500 − $26,500) ÷ 30 years = $30,000

Vat 1:

2011 depreciation ($240,000 × .40) = $96,000

2012 depreciation ($240,000 − $96,000) × .40 = $57,600

Vat 2:

2011 depreciation ($150,000 − $15,000) × .10 = $13,500

2012 depreciation ($150,000 − $15,000) × .10 = $13,500

Vat 3:

2011 depreciation ($350,000 − $30,000) × 8/36 = $71,111

2012 depreciation ($350,000 − $30,000) × 7/36 = $62,222

3. On March 31, 2011, Discovery realized that Vat 2 was inadequate and traded it on a new vat (Vat 4) with a fair value and list price of $250,000. Discovery received a trade-in allowance of $65,000 for Vat 2 and paid the difference of $185,000 in cash.

a. What amount of depreciation will be recorded on March 31 on Vat 2?

b. Will gain or loss be recorded on the trade-in? If so, which? If so, how much?

c. What amount will be recorded in the asset account for Vat 4?

SOLUTION

a. Depreciation for three months = [($150,000 − $15,000) × .10 × 3/12] = $3,375.

b. Losses, but not gains, are recognized. In this case the loss is $54,625:

Trade-in allowance received	$ 65,000
Less: book value of old asset (150,000 − $16,875)	133,125
= Loss on trade-in	$ 68,125

c. Vat 4 cost is deemed to be cash paid ($185,000) + trade-in allowance ($65,000) = $250,000. This is also the fair market value of the new asset.

WORKING PAPERS

Name ______________________

EXERCISE 18.1

	Land	Warehouse

EXERCISE 18.2

EXERCISE 18.3

GENERAL JOURNAL PAGE ______

	DATE		DESCRIPTION	POST. REF.	DEBIT	CREDIT	
1							1
2							2
3							3
4							4
5							5
6							6
7							7

EXTRA FORM

GENERAL JOURNAL PAGE ______

	DATE		DESCRIPTION	POST. REF.	DEBIT	CREDIT	
1							1
2							2
3							3
4							4
5							5

Name ______________________

EXERCISE 18.4

STRAIGHT-LINE METHOD

Year	Acquisition Cost	Salvage Value	Useful Life	Depreciation	Accumulated Depreciation

DOUBLE-DECLINING-BALANCE METHOD

Year	Beginning Book Value	Rate	Depreciation	Accumulated Depreciation

SUM-OF-THE-YEARS'-DIGITS METHOD

Year	Fraction	Cost Less Salvage	Depreciation	Accumulated Depreciation

EXERCISE 18.5

Name

EXERCISE 18.6

EXERCISE 18.7

GENERAL JOURNAL

PAGE

	DATE		DESCRIPTION	POST. REF.	DEBIT	CREDIT	
1							1
2							2
3							3
4							4
5							5
6							6
7							7
8							8
9							9
10							10
11							11
12							12
13							13

EXERCISE 18.8

Name ____________________

EXERCISE 18.8 (continued)

GENERAL JOURNAL PAGE ________

	DATE		DESCRIPTION	POST. REF.	DEBIT	CREDIT	
1							1
2							2
3							3
4							4
5							5
6							6
7							7
8							8
9							9
10							10
11							11
12							12
13							13

EXERCISE 18.9

1. ____________________

2. ____________________

EXERCISE 18.10

Name

EXERCISE 18.11

a.

b.

EXERCISE 18.12

1.

2.

Name

PROBLEM 18.1A or 18.1B

1.

2.

3.

Analyze:

Name ______________________________

PROBLEM 18.2A or 18.2B

STRAIGHT-LINE METHOD

Year	Acquisition Cost	Salvage Value	Useful Life	Annual Depreciation	Accumulated Depreciation

SUM-OF-THE-YEARS'-DIGITS METHOD

Year	Fraction	Cost Less Salvage	Annual Depreciation	Accumulated Depreciation

DOUBLE-DECLINING-BALANCE METHOD

Year	Beginning Book Value	Rate	Annual Depreciation	Accumulated Depreciation

Analyze: ______________________________

____

PROBLEM 18.3A or 18.3B

STRAIGHT-LINE METHOD

Year	Acquisition Cost	Salvage Value	Useful Life	Annual Depreciation	Accumulated Depreciation

UNITS-OF-PRODUCTION METHOD

Year	Acquisition Cost	Salvage Value	Total Expected Units of Production	Actual Units of Production	Cost per Unit	Annual Depreciation	Accumulated Depreciation

Analyze: ______________________________

____

Name

PROBLEM 18.4A or 18.4B

1.

2.

3.

4.

Analyze:

Name ______________________

PROBLEM 18.5A or 18.5B

GENERAL JOURNAL

PAGE ______

DATE		DESCRIPTION	POST. REF.	DEBIT	CREDIT

Analyze: ______________________

Name ______________________

PROBLEM 18.5A or 18.5B (continued)

GENERAL JOURNAL

PAGE ______

	DATE	DESCRIPTION	POST. REF.	DEBIT	CREDIT	
1						1
2						2
3						3
4						4
5						5
6						6
7						7
8						8
9						9
10						10
11						11
12						12
13						13
14						14
15						15
16						16
17						17
18						18
19						19
20						20
21						21
22						22
23						23
24						24
25						25
26						26
27						27
28						28
29						29
30						30
31						31
32						32
33						33
34						34
35						35
36						36

Analyze: ______________________

Name ______________________

PROBLEM 18.6A or 18.6B

GENERAL JOURNAL

PAGE ______

	DATE	DESCRIPTION	POST. REF.	DEBIT	CREDIT	
1						1
2						2
3						3
4						4
5						5
6						6
7						7
8						8
9						9
10						10
11						11
12						12
13						13
14						14
15						15
16						16
17						17
18						18
19						19
20						20
21						21
22						22
23						23
24						24
25						25
26						26
27						27
28						28
29						29
30						30
31						31
32						32
33						33
34						34
35						35
36						36
37						37

Name ____________________

PROBLEM 18.6A or 18.6B (continued)

GENERAL JOURNAL PAGE ______

DATE	DESCRIPTION	POST. REF.	DEBIT	CREDIT

Analyze: ____________________

Name

PROBLEM 18.7A or 18.7B

1.

2. a.

b.

c.

d.

Analyze:

Name

PROBLEM 18.8A or 18.8B

1.

2.

3.

4.

Analyze:

Name ______________________

PROBLEM 18.9A or 18.9B

GENERAL JOURNAL

PAGE ______

DATE		DESCRIPTION	POST. REF.	DEBIT	CREDIT

Name ______________________________

PROBLEM 18.9A or 18.9B (continued)

GENERAL JOURNAL PAGE ______

	DATE		DESCRIPTION	POST. REF.	DEBIT	CREDIT	
1							1
2							2
3							3
4							4
5							5
6							6
7							7
8							8
9							9
10							10
11							11
12							12
13							13
14							14
15							15
16							16
17							17
18							18
19							19
20							20
21							21
22							22
23							23
24							24
25							25
26							26
27							27
28							28
29							29
30							30
31							31
32							32
33							33

Analyze: ______________________________

Name ______________________

CRITICAL THINKING PROBLEM 18.1

GENERAL JOURNAL

PAGE ______

	DATE		DESCRIPTION	POST. REF.	DEBIT	CREDIT	
1							1
2							2
3							3
4							4
5							5
6							6
7							7
8							8
9							9
10							10
11							11
12							12
13							13
14							14
15							15
16							16
17							17
18							18
19							19
20							20
21							21
22							22
23							23
24							24
25							25
26							26

2. a. ______________________

____

____

b. ______________________

Name ______________________

CRITICAL THINKING PROBLEM 18.1 (continued)

3. ______________________

4. ______________________

Name

CRITICAL THINKING PROBLEM 18.2

1.

2.

3.

4.

Chapter 18 Practice Test Answer Key

Part A True-False

1. F	8. F	15. F
2. F	9. T	16. T
3. F	10. F	17. T
4. T	11. T	18. F
5. T	12. T	19. F
6. F	13. T	20. F
7. F	14. T	

Part B Matching

1. b	6. f
2. e	7. a
3. h	8. g
4. j	9. d
5. c	10. i

Part C Exercise

1. Depreciation for 2010 = ($22,000 − $2,000) ÷ 8 years = $2,500
   Depreciation for 2011 = ($22,000 − $2,000) ÷ 8 years = $2,500
2. Depreciation for 2010 = ($22,000 − $2,000) × 8/36 = $4,444
   Depreciation for 2011 = ($22,000 − $2,000) × 7/36 = $3,889
3. Depreciation for 2010 = $22,000 × .25 = $5,500
   Depreciation for 2011 = ($22,000 − $5,500) × .25 = $4,125

CHAPTER 19

Accounting for Partnerships

STUDY GUIDE

STUDY GUIDE

Understanding the Chapter

Objectives

1. Explain the major advantages and disadvantages of a partnership. **2.** State the important provisions that should be included in every partnership agreement. **3.** Account for the formation of a partnership. **4.** Compute and record the division of net income or net loss between partners in accordance with the partnership agreement. **5.** Prepare a statement of partners' equities. **6.** Account for the revaluation of assets and liabilities prior to the dissolution of a partnership. **7.** Account for the sale of a partnership interest. **8.** Account for the investment of a new partner in an existing partnership. **9.** Account for the withdrawal of a partner from a partnership. **10.** Define the accounting terms new to this chapter.

Reading Assignment

Read Chapter 19 in the textbook. Complete the textbook Section Self Review as you finish reading each section of the chapter, and the Comprehensive Self Review at the end of the chapter. Refer to the Chapter 19 Glossary or to the Glossary at the end of the book to find definitions for terms that are not familiar to you.

Activities

- ❑ **Thinking Critically** — Answer the *Thinking Critically* questions for Healthcare Venture Professionals, L.L.C. and Managerial Implications.
- ❑ **Discussion Questions** — Answer each assigned discussion question in Chapter 19.
- ❑ **Exercises** — Complete each assigned exercise in Chapter 19. Use the forms provided in this SGWP. The objectives covered by an exercise are given after the exercise number. If you need help with an exercise, review the portion of the chapter related to the objective(s) covered.
- ❑ **Problems A/B** — Complete each assigned problem in Chapter 19. Use the forms provided in this SGWP. The objectives covered by a problem are given after the problem number. If you need help with a problem, review the portion of the chapter related to the objective(s) covered.
- ❑ **Critical Thinking Problems** — Complete the critical thinking problems as assigned. Use the forms provided in this SGWP.
- ❑ **Business Connections** — Complete the Business Connections activities as assigned to gain a deeper understanding of Chapter 19 concepts.

Practice Tests

Complete the Practice Tests, which cover the main points in your reading assignment. Compare your answers with those in the Practice Test Answer Key for Chapter 19 at the end of this chapter. If you have answered any questions incorrectly, review the related section of the text.

Part A True-False *For each of the following statements, circle T in the answer column if the statement is true or F if the statement is false.*

T F 1. If fixed assets are transferred from an existing sole proprietorship to a partnership, the accumulated balance of the **Allowance for Depreciation** account should be brought forward to the partnership books.

T F 2. Salary allowances to partners are deducted in arriving at net income for financial accounting purposes; however they are not deductible in determining net income for federal income tax purposes.

T F 3. When the assets and liabilities of an existing sole proprietorship are transferred to a partnership, they are recorded on the partnership books at their fair market values.

T F 4. Unless the partnership agreement provides otherwise, profits and losses are shared in proportion to average balances in their capital accounts during the year.

T F 5. A legal partnership may exist without a written partnership agreement.

T F 6. Unless otherwise stated in the partnership agreement, a partnership has a life of 28 years.

T F 7. Limited partners do not, generally, have a voice in operating decisions.

T F 8. General partners have personal liability for all debts of the partnership.

T F 9. Unless the partnership agreement states otherwise, partners share profits and losses equally among the partners.

T F 10. A major advantage of the partnership form of business entity is that it does not pay federal income taxes.

T F 11. If a new partner's investment is greater than the corresponding partnership equity, it may be said that a bonus has been allowed the original partners.

T F 12. A gain or loss on revaluation of assets should be allocated to the partners in accordance with the ratio of the balance of the partners' capital accounts.

T F 13. If a new partner purchases an interest from an old partner, no cash comes into the partnership, and the only entry necessary is one to record the transfer between the capital accounts.

T F 14. The partnership's accounting records should reflect the sales price of an existing partnership interest to a new partner.

T F 15. Salaries allowed a partner must be deducted in arriving at the partnership's net profit or loss for the year.

T F 16. A salary may be allowed to one partner, even though other partners do not receive salary allowances.

T F 17. Salary allowances to partners are considered in dividing net income or loss, even though the partnership may have a loss for the period.

T F 18. Each partner should have a drawing account and a capital account.

Part B Matching *For each numbered item, choose the matching term from the box and write the identifying letter in the answer column.*

a. Bonus
b. Business continuity
c. Dissolution value
d. General partner
e. Liquidation
f. Mutual agency
g. Partner's Drawing
h. Partnership agreement
i. Revaluation
j. Salary allowance
k. Unlimited liability

______ **1.** The amount that may be credited to the old partners' accounts when the amount invested by a new partner is greater than that partner's share of total equity.

______ **2.** A partner who has general liability for losses and debts of a partnership without being limited to that partner's investment in the partnership.

______ **3.** The account that is debited for salary payments to a partner.

______ **4.** A characteristic of partnerships under which a partner is responsible for all debts of the partnership.

______ **5.** A legal contract between the partners creating the partnership.

______ **6.** A factor that may be used in dividing profits and losses.

______ **7.** The value placed on the partnership interest of a partner who dies.

______ **8.** The situation in which a business continues even though an owner dies or transfers ownership to someone else.

______ **9.** The situation in which all assets are sold and cash is distributed to partners.

______ **10.** The adjustment of asset and liability accounts to reflect current value.

______ **11.** The rule that one partner's actions can bind all other partners.

Part C Completion *In the answer column, supply the missing word or words needed to complete each of the following statements.*

______________ **1.** If an incoming partner invests less than the book value of his or her interest, the ______ partner(s) can be said to have received a bonus.

______________ **2.** At the end of the period, each partner's drawing account is closed into the ______ account.

______________ **3.** Payments of salaries to a partner should be charged to the ______ account.

______________ **4.** A partnership ______ occurs when the partnership is completely terminated and the business ceases to exist.

______________ **5.** Assets transferred to a partnership by a sole proprietor in return for a partnership interest should be recorded in the partnership's records at their ______.

______________ **6.** The ______ (partnership, partners) must pay federal income tax on a partnership's profits.

______________ **7.** A partnership is said to lack ______ because the partnership is terminated if a partner dies or is incapacitated.

______________ **8.** Articles of Partnership are commonly referred to as the ______.

______________ **9.** ______ partners have liability for debts of the partnership only to the extent of their investments.

______________ **10.** The ______ is a written contract between the partners containing the major provisions of their agreement.

Demonstration Problem

For several years, Sherrye Cravens has operated the Cravens Hardware Store (there are actually three stores) as a sole proprietor. Near the end of 2010, she agreed to form a partnership with Rhonda Johnson to operate the stores under the name Cravens-Johnson Stores, effective January 1, 2011. Pertinent terms of the partnership agreement follow:

1. Sherrye Cravens is to withdraw all cash from her business on December 31, 2010. She is to transfer to the partnership the accounts receivable, merchandise inventory, furniture and equipment, and all liabilities of the sole proprietorship in return for a partnership interest of 60 percent of the partnership capital. Craven Hardware Store assets are to be appraised and transferred to the partnership at the appraised values.

   Balances in the relevant accounts of Cravens' sole proprietorship at the close of business on December 31, 2010, were:

Accounts Receivable	$253,600 Dr.
Allowance for Doubtful Accounts	16,800 Cr.
Merchandise Inventory	426,000 Dr.
Furniture and Equipment	176,000 Dr.
Allowance for Depreciation of Furniture and Equipment	20,000 Cr.
Accounts Payable	140,000 Cr.

2. The two parties agreed there are $4,000 of additional unrecorded accounts payable and unrecorded accrued expenses of $3,000. They also agreed that $8,000 of the accounts receivable were definitely uncollectible and should not be transferred to the partnership and that the balance for **Allowance for Doubtful Accounts** should be $12,000. The appraised values of the other assets were: Merchandise Inventory, $396,000, and Furniture and Equipment, $216,000.

3. In return for a 40 percent interest in partnership capital, Johnson is to invest cash in an amount equal to two-thirds of Craven's net investment.

4. Each partner is to be allowed a salary, payable on the 15th day of each month. Cravens' salary is to be $16,000 per month and Johnson's is to be $12,000 per month.

5. The partners are to be allowed interest of 10 percent of their beginning Capital balances.

6. The balance of profit or loss after salary and interest allowance is to be divided equally between the two partners.

7. Revenues for 2011 were $4,120,000, expenses were $1,056,000, and cost of goods sold was $2,584,000. Payments for salary allowances were charged to the Drawing accounts.

Instructions

1. Record the general journal entries for the following transactions. Omit descriptions.
   a. Receipt by the partnership of assets and liabilities from Cravens on January 1, 2010.
   b. Investment of cash by Johnson on January 1, 2010.
   c. Summary of cash withdrawals for salaries for the two partners during the year (date entry as December 31, 2010.)
2. Prepare a schedule showing the division of net income to the partners as it would appear on the income statement for 2010.
3. Prepare journal entries to record the following factors related to distribution of net income or loss for the year:
   a. Entry to record salary allowances
   b. Entry to record interest allowances
   c. Entry to close balance of **Income Summary** account

SOLUTION

1.

GENERAL JOURNAL

PAGE 1

DATE		DESCRIPTION	POST. REF.	DEBIT	CREDIT
2010		a.			
Jan.	1	Accounts Receivable		245,600.00	
		Merchandise Inventory		396,000.00	
		Furniture and Equipment		216,000.00	
		Allowance for Doubtful Accounts			12,000.00
		Accounts Payable			144,000.00
		Accrued Expenses			3,000.00
		Sherrye Cravens, Capital			698,600.00
		b.			
	1	Cash		465,733.00	
		Rhonda Johnson, Capital			471,068.00
		c.			
Dec.	31	Sherrye Cravens, Drawing		192,000.00	
		Rhonda Johnson, Drawing		144,000.00	
		Cash			336,000.00

SOLUTION (continued)

2.

Cravens Johnson Stores
Income Statement (Partial)
Year Ended December 31, 2010

	Cravens	Johnson	
Net Income for Year			480,000.00
Salary Allowance	192,000.00	144,000.00	336,000.00
Interest Allowance	70,660.00	47,106.00	117,766.00
Remainder in 50:50 Ratio	13,117.00	13,117.00	26,234.00
	275,777.00	204,223.00	480,000.00

3.

GENERAL JOURNAL PAGE ____

	DATE		DESCRIPTION	POST. REF.	DEBIT	CREDIT	
1	2010		a.				1
2	Dec.	31	Income Summary		336,000.00		2
3			Sherrye Cravens, Capital			192,000.00	3
4			Rhonda Johnson, Capital			144,000.00	4
5							5
6			b.				6
7		31	Income Summary		117,766.00		7
8			Sherrye Cravens, Capital			70,660.00	8
9			Rhonda Johnson, Capital			47,106.00	9
10							10
11			c.				11
12		31	Income Summary		26,234.00		12
13			Sherrye Cravens, Capital			13,117.00	13
14			Rhonda Johnson, Capital			13,117.00	14
15							15
16							16
17							17

WORKING PAPERS

Name ____________________

EXERCISE 19.1

GENERAL JOURNAL

PAGE ______

	DATE		DESCRIPTION	POST. REF.	DEBIT	CREDIT	
1							1
2							2
3							3
4							4

EXERCISE 19.2

GENERAL JOURNAL

PAGE ______

	DATE		DESCRIPTION	POST. REF.	DEBIT	CREDIT	
1							1
2							2
3							3
4							4
5							5
6							6
7							7
8							8
9							9

EXERCISE 19.3

Name ______________________

EXERCISE 19.4

EXERCISE 19.5

EXERCISE 19.6

Name ______________________

EXERCISE 19.7

GENERAL JOURNAL PAGE ______

	DATE	DESCRIPTION	POST. REF.	DEBIT	CREDIT	
1						1
2						2
3						3
4						4
5						5
6						6
7						7
8						8
9						9
10						10
11						11
12						12

EXERCISE 19.8

GENERAL JOURNAL PAGE ______

	DATE	DESCRIPTION	POST. REF.	DEBIT	CREDIT	
1						1
2						2
3						3
4						4
5						5
6						6

EXERCISE 19.9

EXERCISE 19.10

Name ____________________

EXERCISE 19.10 (continued)

GENERAL JOURNAL PAGE ______

	DATE		DESCRIPTION	POST. REF.	DEBIT	CREDIT	
1							1
2							2
3							3
4							4
5							5
6							6

EXERCISE 19.11

GENERAL JOURNAL PAGE ______

	DATE		DESCRIPTION	POST. REF.	DEBIT	CREDIT	
1							1
2							2
3							3
4							4

EXERCISE 19.12

Name ______________________

PROBLEM 19.1A or 19.1B

GENERAL JOURNAL

PAGE ______

	DATE		ACCOUNTS	POST. REF.	DEBIT	CREDIT	
1							1
2							2
3							3
4							4
5							5
6							6
7							7
8							8
9							9
10							10
11							11
12							12
13							13
14							14

Analyze: ______________________

Name ______________________

PROBLEM 19.2A or 19.2B

GENERAL JOURNAL PAGE ______

	DATE		DESCRIPTION	POST. REF.	DEBIT	CREDIT	
1							1
2							2
3							3
4							4
5							5
6							6
7							7
8							8
9							9
10							10
11							11
12							12
13							13
14							14

Analyze: ______________________

Name

PROBLEM 19.3A or 19.3B

GENERAL JOURNAL

PAGE

	DATE		ACCOUNTS	POST. REF.	DEBIT	CREDIT	
1							1
2							2
3							3
4							4
5							5
6							6
7							7
8							8
9							9
10							10
11							11
12							12
13							13
14							14
15							15
16							16
17							17
18							18
19							19
20							20
21							21
22							22
23							23
24							24
25							25
26							26
27							27
28							28
29							29
30							30
31							31
32							32
33							33
34							34
35							35

Analyze:

Name ______________________

PROBLEM 19.4A or 19.4B

GENERAL JOURNAL

PAGE ______

DATE	ACCOUNTS	POST. REF.	DEBIT	CREDIT

Name

PROBLEM 19.4A or 19.4B (continued)

Analyze:

Name ____________________

PROBLEM 19.5A or 19.5B

GENERAL JOURNAL

PAGE ________

DATE		ACCOUNTS	POST. REF.	DEBIT	CREDIT

Name

PROBLEM 19.5A or 19.5B (continued)

GENERAL JOURNAL

PAGE

	DATE		DESCRIPTION	POST. REF.	DEBIT	CREDIT	
1							1
2							2
3							3
4							4
5							5
6							6
7							7
8							8
9							9
10							10
11							11
12							12
13							13
14							14
15							15
16							16
17							17
18							18
19							19
20							20
21							21
22							22
23							23
24							24
25							25
26							26
27							27
28							28
29							29
30							30
31							31
32							32
33							33
34							34
35							35
36							36

Analyze:

Name ______________________

PROBLEM 19.6A or 19.6B

GENERAL JOURNAL

PAGE ______

DATE		ACCOUNTS	POST. REF.	DEBIT	CREDIT

Analyze: ______________________

Name ____________________

CRITICAL THINKING PROBLEM 19.1

GENERAL JOURNAL

PAGE ______

	DATE	ACCOUNTS	POST. REF.	DEBIT	CREDIT	
1						1
2						2
3						3
4						4
5						5
6						6
7						7
8						8
9						9
10						10
11						11
12						12
13						13
14						14
15						15
16						16
17						17
18						18
19						19
20						20
21						21
22						22
23						23
24						24
25						25
26						26
27						27
28						28
29						29
30						30
31						31
32						32
33						33
34						34
35						35
36						36
37						37

Name

CRITICAL THINKING PROBLEM 19.1 (continued)

GENERAL JOURNAL

PAGE

	DATE		DESCRIPTION	POST. REF.	DEBIT	CREDIT	
1							1
2							2
3							3
4							4
5							5
6							6
7							7
8							8
9							9
10							10

Analyze:

GENERAL LEDGER

ACCOUNT ACCOUNT NO.

DATE		DESCRIPTION	POST. REF.	DEBIT	CREDIT	BALANCE	
						DEBIT	CREDIT

ACCOUNT ACCOUNT NO.

DATE		DESCRIPTION	POST. REF.	DEBIT	CREDIT	BALANCE	
						DEBIT	CREDIT

Name ______________________

CRITICAL THINKING PROBLEM 19.1 (continued)

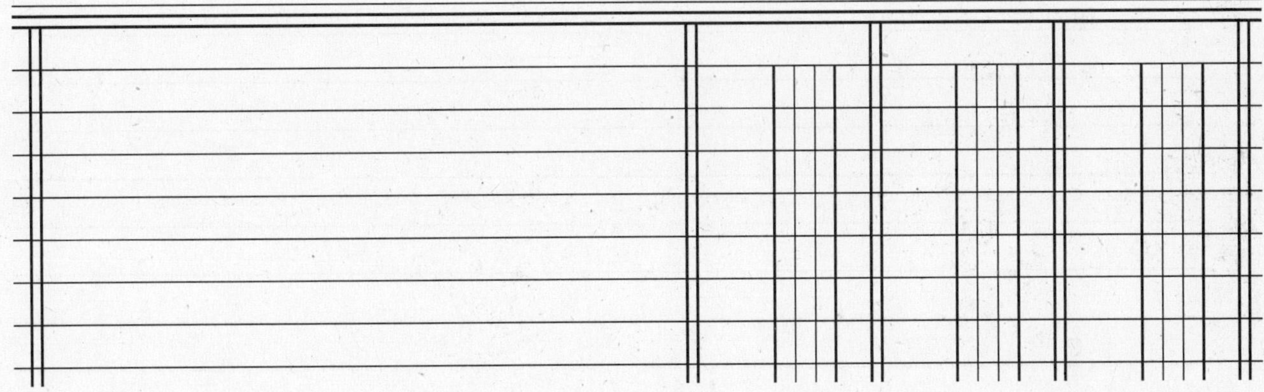

GENERAL JOURNAL PAGE ______

	DATE		ACCOUNTS	POST. REF.	DEBIT	CREDIT	
1							1
2							2
3							3
4							4
5							5
6							6
7							7
8							8
9							9
10							10

Analyze: ______________________

Name

CRITICAL THINKING PROBLEM 19.2

Chapter 19 Practice Test Answer Key

Part A True-False

1. F	**7.** T	**13.** T
2. F	**8.** T	**14.** F
3. T	**9.** T	**15.** F
4. F	**10.** T	**16.** T
5. T	**11.** T	**17.** T
6. F	**12.** F	**18.** T

Part B Matching

1. a	**7.** c
2. d	**8.** b
3. g	**9.** e
4. k	**10.** i
5. h	**11.** f
6. j	

Part C Completion

1. incoming	**6.** partners
2. capital	**7.** continuity
3. partners' drawing	**8.** partnership agreement
4. liquidation	**9.** limited
5. market values	**10.** partnership agreement

CHAPTER 20 Corporations: Formation and Capital Stock Transactions

STUDY GUIDE

Understanding the Chapter

Objectives

1. Explain the characteristics of a corporation. **2.** Describe special "hybrid" organizations that have some characteristics of partnerships and some characteristics of corporations. **3.** Describe the different types of stock. **4.** Compute the number of shares of common stock to be issued on the conversion of convertible preferred stock. **5.** Compute dividends payable on stock. **6.** Record the issuance of capital stock at par value. **7.** Prepare a balance sheet for a corporation. **8.** Record organization costs. **9.** Record stock issued at a premium and stock with no par value. **10.** Record transactions for stock subscriptions. **11.** Describe the capital stock records for a corporation. **12.** Define the accounting terms new to this chapter.

Reading Assignment

Read Chapter 20 in the textbook. Complete the textbook Section Self Review as you finish reading each section of the chapter, and the Comprehensive Self Review at the end of the chapter. Refer to the Chapter 20 Glossary or to the Glossary at the end of the book to find definitions for terms that are not familiar to you.

Activities

❑ **Thinking Critically** — Answer the *Thinking Critically* questions for ConAgra Foods and Managerial Implications.

❑ **Discussion Questions** — Answer each assigned discussion question in Chapter 20.

❑ **Exercises** — Complete each assigned exercise in Chapter 20. Use the forms provided in this SGWP. The objectives covered by an exercise are given after the exercise number. If you need help with an exercise, review the portion of the chapter related to the objective(s) covered.

❑ **Problems A/B** — Complete each assigned problem in Chapter 20. Use the forms provided in this SGWP. The objectives covered by a problem are given after the problem number. If you need help with a problem, review the portion of the chapter related to the objective(s) covered.

❑ **Critical Thinking Problems** — Complete the critical thinking problems as assigned. Use the forms provided in this SGWP.

❑ **Business Connections** — Complete the Business Connections activities as assigned to gain a deeper understanding of Chapter 20 concepts.

Practice Tests

Complete the Practice Tests, which cover the main points in your reading assignment. Compare your answers with those in the Practice Test Answer Key for Chapter 20 at the end of this chapter. If you have answered any questions incorrectly, review the related section of the text.

Part A True-False *For each of the following statements, circle T in the answer column if the answer is true or F if the answer is false.*

T F **1.** A corporate charter specifies the classes and number of shares of stock authorized.

T F **2.** If only one class of stock is issued by a corporation, it is referred to as *normal* stock.

T F **3.** If dividends on participating preferred stock are not paid in one year, they must be paid in the following year before any dividends can be paid on common stock.

T F **4.** Usually a corporation must pay federal income taxes on its net income.

T F **5.** Most preferred stock does not have a par value.

T F **6.** Stockholders are empowered to act for the corporation in most circumstances.

T F **7.** Owners of stock of a corporation are usually personally liable for the corporation's debts.

T F **8.** A corporation is a legal entity, separate and apart from its owners.

T F **9.** It is necessary to obtain a charter from the United States government before a corporation can commence business.

T F **10.** A shareholder generally has the right to sell the shares he or she owns without prior approval of the corporation.

T F **11.** Convertible preferred stock is redeemable for cash by the owner.

T F **12.** Convertible preferred stock must have the same par value as nonconvertible preferred stock.

T F **13.** Preferred stock must have the same par value as the corporation's common stock.

T F **14.** If common stock has a par value, the Common Stock account should be debited for the par value of all common stock issued.

T F **15.** The stock certificate is usually issued as soon as the stock subscription is recorded.

T F **16.** Organization costs are now usually charged to expense when incurred.

T F **17.** Callable preferred stock may be reacquired by the corporation from the stockholders at the option of the corporation, provided pre-established conditions are met.

T F **18.** The conversion ratio establishes the number of shares of common stock into which a share of convertible preferred stock can be converted.

T F **19.** The preemptive right gives the stockholders the right to receive dividends when declared by the directors.

STUDY GUIDE

Part B Completion *In the answer column, supply the missing word or words needed to complete each of the following statements.*

_______________ **1.** A corporation that is generally taxed as a partnership is a(an) ______ corporation.

_______________ **2.** A record of the number of shares owned by each shareholder is kept in the ______.

_______________ **3.** The ______ contains a record of all meetings of stockholders and directors.

_______________ **4.** The paper that serves as evidence of ownership of stock is the ______.

_______________ **5.** The amount above par value or stated value at which stock is issued is the ______.

_______________ **6.** The transfer of stock between shareholders is recorded in the ______ journal.

_______________ **7.** If preferred stock is ______, dividends stated must be paid to preferred stockholders for the current year and all prior years before any dividend can be paid on common stock.

_______________ **8.** A state government issues a ______, which establishes or creates a corporation.

_______________ **9.** An amount known as ______ may be set by the board of directors to be credited to the Capital Stock account for each share.

_______________ **10.** Stock that may have prior claims on profits or on assets in case of liquidation is known as ______ stock.

_______________ **11.** The figure shown in the corporate charter to establish a face value for each share of stock is known as ______.

Demonstration Problem

Just after its formation on July 1, 2010, the ledger accounts of the Waggoner Athletics Corporation showed the following balances.

Account	Balance	Account	Balance
Accrued Expenses	$ 24,000	Merchandise Inventory	69,500
Accounts Payable	80,000	Notes Payable—Short-Term	44,000
Accounts Receivable	72,000	Paid-in Capital in Excess of Par—Common	68,600
Allowance for Doubtful Accounts	14,000	Paid-in Capital in Excess of Par—Preferred	21,500
Building	400,000	Preferred Stock (8%, $25 Par)	100,000
Cash	75,000	Preferred Stock Subscribed	40,000
Common Stock ($50 Par)	400,000	Subscriptions Receivable—Common	17,600
Common Stock Subscribed	16,000	Subscriptions Receivable—Preferred	40,000
Furniture and Fixtures	134,000		

The corporation is authorized to issue 100,000 shares of $50 par common stock and 20,000 shares of 8 percent, $25 par noncumulative and nonparticipating preferred stock.

Instructions

Answer the questions that follow.

1. How many shares of common stock are outstanding?
2. How many shares of common stock are subscribed?
3. How many shares of preferred stock are outstanding?
4. How many shares of preferred stock are subscribed?
5. At what average price has common stock been subscribed or issued?
6. Assume that no dividends are paid in the first year of the corporation's existence. What are the rights of the preferred stockholders?
7. Assuming that all paid-in capital in excess of par on common stock was applicable to the shares of common stock that have been subscribed but not yet issued, what is the subscription price per share of the common stock subscribed?
8. Assuming that the board of directors declared no dividends in 2010, what amount would have to be paid to preferred stockholders in 2011 before any dividend could be paid to common stockholders?
9. Prepare a classified balance sheet for Waggoner Athletics Corporation just after its formation on July 1, 2010.

SOLUTION

1. $400,000 ÷ $50 = 8,000 shares of common stock

2. $ 16,000 ÷ $50 = 320 shares

3. $100,000 ÷ $25 = 4,000 shares

4. $ 40,000 ÷ $25 = 1,600 shares

5. Common Stock	**$400,000**
Common Stock Subscribed	**16,000**
Paid-in Capital in Excess of Par—Common	**68,600**
Total	**$484,600**

$484,600 ÷ 8,320 shares = $58.25 per share

6. None. The preferred stock is noncumulative.

7. ($16,000 + $68,600 = $84,600) ÷ 320 = $264.38 per share

8. $2.00 dividend per share must be paid to preferred stockholders ($25 × 0.08)

SOLUTION (continued)

Waggoner Athletics Corporation

Balance Sheet

July 1, 2010

Assets		
Current Assets		
Cash		75,000.00
Accounts Receivable	72,000.00	
Less Allowance for Doubtful Accounts	14,000.00	58,000.00
Subscriptions Receivable—Common		17,600.00
Subscriptions Receivable—Preferred		40,000.00
Merchandise Inventory		69,500.00
Total Current Assets		260,100.00
Property, Plant, and Equipment		
Building	400,000.00	
Furniture and Fixtures	134,000.00	
Total Property, Plant, and Equipment		534,000.00
Total Assets		794,100.00
Liabilities and Stockholders' Equity		
Current Liabilities		
Accrued Expenses	24,000.00	
Accounts Payable	80,000.00	
Notes Payable—Short-Term	44,000.00	
Total Liabilities		148,000.00
Stockholders' Equity		
Preferred Stock (8%, $25 par, 20,000 sh auth., 4,000 sh iss. and out.)	100,000.00	
Preferred Stock Subscribed (1,600 shares)	40,000.00	
Paid-in Capital in Excess of Par—Preferred	21,500.00	161,500.00
Common Stock ($50 par, 100,000 shares authorized, 8,000 sh. iss. and out.)	400,000.00	
Common Stock Subscribed (320 shares)	16,000.00	
Paid-in Capital in Excess of Par—Common	68,600.00	484,600.00
Total Stockholders' Equity		646,100.00
Total Liabilities and Stockholders' Equity		794,100.00

STUDY GUIDE

WORKING PAPERS

Name

EXERCISE 20.1

EXERCISE 20.2

1.

2.

Name

EXERCISE 20.3

1.

2.

EXERCISE 20.4

EXERCISE 20.5

EXERCISE 20.6

Name ______________________________

EXERCISE 20.7

GENERAL JOURNAL PAGE ______

	DATE		DESCRIPTION	POST. REF.	DEBIT	CREDIT	
1							1
2							2
3							3
4							4
5							5
6							6
7							7
8							8

EXERCISE 20.8

GENERAL JOURNAL PAGE ______

	DATE		DESCRIPTION	POST. REF.	DEBIT	CREDIT	
1							1
2							2
3							3
4							4
5							5
6							6
7							7
8							8

EXERCISE 20.9

GENERAL JOURNAL PAGE ______

	DATE		DESCRIPTION	POST. REF.	DEBIT	CREDIT	
1							1
2							2
3							3
4							4
5							5
6							6
7							7
8							8
9							9
10							10

Name ____________________

EXERCISE 20.10

GENERAL JOURNAL

PAGE ______

	DATE		DESCRIPTION	POST. REF.	DEBIT	CREDIT	
1							1
2							2
3							3
4							4
5							5
6							6
7							7
8							8
9							9
10							10
11							11
12							12
13							13
14							14
15							15
16							16
17							17
18							18
19							19
20							20
21							21
22							22
23							23
24							24
25							25
26							26
27							27
28							28
29							29
30							30
31							31
32							32
33							33
34							34
35							35
36							36
37							37

Name ______________________

PROBLEM 20.1A or 20.1B

	Year	Total Dividends	Preferred Stock Total	Preferred Stock Per Share	Common Stock Total	Common Stock Per Share

Analyze: ______________________

PROBLEM 20.2A or 20.2B

PART I

Name ______________________

PROBLEM 20.2A or 20.2B (continued)

PART II

Analyze: ______________________

PROBLEM 20.3A or 20.3B

GENERAL JOURNAL

PAGE ______

	DATE		DESCRIPTION	POST. REF.	DEBIT	CREDIT	
1							1
2							2
3							3
4							4
5							5
6							6
7							7
8							8
9							9
10							10
11							11
12							12
13							13
14							14
15							15
16							16
17							17
18							18
19							19
20							20
21							21
22							22

Analyze: ______________________

Name

PROBLEM 20.4A or 20.4B

GENERAL JOURNAL

PAGE

	DATE		DESCRIPTION	POST. REF.	DEBIT	CREDIT	
1							1
2							2
3							3
4							4
5							5
6							6
7							7
8							8
9							9
10							10
11							11
12							12
13							13
14							14
15							15
16							16
17							17
18							18
19							19
20							20
21							21
22							22
23							23
24							24
25							25
26							26
27							27
28							28
29							29
30							30
31							31
32							32
33							33
34							34
35							35
36							36

Name

PROBLEM 20.4A or 20.4B (continued)

Analyze:

Name

PROBLEM 20.5A or 20.5B

GENERAL JOURNAL PAGE

DATE	DESCRIPTION	POST. REF.	DEBIT	CREDIT

Name

PROBLEM 20.5A or 20.5B (continued)

GENERAL JOURNAL

PAGE

DATE		DESCRIPTION	POST. REF.	DEBIT	CREDIT

GENERAL LEDGER

ACCOUNT ACCOUNT NO.

DATE		DESCRIPTION	POST. REF.	DEBIT	CREDIT	BALANCE	
						DEBIT	CREDIT

Name ______________________

PROBLEM 20.5A or 20.5B (continued)

GENERAL LEDGER

ACCOUNT ______________________ ACCOUNT NO. ________

DATE		DESCRIPTION	POST. REF.	DEBIT	CREDIT	BALANCE	
						DEBIT	CREDIT

ACCOUNT ______________________ ACCOUNT NO. ________

DATE		DESCRIPTION	POST. REF.	DEBIT	CREDIT	BALANCE	
						DEBIT	CREDIT

ACCOUNT ______________________ ACCOUNT NO. ________

DATE		DESCRIPTION	POST. REF.	DEBIT	CREDIT	BALANCE	
						DEBIT	CREDIT

ACCOUNT ______________________ ACCOUNT NO. ________

DATE		DESCRIPTION	POST. REF.	DEBIT	CREDIT	BALANCE	
						DEBIT	CREDIT

ACCOUNT ______________________ ACCOUNT NO. ________

DATE		DESCRIPTION	POST. REF.	DEBIT	CREDIT	BALANCE	
						DEBIT	CREDIT

Name

PROBLEM 20.5A or 20.5B (continued)

GENERAL LEDGER

ACCOUNT ______________________ ACCOUNT NO. ________

DATE		DESCRIPTION	POST. REF.	DEBIT	CREDIT	BALANCE DEBIT	BALANCE CREDIT

ACCOUNT ______________________ ACCOUNT NO. ________

DATE		DESCRIPTION	POST. REF.	DEBIT	CREDIT	BALANCE DEBIT	BALANCE CREDIT

ACCOUNT ______________________ ACCOUNT NO. ________

DATE		DESCRIPTION	POST. REF.	DEBIT	CREDIT	BALANCE DEBIT	BALANCE CREDIT

Analyze: ______________________

Name

CRITICAL THINKING PROBLEM 20.1

1.

Name

CRITICAL THINKING PROBLEM 20.1 (continued)

2.

Analyze:

Name

CRITICAL THINKING PROBLEM 20.2

Chapter 20 Practice Test Answer Key

Part A True-False

1.	**T**	**11.**	**F**
2.	**F**	**12.**	**F**
3.	**F**	**13.**	**F**
4.	**T**	**14.**	**F**
5.	**F**	**15.**	**F**
6.	**F**	**16.**	**T**
7.	**F**	**17.**	**T**
8.	**T**	**18.**	**T**
9.	**F**	**19.**	**F**
10.	**T**		

Part B Completion

1. Subchapter S (or "S")
2. capital stock ledger
3. minute book
4. stock certificate
5. premium
6. capital stock transfer journal
7. cumulative
8. charter
9. stated value
10. preferred stock
11. par value

CHAPTER 21

Corporate Earnings and Capital Transactions

STUDY GUIDE

Understanding the Chapter

Objectives

1. Estimate the federal corporate income tax and prepare related journal entries. **2.** Complete a worksheet for a corporation. **3.** Record corporate adjusting and closing entries. **4.** Prepare an income statement for a corporation. **5.** Record the declaration and payment of cash dividends. **6.** Record the declaration and issuance of stock dividends. **7.** Record stock splits. **8.** Record appropriations of retained earnings. **9.** Record a corporation's receipt of donated assets. **10.** Record treasury stock transactions. **11.** Prepare financial statements for a corporation. **12.** Define the accounting terms new to this chapter.

Reading Assignment

Read Chapter 21 in the textbook. Complete the textbook Section Self Review as you finish reading each section of the chapter, and the Comprehensive Self Review at the end of the chapter. Refer to the Chapter 21 Glossary or to the Glossary at the end of the book to find definitions for terms that are not familiar to you.

Activities

- ❑ **Thinking Critically** — Answer the *Thinking Critically* questions for McDonald's Corporation and Managerial Implications.
- ❑ **Discussion Questions** — Answer each assigned discussion question in Chapter 21.
- ❑ **Exercises** — Complete each assigned exercise in Chapter 21. Use the forms provided in this SGWP. The objectives covered by an exercise are given after the exercise number. If you need help with an exercise, review the portion of the chapter related to the objective(s) covered.
- ❑ **Problems A/B** — Complete each assigned problem in Chapter 21. Use the forms provided in this SGWP. The objectives covered by a problem are given after the problem number. If you need help with a problem, review the portion of the chapter related to the objective(s) covered.
- ❑ **Critical Thinking Problems** — Complete the critical thinking problems as assigned. Use the forms provided in this SGWP.
- ❑ **Business Connections** — Complete the Business Connections activities as assigned to gain a deeper understanding of Chapter 21 concepts.

Practice Tests

Complete the Practice Tests, which cover the main points in your reading assignment. Compare your answers with those in the Practice Test Answer Key for Chapter 21 at the end of this chapter. If you have answered any questions incorrectly, review the related section of the text.

STUDY GUIDE

Part A True-False

For each of the following statements, circle T in the answer column if the statement is true or F if the statement is false.

T F 1. A stock dividend decreases the Paid-in Capital of the corporation.

T F 2. The entry to record a stock dividend is made on the declaration date.

T F 3. The **Treasury Stock** account is debited for the market value of treasury stock purchased.

T F 4. Extraordinary gains and losses are commonly shown "net of tax."

T F 5. Corporate income taxes may be shown as operating expenses or as a final deduction to arrive at "net income after taxes."

T F 6. When a stock split is declared, the **Retained Earnings** account is debited for the estimated market value of the stock to be issued.

T F 7. The statement of retained earnings shows all changes in the corporate capital during the year.

T F 8. Treasury stock should be shown as a liability on the balance sheet.

T F 9. Property received as a gift should be recorded at its fair market value and credited to an account such as **Donated Capital.**

T F 10. When a stock dividend is declared, the **Retained Earnings** account is debited for the par value of the stock to be issued.

T F 11. Appropriated retained earnings represents cash set aside for specific purposes.

T F 12. Appropriations of retained earnings may reflect contractual requirements or may be purely discretionary.

T F 13. The issuance of a stock dividend decreases the total stockholders' equity of the corporation.

T F 14. Cash dividends are credited to the **Retained Earnings** account.

T F 15. Extraordinary gains and losses should be classified as Other Income or Other Deductions in the income statement.

Part B Matching

For each numbered item, choose the matching term from the box and write the identifying letter in the answer column.

______ 1. An example of an appropriation of retained earnings for a specific project.

______ 2. The issuance of new shares to shareholders with a debit to **Retained Earnings,** a credit to **Paid-in Capital** and **Stock Dividends Distributable.**

______ 3. The section of a balance sheet that contains paid-in capital and retained earnings.

______ 4. The term used to describe the accumulated net income of a corporation.

______ 5. Stock that has been issued and reacquired.

______ 6. The account credited when a gift of property is received by a corporation.

______ 7. An analysis of the equity accounts of a corporation.

a. Stock dividend
b. Treasury Stock
c. Retained Earnings Appropriated for Plant Expansion
d. Statement of stockholders' equity
e. Retained Earnings
f. Stockholders' equity
g. Donated Capital

Part C Exercises

1. Prior to a 10 percent stock dividend, the total stockholders' equity of the Autumn Corporation consists of \$500,000 of common stock (10,000 shares of \$50 par value, issued and outstanding) plus retained earnings of \$250,000. Assets are \$950,000 and liabilities, \$200,000. The estimated market value of the stock to be issued is \$160 per share. Compute the book value per share before and after the dividend is declared.
2. The Paducah Corporation has 1,000 shares of \$50 par value, 10 percent, cumulative, nonparticipating preferred stock authorized and issued. On December 15, 2010, the directors declare a dividend on preferred stock payable on January 12, 2011, to stockholders of record on December 31, 2010. The dividend is the regular dividend for the current year and the dividends in arrears. (No dividend was paid in 2009.) Record the general journal entry for the dividend declaration.

GENERAL JOURNAL PAGE ______

	DATE		DESCRIPTION	POST. REF.	DEBIT	CREDIT	
1							1
2							2
3							3
4							4
5							5

Demonstration Problem

The stockholders' equity section of the balance sheets of the Vandy Landscaping Corporation on December 31, 2009, and December 31, 2010, plus other selected account balances, follows (some information is omitted). During 2010 the following transactions, other than net income or loss after taxes, affected stockholders' equity.

1. A stock dividend was declared on common stock and issued in March. No other common stock was issued during the year.
2. A cash dividend of \$6 a share was declared and paid on common stock in December 2010.
3. Preferred treasury stock was purchased at par value in January.
4. Additional preferred stock was issued for cash in April 2010.
5. The yearly cash dividend of \$4 per share was declared and paid on preferred stock outstanding as of December 2010.

Partial Balance Sheets

Stockholders' Equity	2010	2009
Paid-in Capital		
Preferred Stock (8%, \$50 par, 20,000 shares authorized)	\$ 110,000	\$ 85,000
Paid-in Capital in Excess of Par—Preferred	2,000	-0-
Common Stock (\$25 par value, 200,000 shares authorized)	1,200,000	1,160,000
Paid-In Capital in Excess of Par—Common	80,000	-0-
Total Paid-in Capital	\$1,392,000	\$1,245,000
Retained Earnings		
Appropriated for Plant Expansion	200,000	200,000
Appropriated for Treasury Stock	80,000	-0-
Unappropriated	1,020,000	555,000
Total Retained Earnings	1,300,000	755,000
	\$2,692,000	\$2,000,000
Less Treasury Stock, Preferred	80,000	-0-
Total Stockholders' Equity	\$2,612,000	\$2,000,000

Instructions

Answer these questions.

1. How many shares of preferred stock were outstanding on December 31, 2010?
2. How many shares of common stock were issued as a stock dividend during 2010?
3. What was the market value per share of common stock at the time the stock dividend was declared?
4. How many shares of preferred stock were purchased as treasury stock?
5. How many shares of preferred stock were issued for cash during 2010?
6. What was the sales price per share of the preferred stock issued during the year?
7. What was the total cash dividend on preferred stock during the year?
8. What was the total cash dividend on common stock?
9. What was the corporation's net income or loss after taxes during 2010?

SOLUTION

1. **$110,000 ÷ $50 = 2,200 shares issued; 2,200 shares issued − 1,600 shares treasury stock ($80,000 ÷ $50) = 600 shares outstanding**

2. **$1,200,000 − $1,160,000 = $40,000; $40,000 ÷ $25 = 1,600 shares**

3. **$40,000 par value + $80,000 paid-in capital = $120,000; $120,000 ÷ 1,600 shares = $75 per share**

4. **$80,000 ÷ $50 = 1,600 shares of treasury stock purchased**

5. **$110,000 − $85,000 = $25,000; $25,000 ÷ $50 = 500 shares**

6. **$110,000 − $85,000 = $25,000; $25,000 ÷ $50 per share = 500 shares; $25,000 + $2,000 paid-in capital = $27,000; $27,000 ÷ 500 shares = $54 per share**

7. **2,200 shares preferred stock − 1,600 shares treasury stock = 600 shares for dividends; 600 × $4 = $2,400 in dividends**

8. **$1,200,000 ÷ $25 = 48,000 shares of common stock; 48,000 × $6 = $288,000 in dividends**

9.

Increase in retained earnings, unappropriated	**$465,000**
Stock dividend	**120,000**
Cash dividend, common stock	**288,000**
Cash dividend, preferred stock	**2,400**
Increase in appropriation for treasury stock	**80,000**
Income for year	**$955,400**

WORKING PAPERS

Name ______________________

EXERCISE 21.1

EXERCISE 21.2

GENERAL JOURNAL

PAGE ______

	DATE		DESCRIPTION	POST. REF.	DEBIT	CREDIT	
1							1
2							2
3							3
4							4
5							5
6							6

EXERCISE 21.3

a.

b.

c.

EXERCISE 21.4

GENERAL JOURNAL

PAGE ______

	DATE		DESCRIPTION	POST. REF.	DEBIT	CREDIT	
1							1
2							2
3							3
4							4
5							5
6							6

Name ____________________

EXERCISE 21.5

GENERAL JOURNAL PAGE ______

DATE	DESCRIPTION	POST. REF.	DEBIT	CREDIT

EXERCISE 21.6

GENERAL JOURNAL PAGE ______

DATE	DESCRIPTION	POST. REF.	DEBIT	CREDIT

EXERCISE 21.7

GENERAL JOURNAL PAGE ______

DATE	DESCRIPTION	POST. REF.	DEBIT	CREDIT

EXERCISE 21.8

GENERAL JOURNAL PAGE ______

DATE	DESCRIPTION	POST. REF.	DEBIT	CREDIT

Name ______________________

EXERCISE 21.9

GENERAL JOURNAL

PAGE ______

	DATE	DESCRIPTION	POST. REF.	DEBIT	CREDIT	
1						1
2						2
3						3
4						4
5						5
6						6

EXERCISE 21.10

GENERAL JOURNAL

PAGE ______

	DATE	DESCRIPTION	POST. REF.	DEBIT	CREDIT	
1						1
2						2
3						3
4						4
5						5

EXERCISE 21.11

GENERAL JOURNAL

PAGE ______

	DATE	DESCRIPTION	POST. REF.	DEBIT	CREDIT	
1						1
2						2
3						3
4						4
5						5

EXERCISE 21.12

Name

PROBLEM 21.1A or 21.1B

GENERAL JOURNAL

PAGE

DATE		DESCRIPTION	POST. REF.	DEBIT	CREDIT

Name ______________________

PROBLEM 21.1A or 21.1B (continued)

GENERAL JOURNAL PAGE ______

	DATE	DESCRIPTION	POST. REF.	DEBIT	CREDIT	
1						1
2						2
3						3
4						4
5						5
6						6
7						7
8						8
9						9
10						10
11						11
12						12
13						13
14						14
15						15
16						16
17						17
18						18
19						19
20						20
21						21
22						22
23						23
24						24
25						25
26						26
27						27
28						28
29						29
30						30
31						31
32						32
33						33
34						34

Analyze: ____

Name ____________________

PROBLEM 21.2A or 21.2B

	ACCOUNT NAME	TRIAL BALANCE		ADJUSTMENTS	
		DEBIT	CREDIT	DEBIT	CREDIT
1					
2					
3					
4					
5					
6					
7					
8					
9					
10					
11					
12					
13					
14					
15					
16					
17					
18					
19					
20					
21					
22					
23					
24					
25					
26					
27					
28					
29					
30					
31					
32					
33					
34					
35					

Name ____________________

PROBLEM 21.2A or 21.2B (continued)

INCOME STATEMENT		BALANCE SHEET		
DEBIT	CREDIT	DEBIT	CREDIT	
				1
				2
				3
				4
				5
				6
				7
				8
				9
				10
				11
				12
				13
				14
				15
				16
				17
				18
				19
				20
				21
				22
				23
				24
				25
				26
				27
				28
				29
				30
				31
				32
				33
				34
				35

Name

PROBLEM 21.2A or 21.2B (continued)

Name

PROBLEM 21.2A or 21.2B (continued)

(continued)

Name

PROBLEM 21.2A or 21.2B (continued)

Name

PROBLEM 21.2A or 21.2B (continued)

GENERAL JOURNAL PAGE

DATE		DESCRIPTION	POST. REF.	DEBIT	CREDIT

Name

PROBLEM 21.2A or 21.2B (continued)

GENERAL JOURNAL

PAGE

DATE	DESCRIPTION	POST. REF.	DEBIT	CREDIT

Analyze:

Name ______________________

PROBLEM 21.3A or 21.3B

GENERAL JOURNAL

PAGE ______

DATE		DESCRIPTION	POST. REF.	DEBIT	CREDIT

Name

PROBLEM 21.3A or 21.3B (continued)

GENERAL LEDGER

ACCOUNT ____________________ ACCOUNT NO. 381

DATE		DESCRIPTION	POST. REF.	DEBIT	CREDIT	BALANCE	
						DEBIT	CREDIT

Analyze:

Name ______________________

PROBLEM 21.4A or 21.4B

GENERAL JOURNAL

PAGE ______

DATE		DESCRIPTION	POST. REF.	DEBIT	CREDIT

Name

PROBLEM 21.4A or 21.4B (continued)

GENERAL JOURNAL

PAGE

	DATE		DESCRIPTION	POST. REF.	DEBIT	CREDIT	
1							1
2							2
3							3
4							4
5							5
6							6
7							7
8							8
9							9
10							10
11							11
12							12
13							13
14							14
15							15
16							16
17							17
18							18
19							19
20							20
21							21
22							22

GENERAL LEDGER

ACCOUNT **10% Preferred Stock, $10 Par** ACCOUNT NO. **301**

DATE		DESCRIPTION	POST. REF.	DEBIT	CREDIT	BALANCE	
						DEBIT	CREDIT

ACCOUNT **Paid-in Capital in Excess of Par Value—Preferred** ACCOUNT NO. **305**

DATE		DESCRIPTION	POST. REF.	DEBIT	CREDIT	BALANCE	
						DEBIT	CREDIT

Name ______________________

PROBLEM 21.4A or 21.4B (continued)

GENERAL LEDGER

ACCOUNT **Common Stock, No-Par, Stated Value, $50** ACCOUNT NO. **311**

DATE		DESCRIPTION	POST. REF.	DEBIT	CREDIT	BALANCE DEBIT	BALANCE CREDIT

ACCOUNT **Paid-in Capital in Excess of Stated Value—Common** ACCOUNT NO. **315**

DATE		DESCRIPTION	POST. REF.	DEBIT	CREDIT	BALANCE DEBIT	BALANCE CREDIT

ACCOUNT **Donated Capital** ACCOUNT NO. **371**

DATE		DESCRIPTION	POST. REF.	DEBIT	CREDIT	BALANCE DEBIT	BALANCE CREDIT

ACCOUNT **Treasury Stock—Preferred** ACCOUNT NO. **372**

DATE		DESCRIPTION	POST. REF.	DEBIT	CREDIT	BALANCE DEBIT	BALANCE CREDIT

ACCOUNT **Retained Earnings** ACCOUNT NO. **381**

DATE		DESCRIPTION	POST. REF.	DEBIT	CREDIT	BALANCE DEBIT	BALANCE CREDIT

Name

PROBLEM 21.4A or 21.4B (continued)

GENERAL LEDGER

ACCOUNT **Retained Earnings Appropriated for Treasury Stock** ACCOUNT NO. **382**

DATE		DESCRIPTION	POST. REF.	DEBIT	CREDIT	BALANCE DEBIT	BALANCE CREDIT

Analyze:

Name

CRITICAL THINKING PROBLEM 21.1

Analyze:

Name

CRITICAL THINKING PROBLEM 21.2

Name ____________________

Chapter 21 Practice Test Answer Key

Part A True-False

1.	**F**	**9.**	**T**
2.	**T**	**10.**	**F**
3.	**T**	**11.**	**F**
4.	**T**	**12.**	**T**
5.	**T**	**13.**	**F**
6.	**F**	**14.**	**F**
7.	**F**	**15.**	**F**
8.	**F**		

Part B Matching

1. **c**
2. **a**
3. **f**
4. **e**
5. **b**
6. **g**
7. **d**

Part C Exercises

1. Book value **before** stock dividend:
Stockholders' equity, \$750,000 ÷ 10,000 shares = \$75.00 per share

Book value **after** stock dividend:
Stockholders' equity, \$750,000 ÷ 11,000 shares = \$68.18 per share.

2. Entry to record dividend declaration:

2010			
Dec. 15	Retained Earnings	10,000.00	
	Preferred Stock Dividend Payable		10,000.00
	To record dividends payable on cumulative preferred stock for 2009 and 2010. Payable on January 12, 2011 to holders of record on December 31, 2010.		

CHAPTER 22

Long-Term Bonds

STUDY GUIDE

Understanding the Chapter

Objectives

1. Name and define the various types of bonds. **2.** Explain the advantages and disadvantages of using bonds as a method of financing. **3.** Record the issuance of bonds. **4.** Record the payment of interest on bonds. **5.** Record the accrual of interest on bonds. **6.** Compute and record the periodic amortization of a bond premium. **7.** Compute and record the periodic amortization of a bond discount. **8.** Record the transactions of a bond sinking fund investment. **9.** Record an increase or decrease in retained earnings appropriated for bond retirement. **10.** Record retirement of bonds payable. **11.** Define the accounting terms new to this chapter.

Reading Assignment

Read Chapter 22 in the textbook. Complete the textbook Section Self Review as you finish reading each section of the chapter, and the Comprehensive Self Review at the end of the chapter. Refer to the Chapter 22 Glossary or to the Glossary at the end of the book to find definitions for terms that are not familiar to you.

Activities

- ❑ **Thinking Critically** — Answer the *Thinking Critically* questions for 3M and Managerial Implications.
- ❑ **Discussion Questions** — Answer each assigned discussion question in Chapter 22.
- ❑ **Exercises** — Complete each assigned exercise in Chapter 22. Use the forms provided in this SGWP. The objectives covered by an exercise are given after the exercise number. If you need help with an exercise, review the portion of the chapter related to the objective(s) covered.
- ❑ **Problems A/B** — Complete each assigned problem in Chapter 22. Use the forms provided in this SGWP. The objectives covered by a problem are given after the problem number. If you need help with a problem, review the portion of the chapter related to the objective(s) covered.
- ❑ **Critical Thinking Problems** — Complete the critical thinking problems as assigned. Use the forms provided in this SGWP.
- ❑ **Business Connections** — Complete the Business Connections activities as assigned to gain a deeper understanding of Chapter 22 concepts.

Practice Tests

Complete the Practice Tests, which cover the main points in your reading assignment. Compare your answers with those in the Practice Test Answer Key for Chapter 22 at the end of this chapter. If you have answered any questions incorrectly, review the related section of the text.

Part A True-False *For each of the following statements, circle T in the answer column if the statement is true and F if the statement is false.*

T F 1. The issuance of bonds payable is a method for raising cash.

T F 2. Interest paid on bonds payable is not deductible for federal income tax purposes.

T F 3. In case of liquidation of a corporation, the claims of stockholders take priority over the claims of bondholders.

T F 4. The interest on registered bonds is usually paid by check made payable to the bondholder.

T F 5. The interest on coupon bonds is paid when the bondholders detach the interest coupons from the bonds and submit them for payment.

T F 6. Bonds cannot be issued at a price greater than their par value.

T F 7. A premium on bonds payable is amortized over the remaining life of the bond.

T F 8. The **Discount on Bonds Payable** is shown on the balance sheet as a current liability.

T F 9. Amortization of bond discount increases the bond interest expense.

T F 10. Bond issue costs may be offset against the premium or added to the discount.

T F 11. When bonds are sold between interest payment dates, the purchaser pays the seller for any interest accrued on the bonds.

T F 12. The **Premium on Bonds Payable** account has a debit balance and should be shown on the income statement as an expense.

T F 13. At the end of the year, an adjusting entry is made to record amortization of discount or premium since the last interest payment.

T F 14. A bond sinking fund is another name for retained earnings appropriated for bond retirement.

T F 15. The bond sinking fund represents assets put aside to be used to retire outstanding bonds.

Part B Matching *For each numbered item, choose the matching term from the box and write the identifying letter in the answer column.*

_______ 1. A contract covering the issuance of bonds

_______ 2. Bonds issued upon pledge of property

_______ 3. Cash or other assets set aside for the retirement of bonds

_______ 4. Bonds whose ownership may be transferred by delivery

_______ 5. Bonds issued on the general credit of the corporation

_______ 6. Bonds whose ownership is recorded on the books of the corporation

_______ 7. The amount by which the par value of bonds exceeds their issue price

_______ 8. Bonds secured by the pledge of stocks or bonds of other corporations

_______ 9. The amount by which the issue price of bonds exceeds par

_______ 10. Loans for an extended period, secured by notes given as part of the purchase price of land, building, or equipment

_______ 11. A method of financing for an intermediate period of more than one year, and usually less than five years

a. Debenture bonds
b. Registered bonds
c. Secured bonds
d. Bond indenture
e. Premium
f. Bond sinking fund
g. Discount
h. Long-term notes
i. Collateral trust bonds
j. Unregistered bonds
k. Mortgage loans

Demonstration Problem

On December 31, 2010, the equity accounts of ABCD Inc. contained these balances:

Common Stock ($2 par value, 500,000 shares authorized)	
100,000 shares issued and outstanding	$200,000
Retained Earnings	400,000

For the year 2010, the corporation had net income before income taxes of $325,000, income taxes of $81,250, and net income after taxes of $243,750. The corporation's tax rate is 40 percent.

Construction of a new plant at a cost of $700,000 is planned. The corporation's president estimates that the new plant will generate additional net income of approximately $200,000 before interest and taxes. The financial vice-president is less optimistic and forecasts an increase in net income of about $150,000 before interest and taxes.

Management is considering two possibilities for financing the project:

1. Issuance of 140,000 additional shares of common stock for $5 per share.
2. Issuance of $700,000 face amount, 10-year, 10 percent bonds payable, secured by a mortgage lien on the plant.

Instructions

1. Assuming that profits from existing operations will remain the same and that the president's estimate of net income from the new plant is correct, prepare a table with two columns to show the cumulative effect of each financing plan for the items listed below.

   a. Total net income before interest and taxes

   b. Total bond interest

   c. Total income tax

   d. Total income after taxes

   e. Present income after taxes

   f. Increase (decrease) in total income after bond interest and taxes

   g. Present earnings per share of common stock (compute earnings per share by dividing net income after taxes by the shares of common stock outstanding)

   h. Estimated earnings per share of common stock under the proposed plans

   i. Ratio of net income, after income taxes for 2010 to total stockholders' equity on December 31, 2010 (divide net income by total stockholders' equity on December 31, 2010)

   j. Ratio of net income after income taxes to total stockholders' equity if the plant is constructed

2. Prepare a similar table assuming the financial vice-president's estimate of earnings is correct.

SOLUTION

	STOCK	BONDS
1. a. $325,000 + $200,000	$525,000	$525,000
b. $700,000 × 0.10	–0–	70,000
	$525,000	$455,000
c. Stock $81,250 + (0.40 tax rate × $200,000)	161,250	
Bonds $200,000 − $70,000 = $130,000 (increase in income before tax)		
$81,250 + (0.40 × $130,000)		133,250
d.	$363,750	$321,750
e.	243,750	243,750
f.	$120,000	$ 78,000
g. $243,750 ÷ 100,000 shares	$ 2.44	
h. $363,750 ÷ 240,000 shares; $321,750 ÷ 100,000 shares	$ 1.52	$ 3.22
i. $243,750 ÷ $600,000	40.63%	
j. $363,750 ÷ $1,300,000 ($600,000 + $700,000)	27.98%	
$321,750 ÷ $600,000		53.6%
2. a. $325,000 + $150,000	$475,000	$475,000
b. $700,000 × 0.10		70,000
	$475,000	$405,000
c. Stock $81,250 + (0.40 × $150,000)	141,250	
Bonds $150,000 − $70,000 = $80,000 (increase in income before tax)		
$81,250 + (0.40 × $80,000)		113,250
d.	$333,750	$291,750
e.	243,750	243,750
f.	$ 90,000	$ 48,000
g. $243,750 ÷ 100,000 shares	$ 2.44	
h. $333,750 ÷ 240,000; $291,750 ÷ 100,000 shares	$ 1.39	$ 2.92
i. $243,750 ÷ $600,000	40.63%	
j. $333,750 ÷ $1,300,000 ($600,000 + $700,000)	25.67%	
$291,750 ÷ $600,000		48.6%

WORKING PAPERS

Name ______________________

EXERCISE 22.1

GENERAL JOURNAL — PAGE ______

DATE		DESCRIPTION	POST. REF.	DEBIT	CREDIT

EXERCISE 22.2

GENERAL JOURNAL — PAGE ______

DATE		DESCRIPTION	POST. REF.	DEBIT	CREDIT

EXERCISE 22.3

GENERAL JOURNAL — PAGE ______

DATE		DESCRIPTION	POST. REF.	DEBIT	CREDIT

EXERCISE 22.4

GENERAL JOURNAL — PAGE ______

DATE		DESCRIPTION	POST. REF.	DEBIT	CREDIT

Name

EXERCISE 22.5

GENERAL JOURNAL PAGE

	DATE		DESCRIPTION	POST. REF.	DEBIT	CREDIT	
1							1
2							2
3							3
4							4
5							5
6							6

EXERCISE 22.6

GENERAL JOURNAL PAGE

	DATE		DESCRIPTION	POST. REF.	DEBIT	CREDIT	
1							1
2							2
3							3
4							4
5							5
6							6
7							7

EXERCISE 22.7

GENERAL JOURNAL PAGE

	DATE		DESCRIPTION	POST. REF.	DEBIT	CREDIT	
1							1
2							2
3							3
4							4
5							5
6							6
7							7
8							8
9							9
10							10
11							11
12							12
13							13

Name ______________________

EXERCISE 22.8

GENERAL JOURNAL

PAGE ______

	DATE		DESCRIPTION	POST. REF.	DEBIT	CREDIT	
1							1
2							2
3							3
4							4
5							5

EXERCISE 22.9

GENERAL JOURNAL

PAGE ______

	DATE		DESCRIPTION	POST. REF.	DEBIT	CREDIT	
1							1
2							2
3							3
4							4
5							5
6							6
7							7
8							8
9							9
10							10
11							11
12							12
13							13

EXTRA FORM

GENERAL JOURNAL

PAGE ______

	DATE		DESCRIPTION	POST. REF.	DEBIT	CREDIT	
1							1
2							2
3							3
4							4
5							5
6							6
7							7
8							8

Name ____________________

PROBLEM 22.1A or 22.1B

GENERAL JOURNAL PAGE ______

DATE	DESCRIPTION	POST. REF.	DEBIT	CREDIT

Name ____________________

PROBLEM 22.1A or 22.1B (continued)

GENERAL JOURNAL PAGE ________

	DATE		DESCRIPTION	POST. REF.	DEBIT	CREDIT	
1							1
2							2
3							3
4							4
5							5
6							6
7							7
8							8
9							9
10							10
11							11
12							12
13							13
14							14
15							15
16							16
17							17
18							18
19							19
20							20
21							21
22							22
23							23
24							24
25							25
26							26
27							27
28							28
29							29
30							30
31							31
32							32
33							33
34							34

Analyze: ____

Name ______________________

PROBLEM 22.2A or 22.2B

GENERAL JOURNAL

PAGE ______

DATE	DESCRIPTION	POST. REF.	DEBIT	CREDIT

Name

PROBLEM 22.2A or 22.2B (continued)

Analyze:

	DATE		DESCRIPTION	POST. REF.	DEBIT	CREDIT	
1							1
2							2
3							3
4							4
5							5

EXTRA FORM

Name

PROBLEM 22.3A or 22.3B

GENERAL JOURNAL PAGE

DATE	DESCRIPTION	POST. REF.	DEBIT	CREDIT

Name

PROBLEM 22.3A or 22.3B (continued)

Analyze:

PROBLEM 22.4A or 22.4B

GENERAL JOURNAL

PAGE

	DATE		DESCRIPTION	POST. REF.	DEBIT	CREDIT	
1							1
2							2
3							3
4							4
5							5
6							6
7							7
8							8
9							9
10							10
11							11
12							12
13							13
14							14
15							15
16							16
17							17
18							18
19							19
20							20
21							21
22							22
23							23
24							24

Name

PROBLEM 22.4A or 22.4B (continued)

Analyze:

PROBLEM 22.5A or 22.5B

GENERAL JOURNAL

PAGE

DATE		DESCRIPTION	POST. REF.	DEBIT	CREDIT

Analyze:

Name

CRITICAL THINKING PROBLEM 22.1

	Issuing Common Stock	Issuing Bonds Payable
1. President's estimated net income before interest and taxes =		
a. Net income before interest and taxes		
b. Total bond interest		
Taxable income		
c. Total income tax		
d. Total income after tax		
e. Present income after tax		
f. Increase in net income		
g. Present EPS		
h. Proposed EPS		
2. Financial VP's estimate of net income before interest and taxes =		
a. Net income before interest and taxes		
b. Total bond interest		
Taxable income		
c. Total income tax		
d. Total income after tax		
e. Present income after tax		
f. Increase in net income		
g. Present EPS		
h. Proposed EPS		

3.

Analyze:

Name

CRITICAL THINKING PROBLEM 22.2

1.

2.

Chapter 22 Practice Test Answer Key

Part A True-False		Part B Matching	
1.	T	1.	d
2.	F	2.	c
3.	F	3.	f
4.	T	4.	j
5.	T	5.	a
6.	F	6.	b
7.	T	7.	g
8.	F	8.	i
9.	T	9.	e
10.	T	10.	k
11.	T	11.	h
12.	F		
13.	T		
14.	F		
15.	T		

MINI-PRACTICE SET 3

Name ______________________________

Corporation Accounting Cycle

The Joshua Company

GENERAL JOURNAL

PAGE 1

DATE		DESCRIPTION	POST. REF.	DEBIT	CREDIT

Name

GENERAL JOURNAL

PAGE 2

DATE	DESCRIPTION	POST. REF.	DEBIT	CREDIT

 Name ____________________

GENERAL JOURNAL

PAGE 3

DATE		DESCRIPTION	POST. REF.	DEBIT	CREDIT

Name

GENERAL JOURNAL

PAGE 4

	DATE		DESCRIPTION	POST. REF.	DEBIT	CREDIT	
1							1
2							2
3							3
4							4
5							5
6							6
7							7
8							8
9							9
10							10
11							11
12							12
13							13
14							14
15							15
16							16
17							17
18							18
19							19
20							20
21							21
22							22
23							23
24							24
25							25
26							26
27							27
28							28
29							29
30							30
31							31
32							32
33							33
34							34
35							35
36							36
37							37

MINI-PRACTICE SET 3 (continued)

Name ______________________________

GENERAL JOURNAL

PAGE 5

DATE		DESCRIPTION	POST. REF.	DEBIT	CREDIT

 Name

GENERAL LEDGER

ACCOUNT **Cash** ACCOUNT NO. **101**

DATE		DESCRIPTION	POST. REF.	DEBIT	CREDIT	BALANCE DEBIT	BALANCE CREDIT

ACCOUNT **Accounts Receivable** ACCOUNT NO. **103**

DATE		DESCRIPTION	POST. REF.	DEBIT	CREDIT	BALANCE DEBIT	BALANCE CREDIT

ACCOUNT **Allowance for Doubtful Accounts** ACCOUNT NO. **104**

DATE		DESCRIPTION	POST. REF.	DEBIT	CREDIT	BALANCE DEBIT	BALANCE CREDIT

 Name

GENERAL LEDGER

ACCOUNT **Subscriptions Receivable—Common Stock** ACCOUNT NO. **105**

DATE		DESCRIPTION	POST. REF.	DEBIT	CREDIT	BALANCE DEBIT	BALANCE CREDIT

ACCOUNT **Interest Receivable** ACCOUNT NO. **121**

DATE		DESCRIPTION	POST. REF.	DEBIT	CREDIT	BALANCE DEBIT	BALANCE CREDIT

ACCOUNT **Merchandise Inventory** ACCOUNT NO. **131**

DATE		DESCRIPTION	POST. REF.	DEBIT	CREDIT	BALANCE DEBIT	BALANCE CREDIT

ACCOUNT **Land** ACCOUNT NO. **141**

DATE		DESCRIPTION	POST. REF.	DEBIT	CREDIT	BALANCE DEBIT	BALANCE CREDIT

ACCOUNT **Buildings** ACCOUNT NO. **151**

DATE		DESCRIPTION	POST. REF.	DEBIT	CREDIT	BALANCE DEBIT	BALANCE CREDIT

 Name

GENERAL LEDGER

ACCOUNT **Accumulated Depreciation—Buildings** ACCOUNT NO. **152**

DATE		DESCRIPTION	POST. REF.	DEBIT	CREDIT	BALANCE DEBIT	BALANCE CREDIT

ACCOUNT **Furniture and Equipment** ACCOUNT NO. **161**

DATE		DESCRIPTION	POST. REF.	DEBIT	CREDIT	BALANCE DEBIT	BALANCE CREDIT

ACCOUNT **Accumulated Depreciation—Furniture and Equipment** ACCOUNT NO. **162**

DATE		DESCRIPTION	POST. REF.	DEBIT	CREDIT	BALANCE DEBIT	BALANCE CREDIT

ACCOUNT **Organization Costs** ACCOUNT NO. **181**

DATE		DESCRIPTION	POST. REF.	DEBIT	CREDIT	BALANCE DEBIT	BALANCE CREDIT

ACCOUNT **Accounts Payable** ACCOUNT NO. **202**

DATE		DESCRIPTION	POST. REF.	DEBIT	CREDIT	BALANCE DEBIT	BALANCE CREDIT

 Name ________

GENERAL LEDGER

ACCOUNT **Interest Payable** ACCOUNT NO. **203**

DATE		DESCRIPTION	POST. REF.	DEBIT	CREDIT	BALANCE DEBIT	BALANCE CREDIT

ACCOUNT **Estimated Income Taxes Payable** ACCOUNT NO. **205**

DATE		DESCRIPTION	POST. REF.	DEBIT	CREDIT	BALANCE DEBIT	BALANCE CREDIT

ACCOUNT **Dividends Payable—Preferred Stock** ACCOUNT NO. **206**

DATE		DESCRIPTION	POST. REF.	DEBIT	CREDIT	BALANCE DEBIT	BALANCE CREDIT

ACCOUNT **Dividends Payable—Common Stock** ACCOUNT NO. **207**

DATE		DESCRIPTION	POST. REF.	DEBIT	CREDIT	BALANCE DEBIT	BALANCE CREDIT

ACCOUNT **10-Year, 10% Bonds Payable** ACCOUNT NO. **211**

DATE		DESCRIPTION	POST. REF.	DEBIT	CREDIT	BALANCE DEBIT	BALANCE CREDIT

 Name

GENERAL LEDGER

ACCOUNT Premium on Bonds Payable ACCOUNT NO. 212

DATE		DESCRIPTION	POST. REF.	DEBIT	CREDIT	BALANCE DEBIT	BALANCE CREDIT

ACCOUNT 8% Preferred Stock ($100 par, 10,000 shares authorized) ACCOUNT NO. 301

DATE		DESCRIPTION	POST. REF.	DEBIT	CREDIT	BALANCE DEBIT	BALANCE CREDIT

ACCOUNT Paid-in Capital in Excess of Par—Preferred Stock ACCOUNT NO. 302

DATE		DESCRIPTION	POST. REF.	DEBIT	CREDIT	BALANCE DEBIT	BALANCE CREDIT

ACCOUNT Common Stock ($10 par, 100,000 shares authorized) ACCOUNT NO. 303

DATE		DESCRIPTION	POST. REF.	DEBIT	CREDIT	BALANCE DEBIT	BALANCE CREDIT

ACCOUNT Paid-in Capital in Excess of Par—Common Stock ACCOUNT NO. 304

DATE		DESCRIPTION	POST. REF.	DEBIT	CREDIT	BALANCE DEBIT	BALANCE CREDIT

 Name

GENERAL LEDGER

ACCOUNT **Common Stock Subscribed** ACCOUNT NO. **305**

DATE		DESCRIPTION	POST. REF.	DEBIT	CREDIT	BALANCE DEBIT	BALANCE CREDIT

ACCOUNT **Common Stock Dividend Distributable** ACCOUNT NO. **306**

DATE		DESCRIPTION	POST. REF.	DEBIT	CREDIT	BALANCE DEBIT	BALANCE CREDIT

ACCOUNT **Retained Earnings Appropriated** ACCOUNT NO. **311**

DATE		DESCRIPTION	POST. REF.	DEBIT	CREDIT	BALANCE DEBIT	BALANCE CREDIT

ACCOUNT **Retained Earnings Unappropriated** ACCOUNT NO. **312**

DATE		DESCRIPTION	POST. REF.	DEBIT	CREDIT	BALANCE DEBIT	BALANCE CREDIT

ACCOUNT **Treasury Stock—Preferred** ACCOUNT NO. **343**

DATE		DESCRIPTION	POST. REF.	DEBIT	CREDIT	BALANCE DEBIT	BALANCE CREDIT

 Name

GENERAL LEDGER

ACCOUNT Income Summary ACCOUNT NO. 399

DATE		DESCRIPTION	POST. REF.	DEBIT	CREDIT	BALANCE	
						DEBIT	CREDIT

ACCOUNT Sales ACCOUNT NO. 401

DATE		DESCRIPTION	POST. REF.	DEBIT	CREDIT	BALANCE	
						DEBIT	CREDIT

ACCOUNT Purchases ACCOUNT NO. 501

DATE		DESCRIPTION	POST. REF.	DEBIT	CREDIT	BALANCE	
						DEBIT	CREDIT

ACCOUNT Operating Expenses ACCOUNT NO. 601

DATE		DESCRIPTION	POST. REF.	DEBIT	CREDIT	BALANCE	
						DEBIT	CREDIT

 Name

GENERAL LEDGER

ACCOUNT **Interest Income** ACCOUNT NO. **701**

DATE		DESCRIPTION	POST. REF.	DEBIT	CREDIT	BALANCE DEBIT	BALANCE CREDIT

ACCOUNT **Gain on Early Retirement of Bonds Payable** ACCOUNT NO. **711**

DATE		DESCRIPTION	POST. REF.	DEBIT	CREDIT	BALANCE DEBIT	BALANCE CREDIT

ACCOUNT **Interest Expense** ACCOUNT NO. **751**

DATE		DESCRIPTION	POST. REF.	DEBIT	CREDIT	BALANCE DEBIT	BALANCE CREDIT

ACCOUNT **Amortization of Organization Costs** ACCOUNT NO. **753**

DATE		DESCRIPTION	POST. REF.	DEBIT	CREDIT	BALANCE DEBIT	BALANCE CREDIT

ACCOUNT **Income Tax Expense** ACCOUNT NO. **801**

DATE		DESCRIPTION	POST. REF.	DEBIT	CREDIT	BALANCE DEBIT	BALANCE CREDIT

 Name

	ACCOUNT NAME	TRIAL BALANCE DEBIT	TRIAL BALANCE CREDIT	ADJUSTMENTS DEBIT	ADJUSTMENTS CREDIT
1	Cash				
2	Accounts Receivable				
3	Allowance for Doubtful Accounts				
4	Subscriptions Receivable—Common Stock				
5	Merchandise Inventory				
6	Land				
7	Buildings				
8	Accumulated Depreciation—Bldg				
9	Furniture and Equipment				
10	Accum. Depreciation—Furn. and Equip.				
11	Organization Costs				
12	Accounts Payable				
13	Interest Payable				
14	Estimated Income Tax Payable				
15	Dividends Payable—Preferred Stock				
16	Dividends Payable—Common Stock				
17	10-Year, 10% Bonds Payable				
18	Premium on Bonds Payable				
19	8% Preferred Stock				
20	Paid-in Cap. in Excess of Par—Pref. Stock				
21	Common Stock				
22	Paid-in Cap. in Excess of Par—Com. Stock				
23	Common Stock Subscribed				
24	Common Stock Dividend Distrib.				
25	Retained Earnings Appropriated				
26	Retained Earnings Unappropriated				
27	Treasury Stock—Preferred				
28	Income Summary				
29	Sales				
30	Purchases				
31	Operating Expenses				
32					
33					
34	Totals Carried Forward				
35					

MINI-PRACTICE SET 3 (continued)

Name ______________________

ADJUSTED TRIAL BALANCE		INCOME STATEMENT		BALANCE SHEET	
DEBIT	CREDIT	DEBIT	CREDIT	DEBIT	CREDIT

Name ______________________

ACCOUNT NAME	TRIAL BALANCE DEBIT	TRIAL BALANCE CREDIT	ADJUSTMENTS DEBIT	ADJUSTMENTS CREDIT
Totals Brought Forward				
Gain on Early Retirement of Bonds Payable				
Interest Expense				
Amortization of Organization Costs				
Income Tax Expense				
Totals				
Net Income After Tax				
Totals				

 Name

ADJUSTED TRIAL BALANCE		INCOME STATEMENT		BALANCE SHEET		
DEBIT	CREDIT	DEBIT	CREDIT	DEBIT	CREDIT	
						1
						2
						3
						4
						5
						6
						7
						8
						9
						10
						11
						12
						13
						14
						15
						16
						17
						18
						19
						20
						21
						22
						23
						24
						25
						26
						27
						28
						29
						30
						31
						32

 Name

Summary Income Statement

 Name

Statement of Retained Earnings

 Name

Balance Sheet

(continued)

 Name

Balance Sheet (continued)

EXTRA FORM

Name

CHAPTER 23

Financial Statement Analysis

STUDY GUIDE

Understanding the Chapter

Objectives

1. Use vertical analysis techniques to analyze a comparative income statement and balance sheet. **2.** Use horizontal analysis techniques to analyze a comparative income statement and balance sheet. **3.** Use trend analysis to evaluate financial statements. **4.** Interpret the results of the statement analysis by comparison with industry averages. **5.** Compute and interpret financial ratios that measure profitability, operating results, and efficiency. **6.** Compute and interpret financial ratios that measure financial strength. **7.** Compute and interpret financial ratios that measure liquidity. **8.** Recognize shortcomings in financial statement analysis. **9.** Define the accounting terms new to this chapter.

Reading Assignment

Read Chapter 23 in the textbook. Complete the textbook Section Self Review as you finish reading each section of the chapter, and the Comprehensive Self Review at the end of the chapter. Refer to the Chapter 23 Glossary or to the Glossary at the end of the book to find definitions for terms that are not familiar to you.

Activities

❑ **Thinking Critically** — Answer the *Thinking Critically* questions for Walt Disney Company and Managerial Implications.

❑ **Discussion Questions** — Answer each assigned discussion question in Chapter 23.

❑ **Exercises** — Complete each assigned exercise in Chapter 23. Use the forms provided in this SGWP. The objectives covered by an exercise are given after the exercise number. If you need help with an exercise, review the portion of the chapter related to the objective(s) covered.

❑ **Problems A/B** — Complete each assigned problem in Chapter 23. Use the forms provided in this SGWP. The objectives covered by a problem are given after the problem number. If you need help with a problem, review the portion of the chapter related to the objective(s) covered.

❑ **Critical Thinking Problems** — Complete the critical thinking problems as assigned. Use the forms provided in this SGWP.

❑ **Business Connections** — Complete the Business Connections activities as assigned to gain a deeper understanding of Chapter 23 concepts.

Practice Tests

Complete the Practice Tests, which cover the main points in your reading assignment. Compare your answers with those in the Practice Test Answer Key for Chapter 23 at the end of this chapter. If you have answered any questions incorrectly, review the related section of the text.

Part A True-False *For each of the following statements, circle T if the statement is true or F if the statement is false.*

T F **1.** In horizontal analysis, the items on each line of the statements for two periods are compared to determine the change in dollar amounts and percentages.

T F **2.** The net sales figure of a business is normally used as the base, or 100%, for vertical analysis comparisons on the income statement.

T F **3.** In statement analysis, a small percentage change in a large dollar amount may be more important than a large percentage change in a small dollar amount.

T F **4.** The rate of return on total assets is affected by the source of financing used to acquire assets.

T F **5.** In vertical analysis, the percentages may be added and subtracted.

T F **6.** Common-size statements are statements of companies that sold approximately the same product.

T F **7.** In general, a period of two years is adequate for comparing figures such as net sales.

T F **8.** In vertical analysis of the balance sheet, each liability item is usually expressed as a percent of total liabilities.

T F **9.** Current ratio and acid-test ratio are the same ratio.

T F **10.** In general, the lower the rate of inventory turnover, the better.

T F **11.** The earlier period is considered to be the base period in the horizontal analysis of statements.

T F **12.** The interpretation phase of statement analysis is composed primarily of computing percentages and ratios.

T F **13.** A lender will be more interested in net income than in the acid-test ratio.

T F **14.** The analyst is interested in both the amount of change and the percent of change in an item from year to year.

T F **15.** Having an accounts receivable collection period that exceeds 30 days will have no effect on your cash flow planning for the business.

Part B Matching *For each of the transactions below, decide the effect (or effects) the transaction would have on the corporation's financial statements or ratios. In the space provided, enter the letter or letters corresponding to all effects that apply. If there is no appropriate response among the effects listed, write "none".*

Transaction

_______ **1.** Issued long-term notes payable for cash

_______ **2.** Declared and paid an ordinary cash dividend

_______ **3.** Omitted the payment of a dividend

_______ **4.** Declared a cash dividend due in one month

_______ **5.** Issued new common stock shares on a 4 for 1 stock split

_______ **6.** Purchased a new office desk for cash

Effect

a. Increases working capital
b. Reduces working capital
c. Increases the current ratio
d. Decreases the current ratio
e. Increases the dollar amount of the total capital stock
f. Decreases the dollar amount of the total capital stock
g. Increases total retained earnings
h. Decreases total retained earnings
i. Reduces the book value of each share of common stock
j. Reduces the book value of each common shareholder's interest

Demonstration Problem

A condensed income statement for Way Down Corporation, for the years 2010 and 2009, follows. This report has been condensed and simplified from the corporation's annual Form 10K for 2010, filed with the U.S. Securities and Exchange Commission. Amounts given are in millions of dollars.

Instructions

1. Prepare a combined horizontal and vertical analysis of the comparative income statement of Way Down Corporation.

2. Analyze the data on the Way Down Corporation. What conclusions might be drawn from the following increases or decreases?

a. Sales
b. Cost of goods sold
c. Inventory
d. General administrative expense
e. Interest expense
f. Net income after income taxes

SOLUTION

1.

Way Down Corporation
Comparative Income Statement
Years Ended December 31, 2010 and 2009

	AMOUNTS		PERCENT OF NET SALES		INCREASE OR (DECREASE)	
	2010	2009	2010	2009	AMOUNT	PERCENT
Gross Sales	138120	139500	100.7	101.1	(1380)	(1.0)
Sales Returns and Allowances	1000	1570	0.7	1.1	(570)	(36.3)
Net Sales	137120	137930	100.0	100.0	810	0.6
Cost of Goods Sold						
Beginning Inventory, January 1	27561	27350	20.1	19.8	211	0.8
Merchandise Purchases	54500	51981	39.7	37.7	2519	4.8
Total Goods Available for Sale	82061	79331	59.8	57.5	2730	3.4
Less Ending Inventory, December 31	31842	27561	23.2	20.0	4281	15.5
Cost of Goods Sold	50219	51770	36.6	37.5	(1551)	(3.0)
Gross Profit on Sales	86901	86160	63.4	62.5	741	0.9
Operating Expenses						
Selling Expenses	29623	32526	21.6	23.6	(2903)	(8.9)
General Administrative Expenses	26514	22005	19.3	16.0	4509	20.5
Total Operating Expenses	56137	54531	40.9	39.6	1606	2.9
Net Income from Operations	30764	31629	22.5	22.9	(865)	(2.7)
Interest Expense	520	920	0.4	0.7	(400)	(43.5)
Net Income Before Income Taxes	30244	30709	22.1	22.2	(465)	(1.5)
Income Tax Expense	4537	4606	3.3	3.3	(69)	(1.5)
Net Income After Income Taxes	25707	26103	18.8	18.9	(396)	(1.5)

SOLUTION (continued)

2. Several items on the comparative income statement of Way Down Corporation merit additional investigation.

   a. Sales decreased slightly. Although the amount was small in both dollar amount and percentage, a decrease in sales is generally unfavorable.

   b. At the same time as sales decreased, cost of goods sold decreased by a higher percentage. This decrease is a good indication, resulting in an increase in gross profit percentage from 62.5 percent in 2009 to 63.4 percent in 2010.

   c. Note that even though sales decreased, the merchandise inventory increased. During 2009 the inventory increased by 0.8 percent, and during 2010, it increased by 15.5 percent. This increase needs to be investigated.

   d. The large percentage increase in general administrative expenses should be carefully investigated. At the same time, selling expenses decreased during 2010. It is possible that some selling expenses were improperly classified as general administrative expenses. However, there was an increase of 2.9 percent in total operating expenses.

   e. Interest expense decreased by 43.5 percent during the year, but the dollar amount was not large. This amount could probably be explained easily.

   f. Overall, there was a decrease in net income after income taxes. This decrease is the result of the increase in expenses.

WORKING PAPERS

Name ____________________

EXERCISE 23.1

	2010	2009

EXERCISE 23.2

	2010	2009

Name ____________________

EXERCISE 23.3

	2010	2009	Change	Percent

EXTRA FORM

Name

EXERCISE 23.4

	2010	2009	Difference	Percent

Name ____________________

EXERCISE 23.5

	2010	2009

EXERCISE 23.6

	2010	2009

EXERCISE 23.7

	2010	2009

EXERCISE 23.8

	2010	2009

EXERCISE 23.9

	2010	2009

Name

EXERCISE 23.10

	2010	2009

EXERCISE 23.11

	2010	2009

EXERCISE 23.12

	2010

Name

PROBLEM 23.1A or 23.1B

1.

Comparative Income Statement

	AMOUNTS		PERCENT OF NET SALES		INCREASE OR (DECREASE)	
	2010	2009	2010	2009	AMOUNT	PERCENT

Name ____________________

PROBLEM 23.1A or 23.1B (continued)

Comparative Income Statement (continued)

	AMOUNTS		PERCENT OF NET SALES		INCREASE OR (DECREASE)	
	2010	2009	2010	2009	AMOUNT	PERCENT

Name

PROBLEM 23.1A or 23.1B (continued)

Comparative Balance Sheet

	AMOUNTS		PERCENT OF TOTAL ASSETS		INCREASE OR (DECREASE)	
	2010	2009	2010	2009	AMOUNT	PERCENT

Name ______________________

PROBLEM 23.1A or 23.1B (continued)

Comparative Balance Sheet (continued)

	AMOUNTS		PERCENT OF TOTAL ASSETS		INCREASE OR (DECREASE)	
	2010	2009	2010	2009	AMOUNT	PERCENT

2. ______________________

Analyze: ______________________

Name ______________________________

PROBLEM 23.2A or 23.2B

PART I

2009

2010

1.

2.

3.

4.

5.

6.

7.

8.

9.

10.

Name

PROBLEM 23.2A or 23.2B (continued)

PART II

Analyze:

Name ______________________

PROBLEM 23.3A or 23.3B

1. a.

b.

c.

d.

e.

f.

g.

h.

Name

PROBLEM 23.3A or 23.3B (continued)

2.

3.

4.

Analyze:

Name

CRITICAL THINKING PROBLEM 23.1

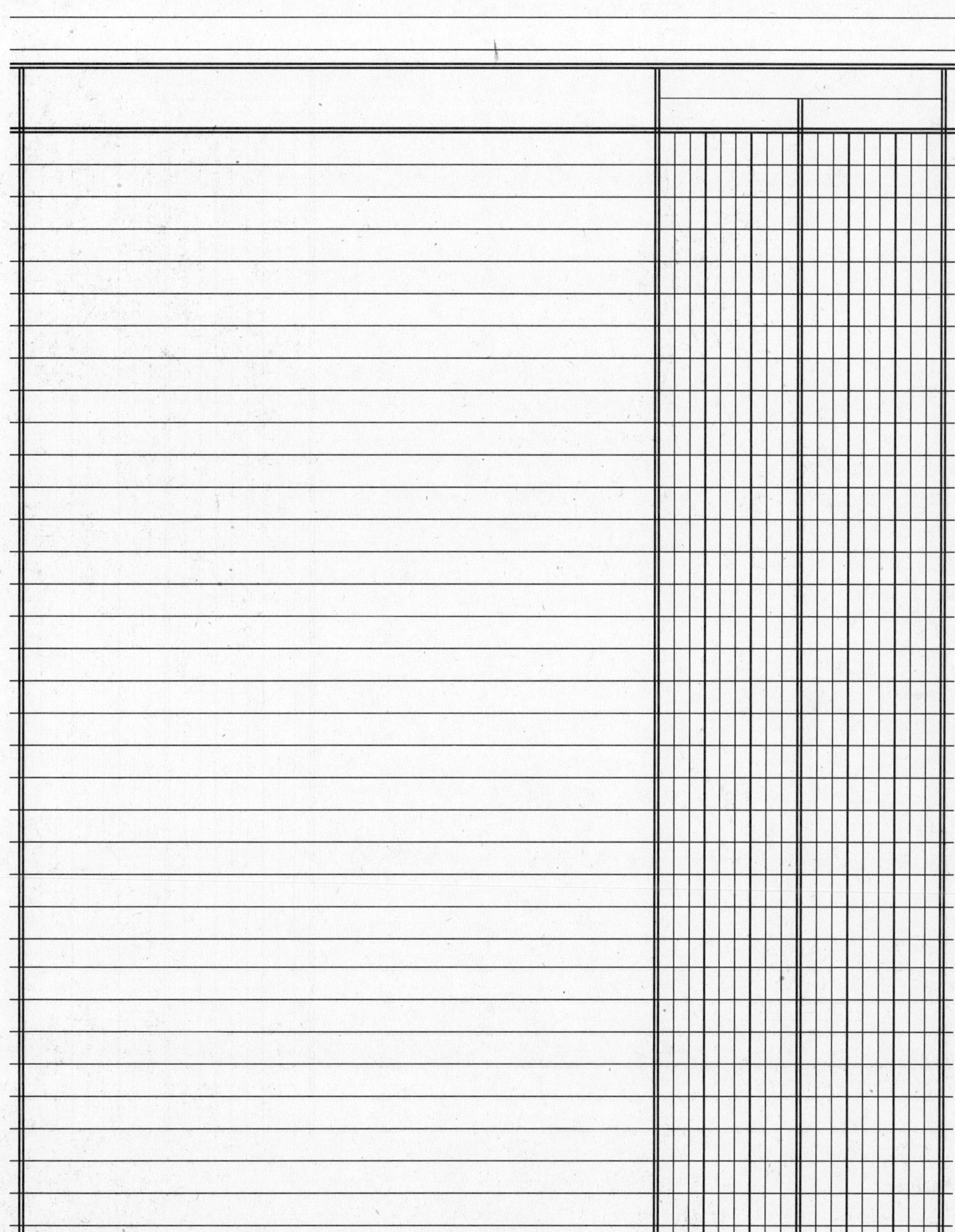

Name ____________________

CRITICAL THINKING PROBLEM 23.1

Analyze: ____________________

Name

CRITICAL THINKING PROBLEM 23.2

Name

EXTRA FORM

Chapter 23 Practice Test Answer Key

Part A True-False

1. T
2. T
3. T
4. F
5. T
6. F
7. F
8. F
9. F
10. F
11. T
12. F
13. F
14. T
15. F

Part B Matching

1. a, c
2. b, d, h
3. i, j
4. b, d, h
5. i
6. b, d

CHAPTER 24

The Statement of Cash Flows

STUDY GUIDE

Understanding the Chapter

Objectives

1. Distinguish between operating, investing, and financing activities. **2.** Compute cash flows from operating activities. **3.** Compute cash flows from investing activities. **4.** Compute cash flows from financing activities. **5.** Prepare a statement of cash flows. **6.** Define the accounting terms new to this chapter.

Reading Assignment

Read Chapter 24 in the textbook. Complete the textbook Section Self Reviews as you finish reading each section of the chapter, and the Comprehensive Self Review at the end of the chapter. Refer to the Chapter 24 Glossary or to the Glossary at the end of the book to find definitions for terms that are not familiar to you.

Activities

- ❑ **Thinking Critically** — Answer the *Thinking Critically* questions for Apple and Managerial Implications.
- ❑ **Discussion Questions** — Answer each assigned discussion question in Chapter 24.
- ❑ **Exercises** — Complete each assigned exercise in Chapter 24. Use the forms provided in this SGWP. The objectives covered by an exercise are given after the exercise number. If you need help with an exercise, review the portion of the chapter related to the objective(s) covered.
- ❑ **Problems A/B** — Complete each assigned problem in Chapter 24. Use the forms provided in this SGWP. The objectives covered by a problem are given after the problem number. If you need help with a problem, review the portion of the chapter related to the objective(s) covered.
- ❑ **Challenge Problem** — Complete the challenge problem as assigned. Use the forms provided in this SGWP.
- ❑ **Critical Thinking Problems** — Complete the critical thinking problems as assigned. Use the forms provided in this SGWP.
- ❑ **Business Connections** — Complete the Business Connections activities as assigned to gain a deeper understanding of Chapter 24 concepts.

Practice Tests

Complete the Practice Tests, which cover the main points in your reading assignment. Compare your answers with those in the Practice Test Answer Key for Chapter 24 at the end of this chapter. If you have answered any questions incorrectly, review the related section of the text.

Part A True-False *For each of the following statements, circle T if the statement is true or F if the statement is false.*

T F 1. A three month CD is an example of a cash equivalent.

T F 2. The statement of cash flows provides an important link between the balance sheet and the income statement.

T F 3. The statement of cash flows is designed to provide information about a corporation's cash position.

T F 4. Interest expense is a cash outflow from an financing activity.

T F 5. The sale of bonds is a financing activity.

T F 6. The statement of cash flows reconciles the beginning and ending balances of cash and cash equivalents.

T F 7. Repayment of a long-term note payable represents an investing activity.

T F 8. The purchase of merchandise inventory for resale is an operating activity.

T F 9. The issue of a mortgage payable for a building is a financing activity.

T F 10. The issue of $50,000 of common stock for land with a fair market value of $50,000 represents an investing activity.

T F 11. Short-term borrowing is classified as a financing activity for purposes of preparing the statement of cash flows.

T F 12. A corporation issued $500,000 of bonds payable, receiving in exchange a building with that value. The transaction would be included in the footnotes of the statement of cash flows.

T F 13. The indirect method of preparing the statement of cash flows is the preferred method of businesses when preparing this statement.

T F 14. The cash received from the sale of equipment represents a cash flow from operating activities.

T F 15. The amortization of premium on bonds payable is added to net income in arriving at the cash flows from operations.

T F 16. The FASB has expressed a preference for the direct method of preparing the statement of cash flows.

T F 17. Depreciation expense is added to the net income figure in arriving at cash flow from operating activities.

Part B Matching *For each numbered item, choose the matching term from the box and write the identifying letter in the answer column.*

______ 1. Paid cash on accounts payable

______ 2. Reacquired common stock as treasury stock

______ 3. Purchased office furniture for cash

______ 4. Paid a cash dividend

______ 5. Paid cash dividend on preferred stock

______ 6. Declared but did not pay a cash dividend

______ 7. Sold land held as a long-term investment

______ 8. Purchased land by issuing common stock

______ 9. Paid interest on a five-year note payable

______ 10. Borrowed $59,000 by issuing a 90-day note payable

a. Operating
b. Investing
c. Financing
d. Not on statement of cash flows

Demonstration Problem

Deli Market, Inc. was formed and began business on December 31, 2009, when Roma Brandon transferred merchandise inventory with a value of $50,000, cash of $30,000, accounts receivable of $20,000, and accounts payable of $20,000 to the corporation in exchange for common stock with a recorded par value of $25 a share.

Information from the company's statement of cash flows for 2010 follows.

Instructions

Based on the data given, prepare the December 31, 2010, balance sheet for the corporation.

Cash Flows from Operating Activities		
Net Income		$ 75,000
Adjustments:		
Depreciation of building	$ 7,500	
Depreciation of equipment	5,000	
Increase in accounts receivable	(33,000)	
Increase in inventory	(10,000)	
Increase in prepaid insurance	(1,300)	
Increase in accounts payable	12,000	
Increase in income tax payable	4,000	
Total Adjustments		(15,800)
Net cash provided by operating activities		$ 59,200
Cash Flows from Investing Activities		
Purchase of land	$(20,000)	
Purchase of building*	(10,000)	
Purchase of equipment	(25,000)	
Net cash used in investing activities		(55,000)
Cash Flows from Financing Activities		
Issuance of common stock at $25	$ 75,000	
Borrowing at bank by issuance of note payable	20,000	
Net cash provided by financing activities		$ 95,000
Net Increase in Cash and Cash Equivalents		$ 99,200
Cash balance, January 1, 2010		30,000
Cash balance, December 31, 2010		$129,200

*A building was acquired at a cost of $75,000. Cash of $10,000 was paid, and a mortgage payable of $65,000 was given for the balance.

SOLUTION

Deli Market, Inc.
Balance Sheet
December 31, 2010

Assets			
Current Assets			
Cash		129,200.00	
Accounts Receivable		53,000.00	
Merchandise Inventory		60,000.00	
Prepaid Insurance		1,300.00	
Total Current Assets			243,500.00
Property, Plant, and Equipment			
Land		20,000.00	
Building	75,000.00		
Less Accumulated Depreciation—Building	7,500.00	67,500.00	
Equipment	25,000.00		
Less Accumulated Depreciation—Equipment	5,000.00	20,000.00	
Total Property, Plant, and Equipment			107,500.00
Total Assets			351,000.00
Liabilities and Stockholders' Equity			
Current Liabilities			
Accounts Payable		32,000.00	
Notes Payable		20,000.00	
Income Tax Payable		4,000.00	
Total Current Liabilities		56,000.00	
Long-Term Liabilities			
Mortgage Payable		65,000.00	
Total Liabilities			121,000.00
Stockholders' Equity			
Common Stock ($25 par, 6,200 shares authorized)		155,000.00	
Retained Earnings		75,000.00	
Total Stockholders' Equity			230,000.00
Total Liabilities and Stockholders' Equity			351,000.00

WORKING PAPERS

Name ______________________

EXERCISE 24.1

1. ______________________

2. ______________________

EXERCISE 24.2

EXERCISE 24.3

Name

EXERCISE 24.4

EXERCISE 24.5

Name ________________________________

EXERCISE 24.6

EXERCISE 24.7

EXERCISE 24.8

EXERCISE 24.9

Name

PROBLEM 24.1A or 24.1B

Analyze:

Name

PROBLEM 24.2A or 24.2B

Analyze:

Name

PROBLEM 24.3A or 24.3B

Analyze:

Name

PROBLEM 24.4A or 24.4B

Analyze:

Name

CRITICAL THINKING PROBLEM 24.1

Analyze:

Name

CRITICAL THINKING PROBLEM 24.2

Name ______________________

EXTRA FORM

Chapter 24 Practice Test Answer Key

Part A True-False

1. T	7. F	13. T
2. T	8. T	14. F
3. T	*9. F	15. F
4. F	*10. F	16. T
5. T	11. T	17. T
6. T	12. T	

*Financing & Investing Activity Not Affecting Cash Flow

Part B Matching

1. a	6. d
2. c	7. b
3. b	8. d
4. c	9. a
5. c	10. c

MINI-PRACTICE SET 4

Name

Financial Analysis and Decision Making

Panama Merchandise, Inc.

Introduction

Panama Merchandise, Inc. sells a variety of consumer products. Its comparative income statement and balance sheet for the years 2010 and 2009 are presented on the following pages.

Instructions

1. Prepare a horizontal and a vertical analysis of the statements. Round all dollar calculations to the nearest whole dollar. Percentage calculations should be rounded to one decimal place (e.g., 11.2%). Remember that some vertical addition of percentages may not equal 100 percent due to rounding.

2. Calculate the following ratios for each year.

   a. The rate of return on net sales.

   b. The rate of return on common stockholders' equity. Preferred dividends are $5,000 for both years. (Remember that dividend requirements on preferred stock must be deducted from net income after taxes to obtain income available to common stockholders.)

   c. The earnings per share of common stock, assuming that the preferred stock is nonparticipating, noncumulative, and has no liquidation value. The number of outstanding shares of common stock remained constant at 100,000 throughout all of 2009 and 2010.

   d. The price-earnings ratio on common stock. The market values were $4.00 in 2010 and $3.00 in 2009.

   e. The rate of return on total assets.

   f. The ratio of stockholders' equity to total liabilities.

   g. The current ratio.

   h. The acid-test ratio.

   i. The merchandise inventory turnover. Inventory was $75,900 at January 1, 2009.

   j. The accounts receivable turnover. Credit sales were $2,000,000 for 2010 and $1,600,000 for 2009. The beginning accounts receivable balance for 2009 was $158,500.

Analyze: Assume that the firm declared and distributed a 5% common stock dividend in 2010. What is the effect on earnings per share in 2010? Assume that market value is equal to par value and all other information is the same.

 Name

Panama Merchandise, Inc.
Comparative Income Statement
Years Ended December 31, 2010 and 2009

	2010	2009
Revenue:		
Sales	2,209,450	1,895,500
Less: Sales Returns and Allowances	(29,450)	(22,500)
Net Sales	2,180,000	1,873,000
Cost of Goods Sold:		
Merchandise Inventory, January 1	72,500	76,500
Purchases	945,650	820,350
Freight In	9,900	7,500
Less: Purchases Discounts	(10,000)	(8,250)
Purchases Returns and Allowances	(8,250)	(5,000)
Total Merchandise Available for Sale	1,009,800	891,100
Less Merchandise Inventory, December 31	(76,500)	(72,500)
Cost of Goods Sold	933,300	818,600
Gross Profit on Sales	1,246,700	1,054,400
Operating Expenses:		
Selling Expenses		
Advertising	23,000	21,000
Sales Salaries	195,000	175,000
Payroll Taxes Sales	19,500	17,500
Supplies Expense	11,825	9,650
Miscellaneous Selling Expenses	9,575	7,950
Insurance Expense	7,700	7,500
Total Selling Expenses	266,600	238,600
Administrative Expenses		
Officers' Salaries	385,000	350,000
Office Employees	137,500	125,000
Payroll Taxes Office Employees	52,250	47,500
Office Supplies	12,250	10,000
Insurance Expense—Administrative	8,000	7,500
Uncollectible Accounts Expense	9,000	8,000
Legal and Accounting	18,000	15,000
Depreciation Expense—Building	15,000	15,000
Depreciation Expense—Furniture	12,000	10,000
Utilities Expense	18,400	16,750
Total Administrative Expenses	667,400	604,750
Total Operating Expenses	934,000	843,350
Other Income:		
Interest and Dividends	4,675	4,500
Total Other Income	4,675	4,500
Other Expenses:		
Bond Interest Expense	6,930	6,930
Interest Expense	6,320	6,070
Total Other Expenses	13,250	13,000
Net Other Expenses	8,575	8,500
Net Income Before Taxes	304,125	202,550
Income Tax Expense	106,444	70,893
Net Income After Taxes	197,681	131,658

 Name ______________________

Panama Merchandise, Inc.
Comparative Balance Sheet
December 31, 2010 and 2009

	2010	2009
Assets		
Current Assets		
Cash	109,025	110,200
Accounts Receivable	193,900	162,500
Merchandise Inventory	76,500	72,500
Prepaid Insurance	600	600
Supplies	975	1,000
Total Current Assets	381,000	346,800
Property, Plant, and Equipment		
Land	105,000	105,000
Building	300,000	300,000
Less: Accumulated Depreciation—Building	(45,000)	(30,000)
Furniture	60,000	50,000
Less: Accumulated Depreciation—Furniture	(22,000)	(10,000)
Total Property, Plant, and Equipment	398,000	415,000
Other Assets		
Marketable Securities (Long-Term)	40,000	40,000
Total Assets	819,000	801,800
Liabilities and Stockholders' Equity		
Current Liabilities		
Accounts Payable	79,889	94,000
Notes Payable	5,000	60,000
Bond Interest Payable	500	500
Income Taxes Payable	15,000	15,000
Sales Salaries Payable	10,000	14,000
Other Payables	5,200	7,500
Total Current Liabilities	115,589	191,000
Long-Term Liabilities		
10% Bonds Payable, due January 1, 2019	70,000	70,000
Premium on Bonds Payable	630	700
Total Long-Term Liabilities	70,630	70,700
Total Liabilities	186,219	261,700
Stockholders' Equity		
5% Preferred Stock, $100 par, 1,000 shares authorized/outstanding	100,000	100,000
Common Stock, $1 par, 500,000 shares authorized, 100,000 shares outstanding	100,000	100,000
Paid-in Capital in Excess of Par—Common Stock	50,000	50,000
Total Paid-in Capital	250,000	250,000
Retained Earnings		
Retained Earnings—Unappropriated	357,781	265,100
Retained Earnings—Appropriated	25,000	25,000
Total Retained Earnings	382,781	290,100
Total Stockholders' Equity	632,781	540,100
Total Liabilities and Stockholders' Equity	819,000	801,800

Name ______________________________

Comparative Balance Sheet

	AMOUNTS		PERCENT OF TOTAL ASSETS		INCREASE OR (DECREASE)	
	2010	2009	2010	2009	AMOUNT	PERCENT

 Name ______________________

Comparative Balance Sheet (continued)

	AMOUNTS		PERCENT OF TOTAL ASSETS		INCREASE OR (DECREASE)	
	2010	2009	2010	2009	AMOUNT	PERCENT

 Name

Comparative Balance Sheet (continued)

	AMOUNTS		PERCENT OF TOTAL ASSETS		INCREASE OR (DECREASE)	
	2010	2009	2010	2009	AMOUNT	PERCENT

MINI-PRACTICE SET 4 (continued) Name

EXTRA FORM

Comparative Statement of Retained Earnings-Unappropriated

	AMOUNTS		PERCENT OF TOTAL ASSETS		INCREASE OR (DECREASE)	
	2010	2009	2010	2009	AMOUNT	PERCENT

Name

Comparative Income Statement

	Amounts 2010	Amounts 2009	Percent of Net Sales 2010	Percent of Net Sales 2009	Increase or (Decrease) Amount	Increase or (Decrease) Percent

 Name

Comparative Income Statement (continued)

	AMOUNTS		PERCENT OF NET SALES		INCREASE OR (DECREASE)	
	2010	2009	2010	2009	AMOUNT	PERCENT

 Name

EXTRA FORM

	AMOUNTS		PERCENT OF NET SALES		INCREASE OR (DECREASE)	
	2010	2009	2010	2009	AMOUNT	PERCENT

Name ______________________

	2009	2010	RATIO
a.			
b.			
c.			
d.			
e.			
f.			
g.			
h.			
i.			
j.			

Name

COMPUTATIONS

Analyze:

CHAPTER 25

Departmentalized Profit and Cost Centers

STUDY GUIDE

Understanding the Chapter

Objectives **1.** Explain profit centers and cost centers. **2.** Prepare the Gross Profit section of a departmental income statement. **3.** Explain and identify direct and indirect departmental expenses. **4.** Choose the basis for allocation of indirect expenses and compute the amounts to be allocated to each department. **5.** Prepare a departmental income statement showing the contribution margin and operating income for each department. **6.** Use a departmental income statement in making decisions such as whether a department should be closed. **7.** Define the accounting terms new to this chapter.

Reading Assignment Read Chapter 25 in the textbook. Complete the textbook Section Self Reviews as you finish reading each section of the chapter, and the Comprehensive Self Review at the end of the chapter. Refer to the Chapter 25 Glossary or to the Glossary at the end of the book to find definitions for terms that are not familiar to you.

Activities

- ❑ **Thinking Critically** Answer the *Thinking Critically* questions for Mattel, Inc. and Managerial Implications.
- ❑ **Discussion Questions** Answer each assigned discussion question in Chapter 25.
- ❑ **Exercises** Complete each assigned exercise in Chapter 25. Use the forms provided in this SGWP. The objectives covered by an exercise are given after the exercise number. If you need help with an exercise, review the portion of the chapter related to the objective(s) covered.
- ❑ **Problems A/B** Complete each assigned problem in Chapter 25. Use the forms provided in this SGWP. The objectives covered by a problem are given after the problem number. If you need help with a problem, review the portion of the chapter related to the objective(s) covered.
- ❑ **Critical Thinking Problems** Complete the critical thinking problems as assigned. Use the forms provided in this SGWP.
- ❑ **Business Connections** Complete the Business Connections activities as assigned to gain a deeper understanding of Chapter 25 concepts.

Practice Tests

Complete the Practice Tests, which cover the main points in your reading assignment. Compare your answers with those in the Practice Test Answer Key for Chapter 25 at the end of this chapter. If you have answered any questions incorrectly, review the related section of the text.

STUDY GUIDE

Part A True-False *For each of the following statements, circle T in the answer column if the statement is true, or F if the statement is false.*

T F **1.** Cost centers are also called profit centers.

T F **2.** Purchases returns and allowances are not normally departmentalized in the accounts.

T F **3.** Sales discounts need not be departmentalized if they are treated as other expense.

T F **4.** Direct expenses are costs shared by all departments.

T F **5.** Responsibility accounting is designed to help management evaluate the performance of each segment of business.

T F **6.** A separate column should be provided in the voucher register for purchases of each sales department.

T F **7.** Semi-direct expenses cannot be allocated to a sales department on any logical basis.

T F **8.** If a business is profitable, it is not important to know how much each department contributed to the overall profit.

T F **9.** Profit centers are usually business segments that sell to customers outside the business.

T F **10.** In a departmental accounting system, sales returns and allowances should be debited to the departmental sales account.

T F **11.** If a department has a negative contribution margin, the business would probably be more profitable if the department were eliminated.

T F **12.** Eliminating a department should eliminate all indirect expenses of that department.

T F **13.** The contribution margin is the difference between gross profit and nonoperating expenses.

T F **14.** Beginning and ending inventories are allocated to the departments on the basis of net sales in each.

T F **15.** The net income of a department should receive more attention than its contribution margin in reaching managerial decisions.

T F **16.** Indirect expenses are allocated to the departments at the time the expense transactions are journalized.

T F **17.** Nonoperating income, such as interest income, should be allocated to departments on the basis of net sales.

T F **18.** Utilities expense should be allocated to departments on the basis of gross sales in each department.

T F **19.** Gross profit and contribution margin have the same meaning.

T F **20.** Payroll taxes applicable to sales salaries may be treated as an indirect expense, or as a direct expense if they are recorded by department.

Part B Matching *For each numbered item, choose the matching term from the box and write the identifying letter in the answer column.*

_______ **1.** The difference between gross profit and direct expense.	**a.** Contribution margin
_______ **2.** Expenses that are closely related to the activities in each department but cannot be allocated to any specific department.	**b.** Direct expenses
_______ **3.** The procedure for dividing indirect expenses among several departments.	**c.** Indirect expenses
_______ **4.** Expenses that can be assigned to a specific department.	**d.** Semi-direct expenses
_______ **5.** Expenses incurred for the benefit of several departments that cannot be assigned directly to any one particular department.	**e.** Allocation

STUDY GUIDE

Demonstration Problem

Your Entertainment is a retail store selling books, music, and videos. The store has three departments: books, music, and videos. Condensed information about the store's revenues and expenses for each department for the year ended December 31, 2010, follows. Indirect expenses have been allocated on bases similar to those discussed in the textbook chapter. The store had interest income of $400 for the year.

Instructions

1. Prepare a departmental income statement showing the contribution margin and the net profit for each department.
2. Based solely on accounting information, would you recommend closing any of the departments? Why or why not?

	Books	Music	DVDs
Allocated indirect expenses	$ 18,000	$12,000	$10,000
Beginning merchandise inventory	19,000	23,000	23,000
Direct expenses	20,000	10,000	17,000
Ending merchandise inventory	17,000	15,000	9,200
Purchases	86,000	41,000	31,500
Purchases returns and allowances	800	200	300
Sales	201,600	96,500	62,500
Sales returns and allowances	3,600	600	1,500

SOLUTION

Your Entertainment
Income Statement
Year Ended December 31, 2010

	BOOKS	MUSIC	DVDs	TOTAL
Sales	201600	96500	62500	360600
Less Sales Returns and Allowances	3600	600	1500	5700
Net Sales	198000	95900	61000	354900
Cost of Goods Sold				
Merchandise Inventory, January 1	19000	23000	23000	65000
Purchases	86000	41000	31500	158500
Less Purchases Returns and Allowances	800	200	300	1300
Net Purchases	85200	40800	31200	157200
Cost of Goods Available for Sale	104200	63800	54200	222200
Less Merchandise Inventory, December 31	17000	15000	9200	41200
Cost of Goods Sold	87200	48800	45000	181000
Gross Profit	110800	47100	16000	173900
Direct Expenses	20000	10000	17000	47000
Contribution Margin	90800	37100	(1000)	126900
Indirect Expenses	18000	12000	10000	40000
Net Income (Loss) from Operations	72800	25100	(11000)	86900
Other Income				
Interest Income				400
Net Income for Year				87300

Based solely on the accounting information, the DVDs Department should be closed. The contribution margin is a loss of $1,000 and the department net loss is $11,000. The department is not generating enough revenue to pay all of its direct expenses. Generally, when this situation presents itself, the management of the firm would suggest closing that department.

WORKING PAPERS

Name ______________________________

EXERCISE 25.1

DEPARTMENT	BASIS: BOOK VALUE OF INVENTORY AND EQUIPMENT	PERCENT	TOTAL INSURANCE EXPENSE	ALLOCATION

EXERCISE 25.2

DEPARTMENT	BASIS: TOTAL SALES	PERCENT	TOTAL OFFICE EXPENSE	ALLOCATION

EXERCISE 25.3

DEPARTMENT	CREDIT SALES	CREDIT SALES RETURNS AND ALLOWANCES	BASIS: NET CREDIT SALES	PERCENT	ALLOCATION

Name

EXERCISE 25.4

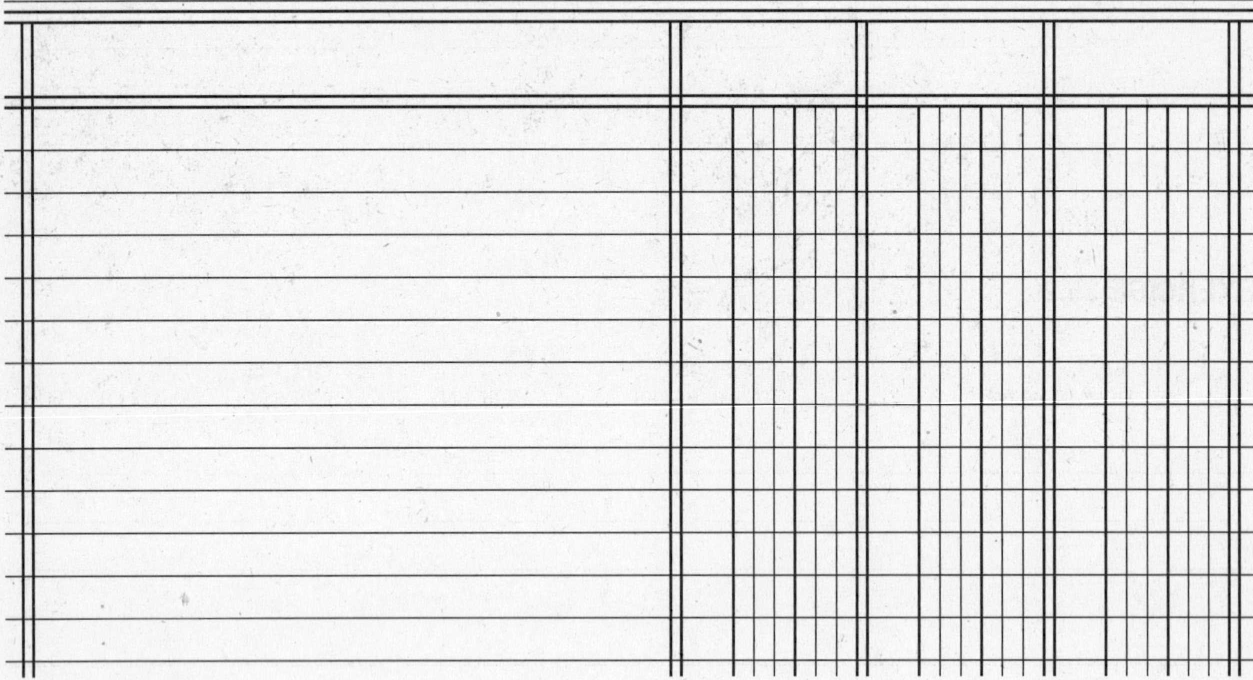

EXTRA FORM

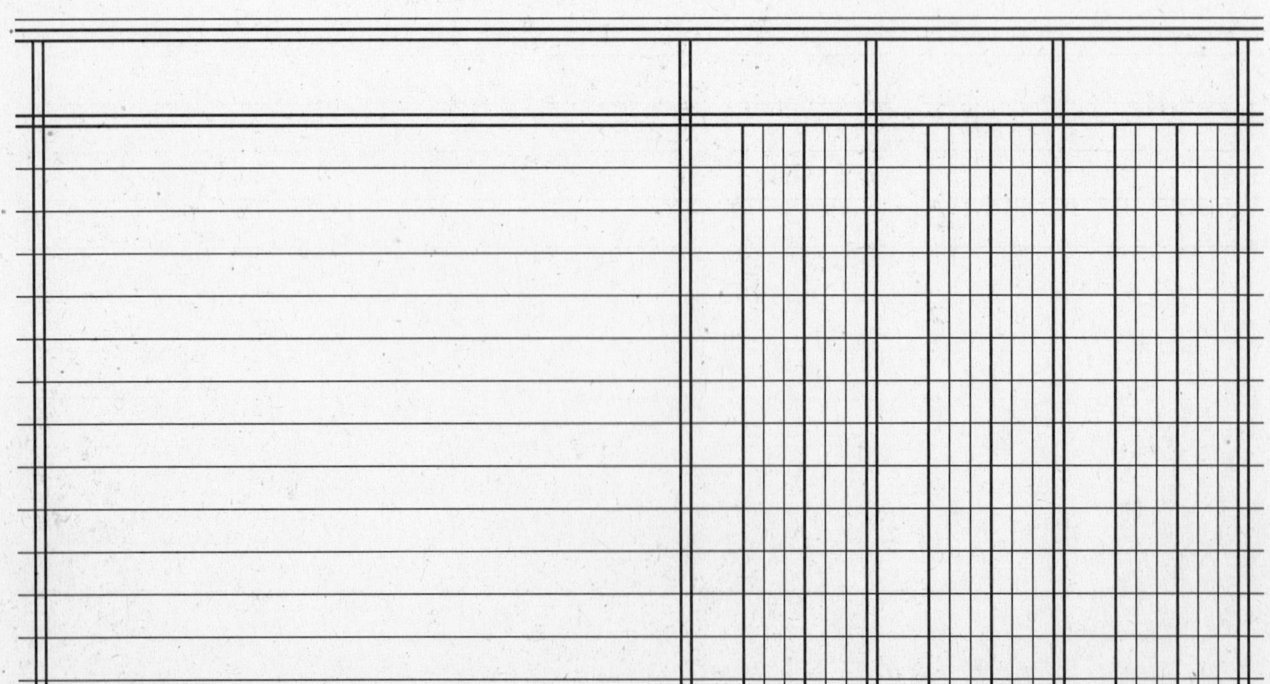

Name

EXERCISE 25.5

EXERCISE 25.6

EXERCISE 25.7

Name

PROBLEM 25.1A or 25.1B

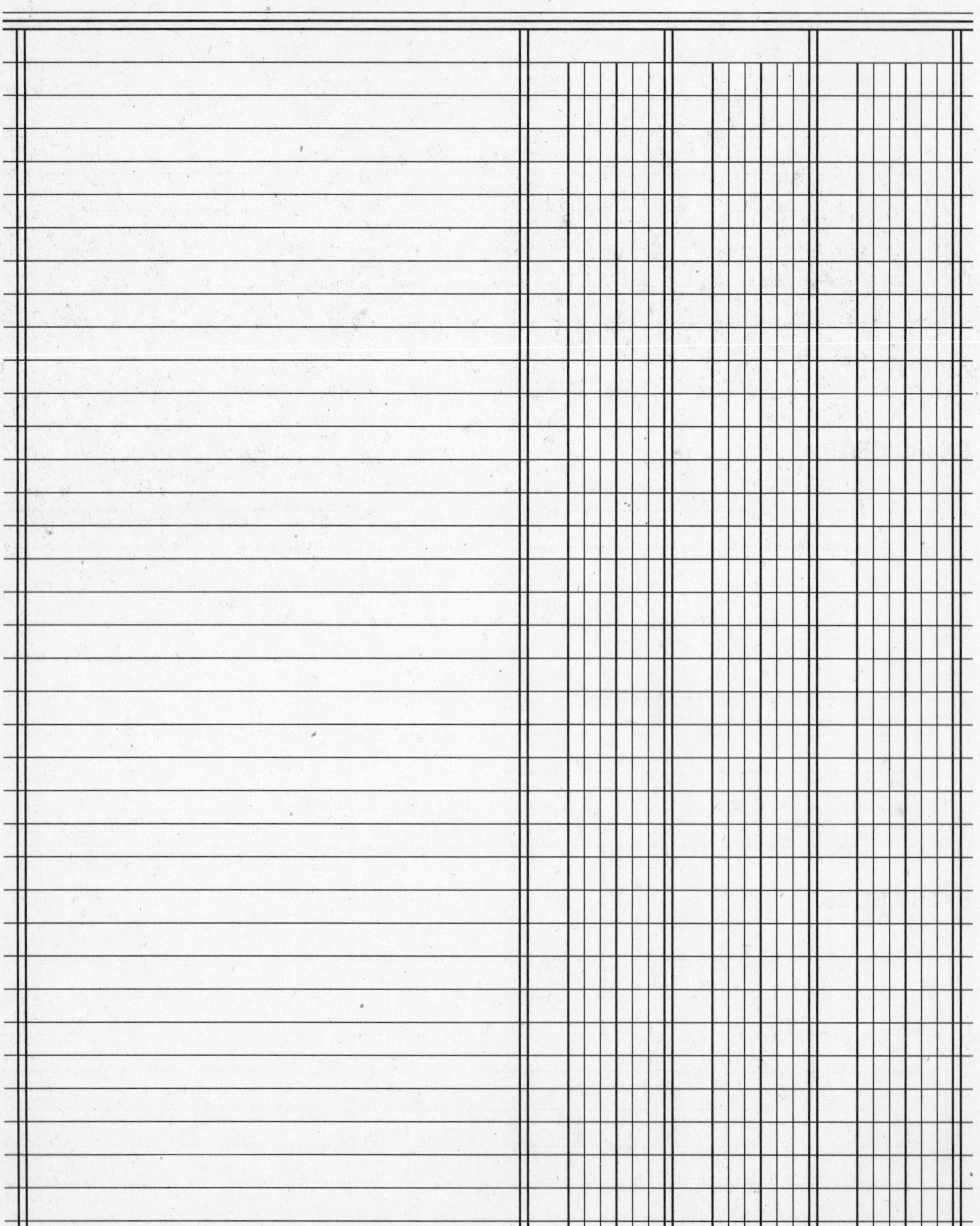

Name

PROBLEM 25.1A or 25.1B (continued)

ALLOCATION OF INDIRECT EXPENSES

Insurance Expense

1.

Rent Expense

2.

Utilities Expense

Name

PROBLEM 25.1A or 25.1B (continued)

ALLOCATION OF INDIRECT EXPENSES (continued)

Office Salaries Expense

3.

Other Office Expenses

Depreciation Expense—Office Equipment

Uncollectible Accounts Expense

4.

Depreciation Expense—Furniture and Fixtures

5.

Analyze:

Name

PROBLEM 25.2A or 25.2B

1.

Income Statement

Name

PROBLEM 25.2A or 25.2B (continued)

2.

3.

Analyze:

Name

CRITICAL THINKING PROBLEM 25.1

Analyze:

Name

CRITICAL THINKING PROBLEM 25.2

Chapter 25 Practice Test Answer Key

Part A True-False

1. F	6. T	11. T	16. F
2. F	7. F	12. F	17. F
3. T	8. F	13. F	18. F
4. F	9. T	14. F	19. F
5. T	10. F	15. F	20. T

Part B Matching

1. a
2. d
3. e
4. b
5. c

CHAPTER 26

Accounting for Manufacturing Activities

STUDY GUIDE

Understanding the Chapter

Objectives

1. Prepare a statement of cost of goods manufactured. **2.** Explain the basic components of manufacturing cost. **3.** Prepare an income statement for a manufacturing business. **4.** Prepare a balance sheet for a manufacturing business. **5.** Prepare a worksheet for a manufacturing business. **6.** Record the end-of-period adjusting entries for a manufacturing business. **7.** Record closing entries for a manufacturing business. **8.** Record reversing entries for a manufacturing business. **9.** Define the accounting terms new to this chapter.

Reading Assignment

Read Chapter 26 in the textbook. Complete the textbook Section Self Reviews as you finish reading each section of the chapter, and the Comprehensive Self Review at the end of the chapter. Refer to the Chapter 26 Glossary or to the Glossary at the end of the book to find definitions for terms that are not familiar to you.

Activities

- ❑ **Thinking Critically** — Answer the *Thinking Critically* questions for Toyota and Managerial Implications.
- ❑ **Discussion Questions** — Answer each assigned discussion question in Chapter 26.
- ❑ **Exercises** — Complete each assigned exercise in Chapter 26. Use the forms provided in this SGWP. The objectives covered by an exercise are given after the exercise number. If you need help with an exercise, review the portion of the chapter related to the objective(s) covered.
- ❑ **Problems A/B** — Complete each assigned problem in Chapter 26. Use the forms provided in this SGWP. The objectives covered by a problem are given after the problem number. If you need help with a problem, review the portion of the chapter related to the objective(s) covered.
- ❑ **Critical Thinking Problems** — Complete the critical thinking problems as assigned. Use the forms provided in this SGWP.
- ❑ **Business Connections** — Complete the Business Connections activities as assigned to gain a deeper understanding of Chapter 26 concepts.

Practice Tests

Complete the Practice Tests, which cover the main points in your reading assignment. Compare your answers with those in the Practice Test Answer Key for Chapter 26 at the end of this chapter. If you have answered any questions incorrectly, review the related section of the text.

Part A True-False *For each of the following statements, circle T in the answer column if the answer is true or F if the answer is false.*

T F 1. The cost of goods manufactured is the total of the direct materials, direct labor, and overhead costs involved in the manufacturing process during the period.

T F 2. Small items, such as glue and nails, that become part of the finished product may be treated either as direct materials or as indirect materials, depending on company policy and cumulative cost of items.

T F 3. The cost of indirect materials used is shown in the Cost of Goods Sold section of the Income Statement.

T F 4. The wages of a worker who saws and forms legs for tables in a furniture factory would be classified as direct labor.

T F 5. In a manufacturing company, it is not necessary to take a physical inventory of the finished goods.

T F 6. In the Cost of Goods Manufactured section of the worksheet, the excess of the total of the Debit column over the total of the Credit column represents the cost of goods manufactured.

T F 7. The entry to set up the ending work in process inventory is part of the adjustments process.

T F 8. The ending inventory of finished goods is entered in the Credit column of the Cost of Goods Manufactured section of the worksheet.

T F 9. On the worksheet of a manufacturing business, the amount of the ending work in process inventory is entered in the Debit column of the Balance Sheet section.

T F 10. Payroll taxes on factory wages should be classified as an administrative expense in the income statement.

Part B Completion *In the answer column, supply the missing word or words needed to complete each of the following statements.*

______________ 1. All materials that become part of the manufactured product are known as ______.

______________ 2. The cost of indirect materials used appears in the ______ section of the statement of cost of goods manufactured.

______________ 3. All raw materials used, direct labor costs incurred, and manufacturing costs incurred during the period make up the total ______.

______________ 4. The adjusted balances of the manufacturing cost accounts are extended from the Adjusted Trial Balance section to the ______ section of a manufacturing company's worksheet.

______________ 5. In the worksheet, the cost of goods manufactured is entered in the ______ column of the Cost of Goods Manufactured section and in the ______ column of the Income Statement section.

______________ 6. The statement on which the beginning and ending inventories of work in process appear is the ______.

______________ 7. The partially completed product at year-end is called ______.

______________ 8. The postclosing trial balance contains the balances of the ______, ______, and ______ accounts.

Demonstration Problem

The Golf Company makes golf equipment. Information about the company's operations follows.

Instructions

1. Prepare a statement of cost of goods manufactured for the year ended December 31, 2010.

	January 1, 2010	December 31, 2010
Finished Goods Inventory	$550,000	$ 475,000
Raw Materials Inventory	300,000	255,000
Work in Process Inventory	100,000	92,500
Direct Labor		900,000
Freight In		25,500
Indirect Labor		150,000
Indirect Materials and Supplies		30,000
Insurance—Factory		18,500
Depreciation—Factory Building and Equipment		50,000
Materials Purchases		1,800,000
Payroll Taxes—Factory		105,000
Utilities—Factory		65,000
Property Taxes—Factory		25,000
Materials Purchases Returns and Allowances		6,900
Repairs and Maintenance—Factory		39,500
Patent Amortization		1,500
Waste Removal—Factory		20,000

SOLUTION

The Golf Company
Statement of Cost of Goods Manufactured
Year Ended December 31, 2010

Raw Materials			
Raw Materials Inventory, January 1, 2010		300,000.00	
Materials Purchases	1,800,000.00		
Freight In	25,500.00		
Delivered Cost of Material Purchases	1,825,500.00		
Less Materials Purchases Returns and Allowances	6,900.00		
Net Material Purchases		1,818,600.00	
Total Materials Available for Use		2,118,600.00	
Less Raw Materials Inventory, December 31, 2010		255,000.00	
Raw Materials Used			1,863,600.00
Direct Labor			900,000.00
Manufacturing Overhead			
Indirect Materials and Supplies		30,000.00	
Indirect Labor		150,000.00	
Payroll Taxes—Factory		105,000.00	
Utilities—Factory		65,000.00	
Repairs and Maintenance—Factory		39,500.00	
Depreciation—Factory Building and Equipment		50,000.00	
Insurance—Factory		18,500.00	
Property Taxes—Factory		25,000.00	
Patent Amortization		1,500.00	
Waste Removal—Factory		20,000.00	
Total Manufacturing Overhead			504,500.00
Total Manufacturing Costs			3,268,100.00
Add Work in Process Inventory, January 1, 2010			100,000.00
			3,368,100.00
Less Work in Process Inventory, December 31, 2010			92,500.00
Cost of Goods Manufactured			3,275,600.00

WORKING PAPERS

Name ______________________________

EXERCISE 26.1

EXERCISE 26.2

GENERAL JOURNAL

PAGE ______

	DATE		DESCRIPTION	POST. REF.	DEBIT	CREDIT	
1							1
2							2
3							3
4							4
5							5
6							6
7							7
8							8
9							9
10							10
11							11
12							12
13							13
14							14
15							15
16							16
17							17
18							18
19							19
20							20

Name

EXERCISE 26.3

EXERCISE 26.4

EXERCISE 26.5

EXERCISE 26.6

Name

EXERCISE 26.7

EXERCISE 26.8

EXERCISE 26.9

Name

EXERCISE 26.10

GENERAL JOURNAL

PAGE

	DATE		DESCRIPTION	POST. REF.	DEBIT	CREDIT	
1							1
2							2
3							3
4							4
5							5
6							6
7							7
8							8
9							9
10							10
11							11
12							12
13							13
14							14
15							15
16							16
17							17
18							18
19							19
20							20
21							21
22							22
23							23
24							24
25							25
26							26
27							27
28							28
29							29
30							30
31							31
32							32
33							33
34							34
35							35
36							36
37							37

Name

EXERCISE 26.10 (continued)

GENERAL JOURNAL

PAGE

DATE		DESCRIPTION	POST. REF.	DEBIT	CREDIT

Name

PROBLEM 26.1A or 26.1B

Statement of Cost of Goods Manufactured

Name

PROBLEM 26.1A or 26.1B (continued)

Income Statement

Analyze:

Name ____________________

PROBLEM 26.2A or 26.2B

	ACCOUNT NAME	TRIAL BALANCE		ADJUSTMENTS	
		DEBIT	CREDIT	DEBIT	CREDIT
1					
2					
3					
4					
5					
6					
7					
8					
9					
10					
11					
12					
13					
14					
15					
16					
17					
18					
19					
20					
21					
22					
23					
24					
25					
26					
27					
28					
29					
30					
31					
32					
33					
34					

Name

PROBLEM 26.2A or 26.2B (continued)

ADJUSTED TRIAL BALANCE		COST OF GOODS MANUFACTURED		INCOME STATEMENT		BALANCE SHEET	
DEBIT	CREDIT	DEBIT	CREDIT	DEBIT	CREDIT	DEBIT	CREDIT

Name

PROBLEM 26.2A or 26.2B (continued)

ACCOUNT NAME	TRIAL BALANCE		ADJUSTMENTS	
	DEBIT	CREDIT	DEBIT	CREDIT

Name

PROBLEM 26.2A or 26.2B (continued)

ADJUSTED TRIAL BALANCE		COST OF GOODS MANUFACTURED		INCOME STATEMENT		BALANCE SHEET	
DEBIT	CREDIT	DEBIT	CREDIT	DEBIT	CREDIT	DEBIT	CREDIT

Name

PROBLEM 26.2A or 26.2B (continued)

Statement of Cost of Goods Manufactured

Name

PROBLEM 26.2A or 26.2B (continued)

Income Statement

Name

PROBLEM 26.2A or 26.2B (continued)

Statement of Retained Earnings

EXTRA FORM

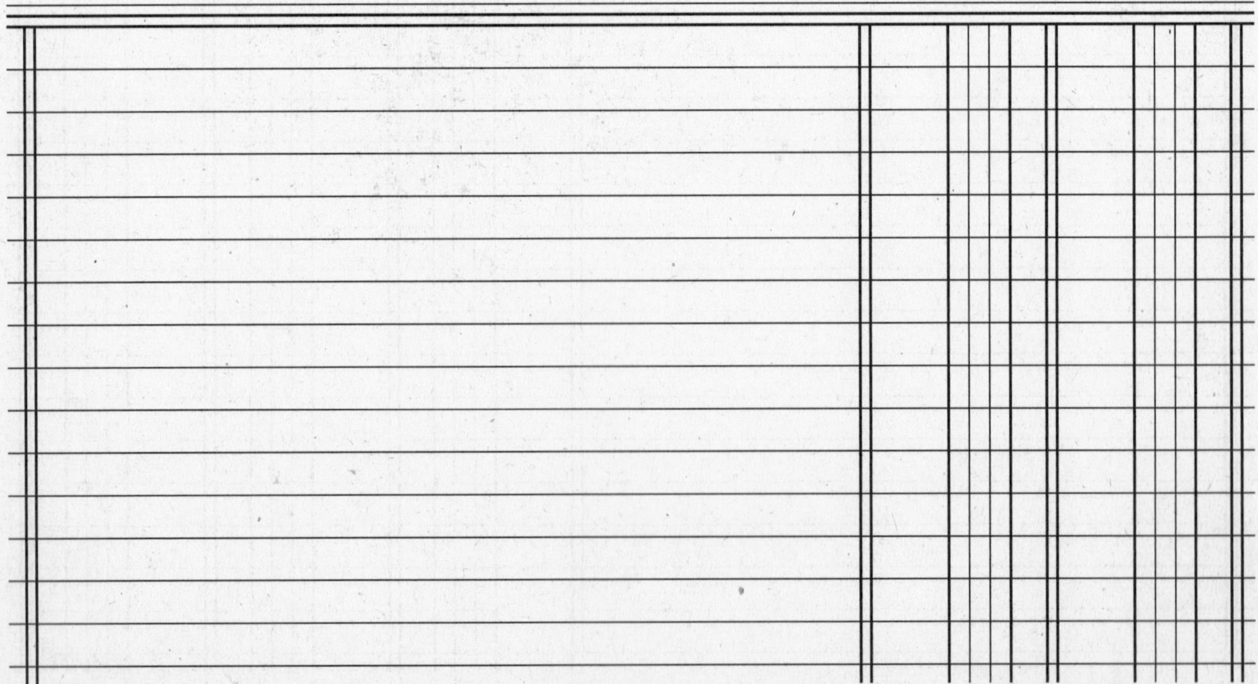

Name

PROBLEM 26.2A or 26.2B (continued)

Balance Sheet

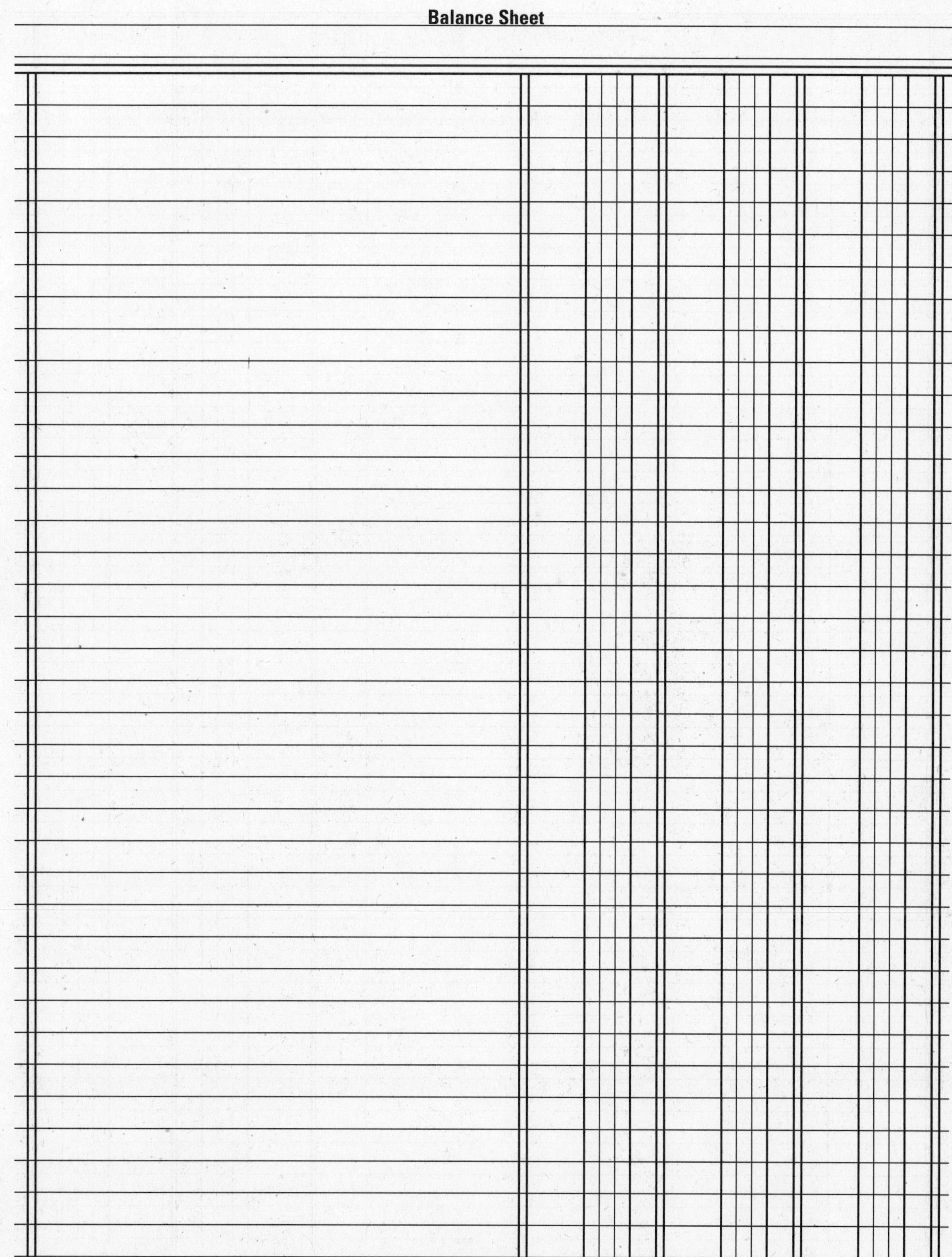

Name ______________________

PROBLEM 26.2A or 26.2B (continued)

GENERAL JOURNAL PAGE ______

DATE		DESCRIPTION	POST. REF.	DEBIT	CREDIT

Name ______________________

PROBLEM 26.2A or 26.2B (continued)

GENERAL JOURNAL

PAGE ______

DATE	DESCRIPTION	POST. REF.	DEBIT	CREDIT

Name ______________________

PROBLEM 26.2A or 26.2B (continued)

GENERAL JOURNAL PAGE ________

DATE	DESCRIPTION	POST. REF.	DEBIT	CREDIT

Name

PROBLEM 28.2A or 28.2B (continued)

GENERAL JOURNAL PAGE

DATE		DESCRIPTION	POST. REF.	DEBIT	CREDIT

Analyze:

Name

CRITICAL THINKING PROBLEM 26.1

Statement of Cost of Goods Manufactured

Income Statement

Name

CRITICAL THINKING PROBLEM 26.1 (continued)

NOTES

Analyze:

Name

CRITICAL THINKING PROBLEM 26.2

Chapter 26 Practice Test Answer Key

Part A True-False

1. F	**6.** T
2. T	**7.** T
3. F	**8.** F
4. T	**9.** T
5. F	**10.** F

Part B Completion

1. direct materials
2. manufacturing overhead
3. manufacturing costs
4. cost of goods manufactured
5. credit; debit
6. statement of cost of goods manufactured
7. work in process
8. asset; liability; stockholders' equity

CHAPTER 27

Job Order Cost Accounting

STUDY GUIDE

Understanding the Chapter

Objectives

1. Explain how a job order cost accounting system operates. **2.** Journalize the purchase and issuance of direct and indirect materials. **3.** Maintain perpetual inventory records. **4.** Record labor costs incurred and charge labor into production. **5.** Compute overhead rates and apply overhead to jobs. **6.** Compute overapplied or underapplied overhead and report it in the financial statements. **7.** Maintain job order cost sheets. **8.** Record the cost of jobs completed and the cost of goods sold under a perpetual inventory system. **9.** Define the accounting terms new to this chapter.

Reading Assignment

Read Chapter 27 in the textbook. Complete the textbook Section Self Reviews as you finish reading each section of the chapter, and the Comprehensive Self Review at the end of the chapter. Refer to the Chapter 27 Glossary or to the Glossary at the end of the book to find definitions for terms that are not familiar to you.

Activities

- ❑ **Thinking Critically** — Answer the *Thinking Critically* questions for The Spring Air Company and Managerial Implications.
- ❑ **Discussion Questions** — Answer each assigned discussion question in Chapter 27.
- ❑ **Exercises** — Complete each assigned exercise in Chapter 27. Use the forms provided in this SGWP. The objectives covered by an exercise are given after the exercise number. If you need help with an exercise, review the portion of the chapter related to the objective(s) covered.
- ❑ **Problems A/B** — Complete each assigned problem in Chapter 27. Use the forms provided in this SGWP. The objectives covered by a problem are given after the problem number. If you need help with a problem, review the portion of the chapter related to the objective(s) covered.
- ❑ **Critical Thinking Problems** — Complete the critical thinking problems as assigned. Use the forms provided in this SGWP.
- ❑ **Business Connections** — Complete the Business Connections activities as assigned to gain a deeper understanding of Chapter 27 concepts.

Practice Tests

Complete the Practice Tests, which cover the main points in your reading assignment. Compare your answers with those in the Practice Test Answer Key for Chapter 27 at the end of this chapter. If you have answered any questions incorrectly, review the related section of the text.

Part A True-False *For each of the following statements, circle T in the answer column if the statement is true or F if the statement is false.*

T	F	**1.** The job order cost system is often used by businesses that produce many units of the same product.
T	F	**2.** Applied overhead is usually posted each day to the job order cost sheets.
T	F	**3.** Perpetual inventory accounts for raw materials, work in process, and finished goods are commonly used in a job order system.
T	F	**4.** Underapplied or overapplied overhead may be closed into the **Cost of Goods Sold** account at the end of the year.
T	F	**5.** Purchases of raw materials are debited to the **Work in Process Inventory** account.
T	F	**6.** Idle time is generally treated as manufacturing overhead.
T	F	**7.** In a job order cost system, the individual job order cost sheets form a subsidiary ledger for the **Work in Process Inventory** account.
T	F	**8.** Under the job order system, unit costs of production are determined for all orders simultaneously.
T	F	**9.** A widely used method of applying manufacturing overhead to individual jobs is based on a percentage of direct labor costs.
T	F	**10.** A just-in-time ordering system reduces the need for inventory storage space.
T	F	**11.** Charging manufacturing overhead to jobs on the basis of a predetermined rate usually results in overapplied or underapplied overhead.
T	F	**12.** The materials requisition provides the information needed to enter receipt of raw materials on the raw materials ledger cards.
T	F	**13.** The posting of labor costs to the individual job order cost sheets is made from the payroll register at the end of the week.
T	F	**14.** Under a job order cost system, the selling price of goods sold will be entered on the finished goods ledger sheet for the products sold.

Part B Completion *In the answer column, supply the missing word or words needed to complete each of the following statements.*

______________________ **1.** The ______ shows the costs incurred for materials, labor, and overhead on a job.

______________________ **2.** Materials are issued by the storeroom clerk only on presentation of a(n) ______ signed by an authorized person.

______________________ **3.** When more overhead costs are incurred than are applied to individual jobs, overhead is said to be ______.

______________________ **4.** The three major inventories of a manufacturing business are generally maintained on a(n) ______ basis.

______________________ **5.** If idle time is caused by a breakdown of factory equipment, the related cost will probably be charged to ______.

______________________ **6.** Depreciation of factory equipment, indirect labor, and indirect materials are examples of ______.

______________________ **7.** The receipt of materials from a supplier is reported by preparing a(n) ______.

______________________ **8.** Under the ______ method of inventory pricing, the quantities issued are priced from the oldest inventory items available in the order they were received.

Demonstration Problem

The cost data that follows is for Roma Leather Products, Inc., a maker of shoes and boots. This data covers the month of December 2010.

a. Materials purchases, $80,000.

b. Materials issued to production, $60,000; direct materials, $59,000; indirect materials, $1,000.

c. Payroll: direct labor, $20,000; indirect labor, $2,000; social security tax deducted, $1,364; medicare tax deducted, $319; income tax deducted, $3,000.

d. Manufacturing overhead of $10,000 was incurred in addition to indirect materials and indirect labor. (Credit **Accounts Payable.**)

e. Manufacturing overhead is applied to production at a predetermined rate of 60 percent of direct labor costs.

f. Jobs costing $70,000 were completed and transferred to finished goods.

g. Finished goods costing $60,000 were sold and billed to customers at $120,000.

Instructions

1. Prepare general journal entries to record each item of cost data given (the general journal is on page 667). Use the account names given in the textbook chapter. Omit explanations.
2. Compute the amount of overapplied or underapplied overhead for the month.
3. Prepare a partial income statement for the month of December, adjusted for any overapplied or underapplied overhead.

STUDY GUIDE

SOLUTION

OVERHEAD COMPUTATIONS

Manufacturing Overhead (Debit Balance)		
Indirect Materials	$ 1,000	
Indirect Labor	2,000	
Other Overhead Costs	10,000	
Total Charged to Manufacturing Overhead		$13,000
Manufacturing Overhead Applied (Credit Balance)		12,000
Underapplied Overhead in December (Net Credit Balance)		$ 1,000

Roma Leather Products, Inc.
Partial Income Statement
Month Ended December 31, 2010

Sales		120 0 0 0 00
Cost of Goods Sold (per ledger account)	60 0 0 0 00	
Add Underapplied Manufacturing Overhead	1 0 0 0 00	
Cost of Goods Sold (adjusted to actual)		61 0 0 0 00
Gross Profit on Sales		59 0 0 0 00

SOLUTION (continued)

GENERAL JOURNAL

PAGE ______

DATE		DESCRIPTION	POST. REF.	DEBIT	CREDIT
2010					
Dec.	31	Raw Materials Inventory		80,000.00	
		Accounts Payable			80,000.00
	31	Work in Process Inventory (Direct Materials)		59,000.00	
		Manufacturing Overhead (Indirect Materials)		1,000.00	
		Raw Materials Inventory			60,000.00
	31	Work in Process Inventory (Direct Labor)		20,000.00	
		Manufacturing Overhead (Indirect Labor)		2,000.00	
		Social Security Tax Payable			1,364.00
		Medicare Tax Payable			319.00
		Employee Income Tax Payable			3,000.00
		Salaries and Wages Payable			17,317.00
	31	Manufacturing Overhead		10,000.00	
		Accounts Payable			10,000.00
	31	Work in Process Inventory		12,000.00	
		Manufacturing Overhead Applied			12,000.00
	31	Finished Goods Inventory		70,000.00	
		Work in Process Inventory			70,000.00
	31	Cost of Goods Sold		60,000.00	
		Finished Goods Inventory			60,000.00
	31	Accounts Receivable		120,000.00	
		Sales			120,000.00

WORKING PAPERS

Name

EXERCISE 27.1

GENERAL JOURNAL PAGE

	DATE		DESCRIPTION	POST. REF.	DEBIT	CREDIT	
1							1
2							2
3							3
4							4
5							5

EXERCISE 27.2

GENERAL JOURNAL PAGE

	DATE		DESCRIPTION	POST. REF.	DEBIT	CREDIT	
1							1
2							2
3							3
4							4
5							5

EXERCISE 27.3

GENERAL JOURNAL PAGE

	DATE		DESCRIPTION	POST. REF.	DEBIT	CREDIT	
1							1
2							2
3							3
4							4
5							5

EXERCISE 27.4

GENERAL JOURNAL PAGE

	DATE		DESCRIPTION	POST. REF.	DEBIT	CREDIT	
1							1
2							2
3							3
4							4
5							5

Name ______________________________

EXERCISE 27.5

GENERAL JOURNAL PAGE ________

DATE	DESCRIPTION	POST. REF.	DEBIT	CREDIT

EXERCISE 27.6

EXERCISE 27.7

GENERAL JOURNAL PAGE ________

DATE	DESCRIPTION	POST. REF.	DEBIT	CREDIT

Name

EXERCISE 27.8

EXERCISE 27.9

EXERCISE 27.10

GENERAL JOURNAL

PAGE

	DATE		DESCRIPTION	POST. REF.	DEBIT	CREDIT	
1							1
2							2
3							3
4							4
5							5
6							6
7							7
8							8
9							9
10							10
11							11
12							12
13							13
14							14
15							15
16							16
17							17
18							18

Name ______________________

PROBLEM 27.1A or 27.1B

GENERAL JOURNAL

PAGE ________

DATE	DESCRIPTION	POST. REF.	DEBIT	CREDIT

Name

PROBLEM 27.1A or 27.1B (continued)

Manufacturing Overhead Computations

Partial Income Statement

Analyze:

Name

PROBLEM 27.2A or 27.2B

JOB ORDER COST SHEET

For Stock ______ Job No. ______ Date ______

Customer's Name ______ Started ______

Address ______ Completed ______

Item ______ Quantity ______ (ordered) (completed)

MATERIAL		LABOR		OVERHEAD APPLIED			SUMMARY	
Date	Amount	Date	Amount	Date	Rate	Amount	Item	Amount
							Materials	
							Labor	
							Overhead	
							Total	
							Unit Cost	
Totals							Comments:	

JOB ORDER COST SHEET

For Stock ______ Job No. ______ Date ______

Customer's Name ______ Started ______

Address ______ Completed ______

Item ______ Quantity ______ (ordered) (completed)

MATERIAL		LABOR		OVERHEAD APPLIED			SUMMARY	
Date	Amount	Date	Amount	Date	Rate	Amount	Item	Amount
							Materials	
							Labor	
							Overhead	
							Total	
							Unit Cost	
Totals							Comments:	

JOB ORDER COST SHEET

For Stock ______ Job No. ______ Date ______

Customer's Name ______ Started ______

Address ______ Completed ______

Item ______ Quantity ______ (ordered) (completed)

MATERIAL		LABOR		OVERHEAD APPLIED			SUMMARY	
Date	Amount	Date	Amount	Date	Rate	Amount	Item	Amount
							Materials	
							Labor	
							Overhead	
							Total	
							Unit Cost	
Totals							Comments:	

Name ______________________

PROBLEM 27.2A or 27.2B (continued)

GENERAL JOURNAL PAGE ______

	DATE	DESCRIPTION	POST. REF.	DEBIT	CREDIT	
1						1
2						2
3						3
4						4
5						5
6						6
7						7
8						8
9						9
10						10

OVERHEAD COMPUTATIONS

Analyze:

Name ______________________

CRITICAL THINKING PROBLEM 27.1

	Job DE31	Job JA01	Job JA02
Materials			
Labor			
Overhead (1)			
Total Costs			

Cost of Goods Sold

Notes:

Analyze:

Name

CRITICAL THINKING PROBLEM 27.2

a.

b.

c.

d.

e.

f.

Chapter 27 Practice Test Answer Key

Part A True-False

1.	**F**	**8.**	**F**
2.	**F**	**9.**	**T**
3.	**T**	**10.**	**T**
4.	**T**	**11.**	**T**
5.	**F**	**12.**	**F**
6.	**T**	**13.**	**F**
7.	**T**	**14.**	**F**

Part B Completion

1. job order cost sheet
2. materials requisition
3. underapplied
4. perpetual
5. manufacturing overhead
6. manufacturing overhead
7. receiving report
8. FIFO

Condensed Income Statement

CHAPTER 28 Process Cost Accounting

STUDY GUIDE

Understanding the Chapter

Objectives

1. Compute equivalent units of production with no beginning work in process inventory. **2.** Prepare a cost of production report with no beginning work in process inventory. **3.** Compute the unit cost of manufacturing under the process cost accounting system. **4.** Record costs incurred and the flow of costs as products move through the manufacturing process and are sold. **5.** Compute equivalent production and prepare a cost of production report with a beginning work in process inventory. **6.** Define the accounting terms new to this chapter.

Reading Assignment

Read Chapter 28 in the textbook. Complete the textbook Section Self Reviews as you finish reading each section of the chapter, and the Comprehensive Self Review at the end of the chapter. Refer to the Chapter 28 Glossary or to the Glossary at the end of the book to find definitions for terms that are not familiar to you.

Activities

- ❑ **Thinking Critically** — Answer the *Thinking Critically* questions for ConocoPhillips and Managerial Implications.
- ❑ **Discussion Questions** — Answer each assigned discussion question in Chapter 28.
- ❑ **Exercises** — Complete each assigned exercise in Chapter 28. Use the forms provided in this SGWP. The objectives covered by an exercise are given after the exercise number. If you need help with an exercise, review the portion of the chapter related to the objective(s) covered.
- ❑ **Problems A/B** — Complete each assigned problem in Chapter 28. Use the forms provided in this SGWP. The objectives covered by a problem are given after the problem number. If you need help with a problem, review the portion of the chapter related to the objective(s) covered.
- ❑ **Critical Thinking Problems** — Complete the critical thinking problems as assigned. Use the forms provided in this SGWP.
- ❑ **Business Connections** — Complete these Business Connections activities as assigned to gain a deeper understanding of Chapter 28 concepts.

Practice Tests

Complete the Practice Tests, which cover the main points in your reading assignment. Compare your answers with those in the Practice Test Answer Key for Chapter 28 at the end of this chapter. If you have answered any questions incorrectly, review the related section of the text.

STUDY GUIDE

Part A True-False *For each of the following statements, circle T in the answer column if the statement is true or F if the statement is false.*

T F 1. The balance of the **Raw Materials Inventory** account at the end of any accounting period should reflect the cost of raw materials, supplies on hand, and work in process at that time.

T F 2. In a process cost system, the cost of service departments are allocated to the producing departments and charged to the work in process inventory accounts.

T F 3. Separate cost records are kept for the various producing and service departments.

T F 4. Raw materials are always added at the start of production.

T F 5. In a process cost system, production costs are not recorded on job order cost sheets.

T F 6. The Quantity Schedule section of a cost of production report shows the total quantities to be accounted for and explains what happened to them.

T F 7. A single **Raw Materials Inventory** account can be used for both direct materials and manufacturing supplies in a process cost system.

T F 8. The equivalent units for materials in a department are always the same as the equivalent units for labor in that department.

T F 9. If the figures from a physical inventory do not agree with the figures in the perpetual inventory records, then the records must be adjusted.

T F 10. A physical inventory should be taken at least once a year to check the accuracy of the perpetual inventory figures.

T F 11. A department had no beginning work in process. During the month, 500 units were started into production and 400 were completed. On the other 100 units, 50 percent of the labor had been performed. The equivalent unit production for labor is 450 units for the month.

T F 12. A process cost system may be viewed as an average cost system.

T F 13. The beginning work in process inventory of one accounting period is the same as the ending work in process of the prior period.

T F 14. The ending work in process inventory of one department becomes the beginning work in process inventory of the next department in the manufacturing process.

T F 15. The entry to record the sale of finished goods is a debit to **Accounts Receivable** and a credit to **Work in Process Inventory** for the selling price.

Part B Completion *In the answer column, supply the missing word or words needed to complete each of the following statements.*

______________________ **1.** In a(n) ______ department, work is performed directly on the product.

______________________ **2.** The number of units to be accounted for and the number actually accounted for are shown in the ______ section of the cost of production report.

______________________ **3.** In a(n) ______ system, the total cost of a unit of production is found by adding the unit costs in each department through which the product passes as it is being manufactured.

______________________ **4.** The ______ report shows the costs incurred in a department, the unit cost of each element of manufacturing costs, and the cost accounted for in the department.

______________________ **5.** A(n) ______ system is normally used in situations where different products are manufactured and are started in batches or by jobs.

______________________ **6.** The ______ technique is used to express the amount of work accomplished in terms of equivalent whole units.

______________________ **7.** The maintenance department is an example of a(n) ______ department that assists in production but does not perform work on the actual product.

______________________ **8.** ______ is a control account with a supporting subsidiary ledger showing the detail of overhead items.

Part C Exercises *Compute the following units.*

______________________ **1.** The assembly department of a manufacturing business had no beginning inventory. During May, 1,000 units of product were started. All materials are added at the beginning of the manufacturing process. During the month, 900 units were transferred to the next department and 100 units were still in work in process. Compute the equivalent units of materials for May.

______________________ **2.** A producing department had no beginning inventory. During the month, 5,000 units of product were begun in the department, of which 4,500 units were transferred to the next department and 500 units were in process at the end of the month. The 500 units were 50 percent complete as to labor. Compute the equivalent units for labor for the month.

______________________ **3.** The beginning inventory in a department was 1,000 units, which were 25 percent complete as to overhead. During June, 5,000 units were placed in process, 5,000 units were transferred to the next department, and 1,000 units were in the ending work in process inventory. The ending inventory was 40 percent complete as to overhead. Compute the equivalent units of overhead for June.

Demonstration Problem

Bat Products, Inc. began business in August 2010. The company manufactures baseballs and softballs. The product is started in the cutting and assembly department and is completed in the stitching and printing department. Data for the month of August follows.

Instructions

1. Prepare equivalent production computations for the cutting and assembly department.
2. Prepare a cost of production report for the cutting and assembly department.

	Cutting and Assembly Department
Costs	
Materials	$51,450
Labor	35,190
Manufacturing Overhead	17,112
Total Costs	$103,752
Quantities	
Started in production	15,000 units
Transferred out to next department	12,000
Work in Process—ending	3,000
Stage of Completion—Ending Work in Process	
Materials	100%
Labor	60%
Manufacturing Overhead	60%

SOLUTION

1.

Bat Products, Inc.

Equivalent Unit Production Computations

Month Ended August 31, 2010

Cutting and Assembly Department	
Materials: Units Transferred Out	
To next department: 100% × 12,000 units	12,000 00
Work in Process: 100% × 3,000 units	3,000 00
Equivalent units of Production for Materials	15,000 00
Labor and Manufacturing Overhead	
Units Transferred Out	
To next department: 100% × 12,000 units	12,000 00
Work in Process: 60% × 3,000 units	1,800 00
Equivalent units of Production for Labor and Overhead	13,800 00

SOLUTION (continued)

2.

Bat Products, Inc.

Equivalent Unit Production Computations Month Ended August 31, 2010

Cutting and Assembly Department

QUANTITY SCHEDULE		UNITS	
(a) Quantity to Be Accounted For:			
Work in Process–Beginning		0.00	
Started in Production		15,000.00	
Total to Be Accounted For		15,000.00	
(b) Quantity accounted for:			
Transferred out to next department		12,000.00	
Work In Process—Ending		3,000.00	
Total Accounted For		15,000.00	

COST SCHEDULE	TOTAL COST	E.P. UNITS*	UNIT COST
(c) Costs to Be Accounted For:			
Costs in Current Department			
Materials	51,450.00	÷ 15,000 =	3.43
Labor	35,190.00	÷ 13,800 =	2.55
Manufacturing Overhead	17,112.00	÷ 13,800 =	1.24
Cummulative Cost Total	103,752.00		7.22
(d) Costs Accounted For:			
Transferred out to next department	86,640.00	= 12,000 ×	7.22
Work in Process—Ending			
Materials	10,290.00	= 3,000 ×	3.43
Labor	4,590.00	= 1,800 ×	2.55
Manufacturing Overhead	2,232.00	= 1,800 ×	1.24
Total Work in Process—Ending	17,112.00		
Total Cost Accounted For	103,752.00		

***Equivalent Production Units or**
Equivalent Units of Production

WORKING PAPERS

Name

EXERCISE 28.1

EXERCISE 28.2

EXERCISE 28.3

EXERCISE 28.4

Name

EXERCISE 28.5

EXERCISE 28.6

Name ______________________

EXERCISE 28.7

GENERAL JOURNAL PAGE ______

DATE	DESCRIPTION	POST. REF.	DEBIT	CREDIT

EXERCISE 28.8

GENERAL JOURNAL PAGE ______

DATE	DESCRIPTION	POST. REF.	DEBIT	CREDIT

EXERCISE 28.9

GENERAL JOURNAL PAGE ______

DATE	DESCRIPTION	POST. REF.	DEBIT	CREDIT

Name

PROBLEM 28.1A or 28.1B

Equivalent Production Computations

Analyze:

Name ____________________

PROBLEM 28.2A or 28.2B

GENERAL JOURNAL PAGE ______

DATE		DESCRIPTION	POST. REF.	DEBIT	CREDIT

Name

PROBLEM 28.2A or 28.2B (continued)

Computation of Equivalent Unit Production

Name

PROBLEM 28.2A or 28.2B (continued)

Cost of Production Report—Fabricating Department

QUANTITY SCHEDULE		UNITS	
COST SCHEDULE	TOTAL COST	E.P. UNITS*	UNIT COST

Name

PROBLEM 28.2A or 28.2B (continued)

Cost of Production Report—Assembly Department

QUANTITY SCHEDULE		UNITS	
COST SCHEDULE	TOTAL COST	E.P. UNITS*	UNIT COST

Analyze:

Name

PROBLEM 28.3A or 28.3B

Equivalent Unit Production Computations

Name

PROBLEM 28.3A or 28.3B (continued)

Cost of Production Report

QUANTITY SCHEDULE		UNITS	
COST SCHEDULE	**TOTAL COST**	**E.P. UNITS***	**UNIT COST**

Analyze:

Name

CRITICAL THINKING PROBLEM 28.1

Equivalent Unit Production Computations

Name

CRITICAL THINKING PROBLEM 28.1 (continued)

Cost of Production Report

		Mixing Department	
QUANTITY SCHEDULE		UNITS	
COST SCHEDULE	TOTAL COST	E.P. UNITS*	UNIT COST

Name

CRITICAL THINKING PROBLEM 28.1 (continued)

Equivalent Unit Production Computations

Analyze:

Name

CRITICAL THINKING PROBLEM 28.2

Raw Materials Inventory	Work in Process Mixing Department	Work in Process Cooking Department	Work in Process Cooling and Packaging Department

Labor Costs

Manufacturing Overhead	Finished Goods Inventory	Cost of Goods Sold

Chapter 28 Practice Test Answer Key

Part A True-False

1. F
2. T
3. T
4. F
5. T
6. T
7. T
8. F
9. T
10. T
11. T
12. T
13. T
14. F
15. F

Part B Completion

1. producing (or production)
2. quantity schedule
3. process cost
4. cost of production
5. job order cost
6. equivalent production
7. service
8. Manufacturing Overhead (Control)

Part C Exercises

1.

Transferred to next department (900 × 100%)	=	900
Ending inventory of work in process (100 × 100%)	=	100
Total equivalent units—materials	=	1,000

2.

Transferred to next department (4,500 × 100%)	=	4,500
Ending inventory of work in process (500 × 50%)	=	250
Total equivalent units—labor	=	4,750

3.

Transferred to next department (5,000 × 100%)	=	5,000
Ending inventory of work in process (1,000 × 40%)	=	400
Total equivalent units—overhead	=	5,400

Name

EXTRA FORM

QUANTITY SCHEDULE		UNITS	
COST SCHEDULE	**TOTAL COST**	**E.P. UNITS**	**UNIT COST**

Name

EXTRA FORM

QUANTITY SCHEDULE		UNITS	

COST SCHEDULE	TOTAL COST	E.P. UNITS	UNIT COST

CHAPTER 29

Controlling Manufacturing Costs: Standard Costs

STUDY GUIDE

STUDY GUIDE

Understanding the Chapter

Objectives

1. Explain how fixed, variable, and semivariable costs change as the level of manufacturing activity changes. **2.** Use the high-low point method to determine the fixed and variable components of a semivariable cost. **3.** Prepare a fixed budget for manufacturing costs. **4.** Develop a flexible budget for manufacturing costs. **5.** Develop standard costs per unit of product. **6.** Compute the standard costs of products manufactured during the period and determine cost variances between actual costs and standard costs. **7.** Compute the amounts and analyze the nature of variances from standard for raw materials, labor, and manufacturing overhead. **8.** Define the accounting terms new to this chapter.

Reading Assignment

Read Chapter 29 in the textbook. Complete the textbook Section Self Reviews as you finish reading each section of the chapter, and the Comprehensive Self Review at the end of the chapter. Refer to the Chapter 29 Glossary or to the Glossary at the end of the book to find definitions for terms that are not familiar to you.

Activities

- ❑ **Thinking Critically** — Answer the *Thinking Critically* questions for Harley-Davidson and Managerial Implications.
- ❑ **Discussion Questions** — Answer each assigned discussion question in Chapter 29.
- ❑ **Exercises** — Complete each assigned exercise in Chapter 29. Use the forms provided in this SGWP. The objectives covered by an exercise are given after the exercise number. If you need help with an exercise, review the portion of the chapter related to the objective(s) covered.
- ❑ **Problems A/B** — Complete each assigned problem in Chapter 29. Use the forms provided in this SGWP. The objectives covered by a problem are given after the problem number. If you need help with a problem, review the portion of the chapter related to the objective(s) covered.
- ❑ **Critical Thinking Problems** — Complete the critical thinking problems as assigned. Use the forms provided in this SGWP.
- ❑ **Business Connections** — Complete the Business Connections activities as assigned to gain a deeper understanding of chapter concepts.

Practice Tests

Complete the Practice Tests, which cover the main points in your reading assignment. Compare your answers with those in the Practice Test Answer Key for Chapter 29 at the end of this chapter. If you have answered any questions incorrectly, review the related section of the text.

STUDY GUIDE

Part A True-False *For each of the following statements, circle T in the answer column if the statement is true or F if the statement is false.*

T F **1.** To properly budget manufacturing costs, those costs must be separated into their fixed and variable components.

T F **2.** The variable costs per unit change in direct proportion to changes in the volume of activity.

T F **3.** A fixed budget for manufacturing costs is ideal for controlling such costs.

T F **4.** Direct materials is a good example of a cost that generally is classified as a variable cost.

T F **5.** The high-low point method may be inappropriate in determining fixed and variable costs in some circumstances.

T F **6.** Power and utility costs are likely to be semivariable costs.

T F **7.** In a factory, if fixed costs per unit are $50 when 500 units are produced, the fixed costs per unit should be $20 per unit if 250 units are produced.

T F **8.** A flexible budget shows expected costs at several levels of production activity.

T F **9.** It is standard practice for a company to prepare monthly budgets of manufacturing costs.

T F **10.** Standard costs are "ideal" costs that should generally be unattainable.

T F **11.** A fixed manufacturing budget is given that name because it is a budget of fixed costs.

T F **12.** Indirect labor costs in a factory consist of $25,000 per month of fixed costs and $10 per direct labor hour for variable costs. If 3,000 direct labor hours are used, the budget for indirect labor will be $55,000.

T F **13.** A materials quantity variance is computed by multiplying the difference between the standard quantity of materials and the actual quantity consumed by the actual costs per unit.

T F **14.** The labor rate variance is determined by multiplying the standard quantity of labor by the difference between the actual rate per hour and the standard rate per hour.

T F **15.** Standard costs may actually be entered into the accounts.

T F **16.** The human resources department should generally be held responsible for labor quantity variances.

T F **17.** It is possible to compute the materials quantity variance for an individual job under the job order cost accounting system if standard costs have been established.

Part B Completion

Answer each question below based on the information given for Pro Industries. Pro has set manufacturing overhead standard costs at $3.50 per unit, based on an expected volume of 100,000 units requiring 100,000 hours of direct labor, fixed costs of $100,000 per year, and variable costs of $2.50 per hour. During the year, actual production was 90,000 units requiring 96,000 hours, actual fixed costs were $110,000 and variable costs were $2.10 per hour.

______________ **1.** What are the standard manufacturing overhead costs of the units produced during the year?

______________ **2.** What are the total actual costs for the year?

______________ **3.** What is the amount of variable costs budgeted for the actual hours worked?

______________ **4.** What is the amount of variable costs budgeted for the standard hours for the work performed?

______________ **5.** What is the amount of fixed costs budgeted for the actual hours worked?

______________ **6.** What are the budgeted costs for the standard hours allowed for the work?

______________ **7.** What is the total manufacturing overhead variance for the year?

Demonstration Problem

The Santa Fe Company manufactures one product. Standard costs for each unit of the product are:

Direct materials, 10 gallons @ $1.80	$18.00
Direct labor, 2 hours @ $15	30.00
Manufacturing Overhead, 1 hour @ $10	10.00
Total Standard Cost per unit	$58.00

Actual production costs for the month are given below for the 2,000 units:

Direct materials, 20,500 gallons @ $1.81	$ 37,105.00
Direct labor, 3,900 hours @ $15.05	58,695.00
Manufacturing Overhead	20,500.00
Total Actual Costs	$116,300.00

Instructions

Compute the following variances:

1. Direct material price variance.
2. Direct material quantity variance.
3. Direct labor rate variance.
4. Direct labor efficiency variance.
5. Total manufacturing overhead variance.

SOLUTION

1. **Direct material price variance:** **($1.81 − $1.80) × 20,500 gallons = $205 unfavorable**
2. **Direct material quantity variance:** **(20,500 − 20,000) × $1.80 = $900 unfavorable**
3. **Direct labor rate variance:** **($15.05 − $15.00) × 3,900 hours = $195 unfavorable**
4. **Direct labor efficiency variance:** **(4,000 − 3,900) × $15.00 = $1,500 favorable**
5. **Total manufacturing overhead variance:** **$20,500 − $20,000 = $500 unfavorable**

WORKING PAPERS

Name

EXERCISE 29.1

Quarter	Direct Labor Hours	Utilities Cost

EXERCISE 29.2

Percent of Budgeted Hours

EXERCISE 29.3

Name

EXERCISE 29.4

Cost Element	Standard Cost	Actual Cost

EXERCISE 29.5

EXERCISE 29.6

EXERCISE 29.7

Name

EXERCISE 29.8

EXERCISE 29.9

EXERCISE 29.10

EXERCISE 29.11

Name

PROBLEM 29.1A or 29.1B

Analyze:

Name

PROBLEM 29.2A or 29.2B

1.

Flexible Budget for Manufacturing Overhead

2.

Manufacturing Overhead Budget Performance Report

Analyze:

Name

PROBLEM 29.3A or 29.3B

1.

Analysis of Materials Variance

2.

Analyze:

Name

PROBLEM 29.4A or 29.4B

1.

Analysis of Materials Variances

2.

Analysis of Labor Variances

Analyze:

Name

CRITICAL THINKING PROBLEM 29.1

Analyze:

Name

CRITICAL THINKING PROBLEM 29.2

Chapter 29 Practice Test Answer Key

Part A True-False

1.	**T**	**10.**	**F**
2.	**F**	**11.**	**F**
3.	**F**	**12.**	**T**
4.	**T**	**13.**	**F**
5.	**T**	**14.**	**F**
6.	**T**	**15.**	**T**
7.	**F**	**16.**	**F**
8.	**T**	**17.**	**T**
9.	**T**		

Part B Completion

1. $325,000
2. $311,600
3. $240,000
4. $225,000
5. $100,000
6. $325,000
7. $13,400 F

CHAPTER 30

Cost-Revenue Analysis for Decision Making

STUDY GUIDE

STUDY GUIDE

Understanding the Chapter

Objectives

1. Explain the basic steps in the decision-making process. **2.** Prepare income statements using the absorption costing and direct costing methods. **3.** Using the contribution approach, analyze the profits of segments of a business. **4.** Determine relevant cost and revenue data for decision-making purposes. **5.** Apply an appropriate decision process in three situations: **(a)** Pricing products in special cases, **(b)** Deciding whether to purchase new equipment, and **(c)** Deciding whether to make or to buy a part. **6.** Define the accounting terms new to this chapter.

Reading Assignment

Read Chapter 30 in the textbook. Complete the textbook Section Self Reviews as you finish reading each section of the chapter, and the Comprehensive Self Review at the end of the chapter. Refer to the Chapter 30 Glossary or to the Glossary at the end of the book to find definitions for terms that are not familiar to you.

Activities

❏ **Thinking Critically** — Answer the *Thinking Critically* questions for Bristol-Myers Squibb and Managerial Implications.

❏ **Discussion Questions** — Answer each assigned discussion question in Chapter 30.

❏ **Exercises** — Complete each assigned exercise in Chapter 30. Use the forms provided in this SGWP. The objectives covered by an exercise are given after the exercise number. If you need help with an exercise, review the portion of the chapter related to the objective(s) covered.

❏ **Problems A/B** — Complete each assigned problem in Chapter 30. Use the forms provided in this SGWP. The objectives covered by a problem are given after the problem number. If you need help with a problem, review the portion of the chapter related to the objective(s) covered.

❏ **Critical Thinking Problems** — Complete the critical thinking problems as assigned. Use the forms provided in this SGWP.

❏ **Business Connections** — Complete the Business Connections activities as assigned to gain a deeper understanding of Chapter 30 concepts.

Practice Tests

Complete the Practice Tests, which cover the main points in your reading assignment. Compare your answers with those in the Practice Test Answer Key for Chapter 30 at the end of this chapter. If you have answered any questions incorrectly, review the related section of the text.

STUDY GUIDE

Part A True-False *For each of the following statements, circle T in the answer column if the statement is true or F if the statement is false.*

T F 1. In the decision-making process, the first step is to define the problem.

T F 2. In managerial decisions, sunk costs can be ignored.

T F 3. Historical costs are usually sunk costs.

T F 4. Fixed costs are rarely controllable.

T F 5. All manufacturing costs, both fixed and variable, are assigned to the cost of goods manufactured under direct costing.

T F 6. Absorption costing concentrates attention on the contribution margin.

T F 7. When a business decision is being made, only those costs that will change as a result of the decision are relevant.

T F 8. Contribution margin is the difference between sales and fixed costs.

T F 9. Assuming no beginning inventory, if the units produced and the units sold are equal, both direct costing and absorption costing will yield the same net income.

T F 10. In general, managerial decisions such as whether or not to purchase new equipment or to drop a product line can be made using only accounting and other quantitative data.

T F 11. If a segment of a business is not producing a positive contribution margin, management should consider eliminating that segment.

T F 12. Direct costing does not follow GAAP financial reporting.

T F 13. It may be profitable for a company to accept an offer to sell some of its product at an amount less than the total cost per unit computed under absorption costing.

T F 14. Under direct costing, all variable costs are treated as part of the cost of goods manufactured in the period when the costs are incurred.

T F 15. In considering whether to replace equipment, the book value of the existing equipment must be considered.

T F 16. When one is deciding whether to drop a product, the contribution margin of the product is probably the most important factor to consider.

T F 17. If the variable cost per unit remains constant, but total fixed cost increases, the contribution margin will decrease.

T F 18. Income taxes can be ignored in making decisions such as to replace equipment, discontinue a product line, etc.

Part B Matching *For each numbered item, choose the matching definition from the box and write the identifying letter in the answer column.*

_______ **1.** relevant

_______ **2.** incremental

_______ **3.** sunk

_______ **4.** manufacturing margin

_______ **5.** differential

_______ **6.** controllable

_______ **7.** common or indirect

a. The difference in cost between one alternative and another

b. Future or expected costs that will change only as a result of a decision

c. Costs that have been incurred in the past

d. Also known as differential costs

e. Costs that depend largely on the actions of the segment manager

f. Costs not traceable to any one segment of the business

g. Excess of sales over variable cost of goods sold

Demonstration Problem

Perma Tool, Inc. distributes small tools to retail hardware stores. Early in 2010, management of the business decided to develop and market a private brand line of tools. They contracted with a manufacturer to make the products and began distribution. After several months, the board of directors is rethinking the decision and has asked you to analyze the following information for the July 2010 sales.

	Fixed Costs per Month	Percent of Selling Price per Unit
Average cost of products		40%
Average cost of packaging		1%
Average freight in		2%
Average delivery costs		3%
Sales commissions		7.5%
Advertising		
Variable		9%
Fixed	$2,500	
Warehousing		
Variable		2%
Fixed	$ 500	
Other		
Variable		1%
Fixed	$ 600	

July sales were $15,000. Several of the directors think the private product line should be discontinued.

Instructions

1. Based on the information provided, what is the amount of income or loss on July sales of these products?

2. Based on the accounting analysis, should the private brand be eliminated?

3. Are there other considerations that bear on this decision to eliminate or keep the product line?

SOLUTION

1. Income for July 2010 is calculated:

	AMOUNTS	
Sales		15 000 00
Cost and Expenses		
Variable Costs		
Product cost (40% of sales)	6 000 00	
Packaging (1% of sales)	150 00	
Freight-In (2% of sales)	300 00	
Delivery Costs (3% of sales)	450 00	
Sales Commission (7.5% of sales)	1 125 00	
Advertising (9% of sales)	1 350 00	
Warehousing (2% of sales)	300 00	
Other Variable (1% of sales)	150 00	
Total Variable		9 825 00
Contribution Margin		5 175 00
Advertising	2 500 00	
Warehousing	500 00	
Other fixed costs	600 00	
Total fixed Costs		3 600 00
Net Income		(1 575 00)

2. Based only on the calculations shown, it would be appropriate to continue the product because it contributes $5,175 toward paying the fixed costs. However, if the directors consider only net income, they will suggest the product be eliminated.

3. Some of the questions to be asked include: Can sales be increased? Do buyers purchase other products as a result of our carrying this item? Are our advertising techniques effective for this product? How does this product fit into our total product offering?

WORKING PAPERS

Name ______________________________

EXERCISE 30.1

1. ______________________________

2. ______________________________

3. ______________________________

4. ______________________________

Name

EXERCISE 30.2

1.

2.

3.

EXERCISE 30.3

Name

EXERCISE 30.4

EXERCISE 30.5

1.

2.

Name

EXERCISE 30.6

EXERCISE 30.7

EXERCISE 30.8

Name

PROBLEM 30.1A or 30.1B

1.

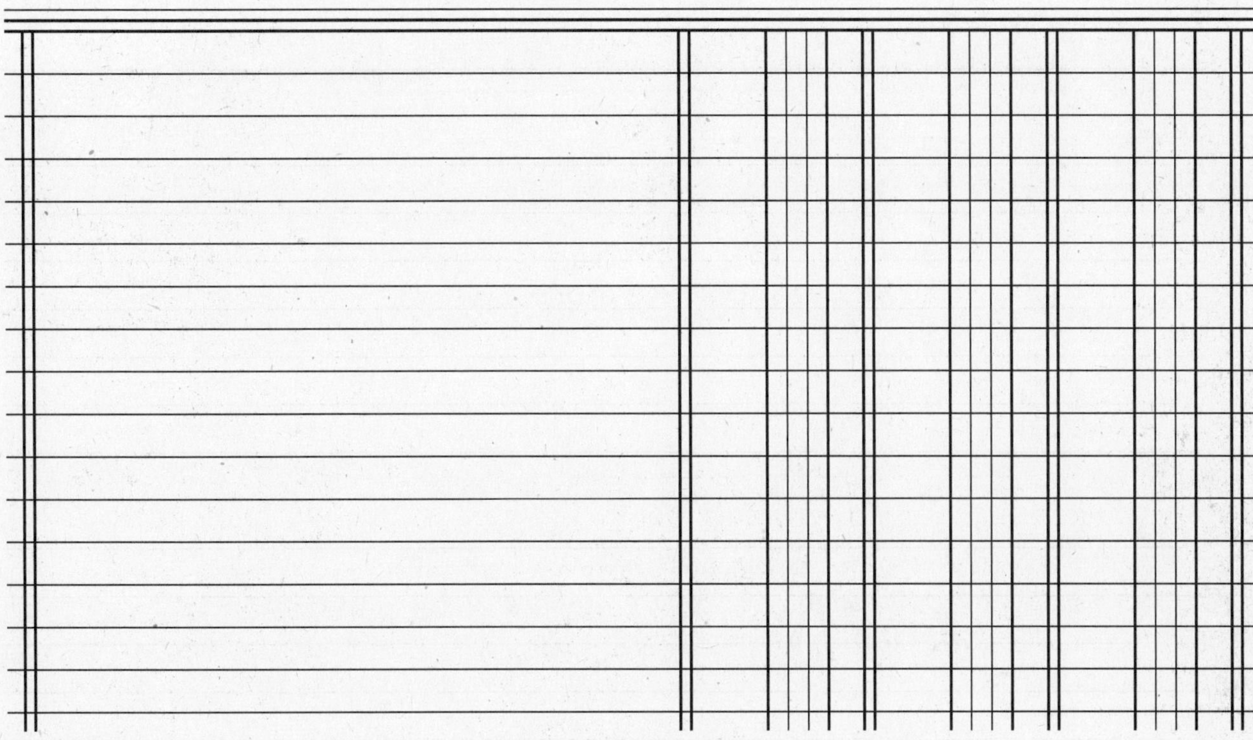

Income Statement (Absorption Costing)

2.

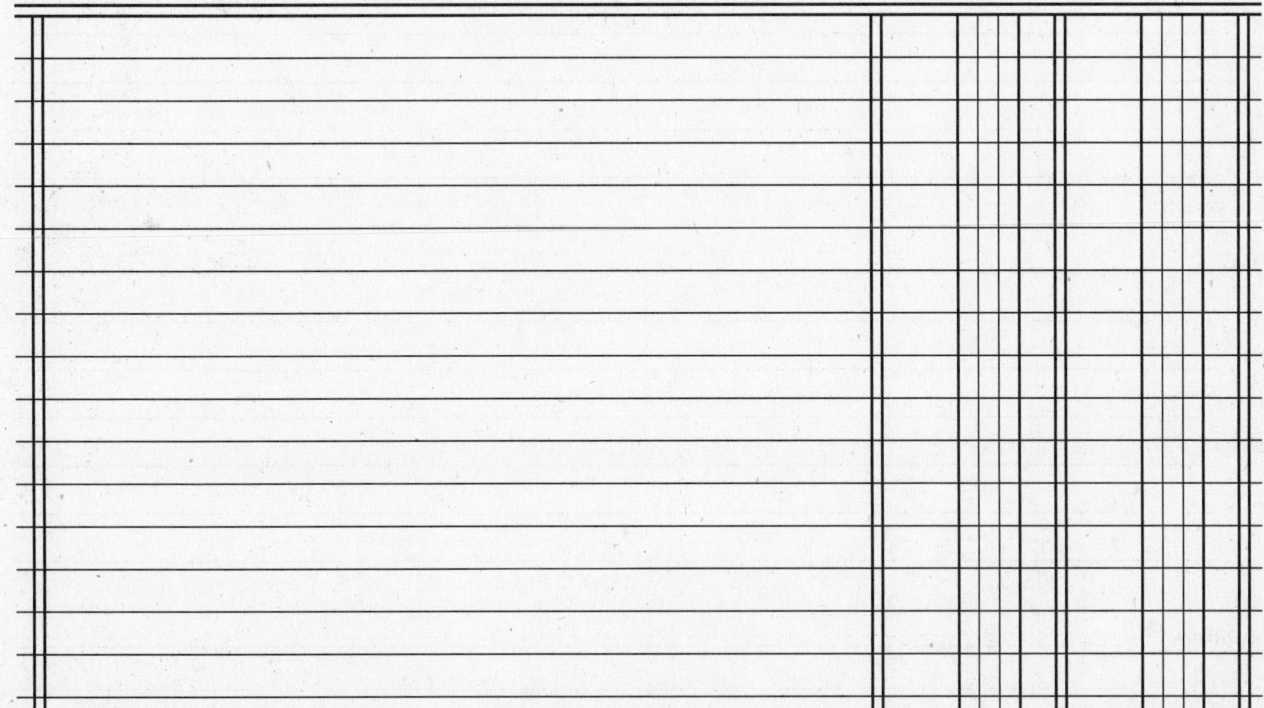

Income Statement (Direct Costing)

Name

PROBLEM 30.1A or 30.1B (continued)

3.

Analyze:

Name ______________________

PROBLEM 30.2A or 30.2B

1.

Income Statement (Direct Costing)

2.

Computations

Analyze:

Name

PROBLEM 30.3A or 30.3B

1. ANALYSIS OF EFFECTS OF PURCHASING MACHINE

2.

Analyze:

Name

PROBLEM 30.4A or 30.4B

1.

Analysis of Effects of Making or Buying a Part

2.

Analyze:

Name

CRITICAL THINKING PROBLEM 30.1

Name

CRITICAL THINKING PROBLEM 30.1 (continued)

Analyze:

Name

CRITICAL THINKING PROBLEM 30.2

	ITEM 101	ITEM 102	ITEM 103	TOTAL

Name

CRITICAL THINKING PROBLEM 30.2 (continued)

Chapter 30 Practice Test Answer Key

Part A True-False

1. T	7. T	13. T
2. T	8. F	14. F
3. T	9. T	15. F
4. F	10. F	16. T
5. F	11. T	17. F
6. F	12. T	18. F

Part B Matching

1. b
2. d
3. c
4. g
5. a
6. e
7. f

Name

EXTRA FORMS

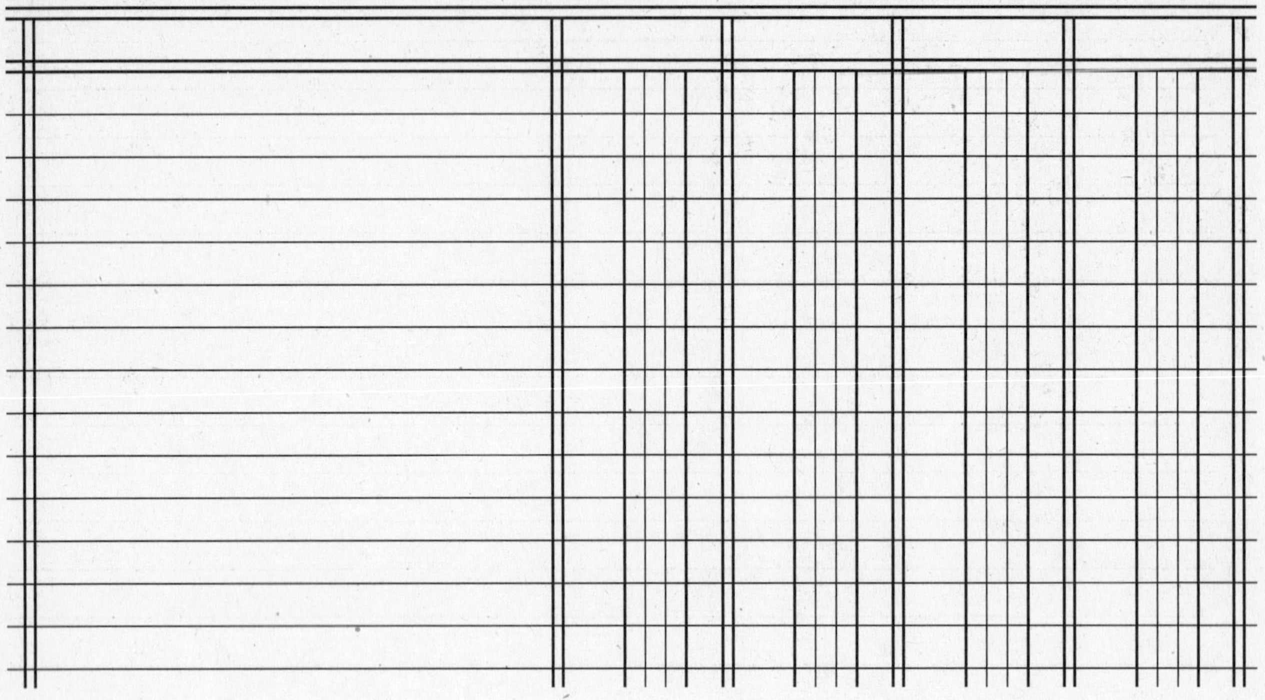

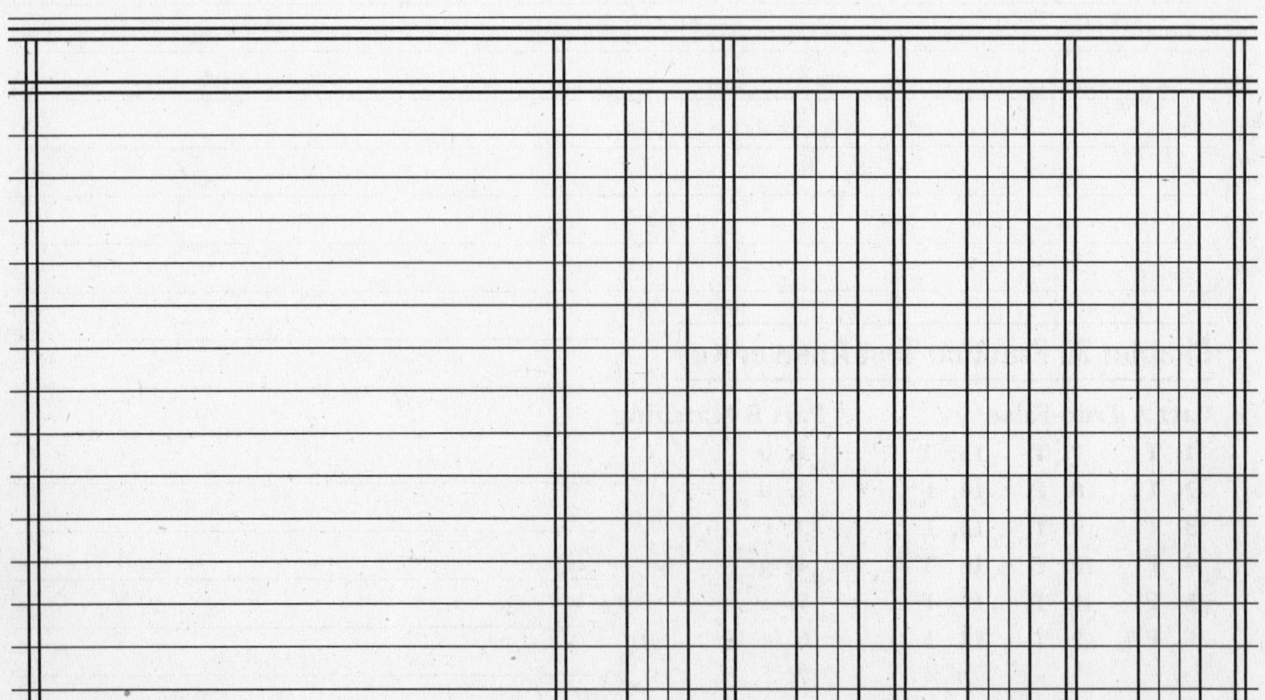